CONCEPT OF DHARMA
Corpus Juris of Law and Morality

A Comparative Study of Legal Cosmology

CONCEPT OF DHARMA

Corpus Juris of Law and Morality

A Comparative Study of Legal Cosmology

Professor Dr. K.L. Bhatia
B.A. (Hons.); LL.M., Ph.D. (Pune)
DAAD and Max Planck Fellow and Alumni
Emeritus Professor of Law,
College of Legal Studies
University of Petroleum and Energy Studies
[Former Head & Dean, Faculty of Law, and Director
The Law School, University of Jammu and Director, Amity Law School]

Foreword by

Justice R.C. Lahoti
Former Chief Justice of India

DEEP & DEEP PUBLICATIONS PVT. LTD.
F-159, Rajouri Garden, New Delhi - 110027

CONCEPT OF DHARMA
Corpus Juris of Law and Morality

ISBN 978-81-8450-261-9

Typeset by THE LASER PRINTERS
8/15, 3rd Floor, Subhash Nagar, New Delhi-110027

Printed in India at MAYUR ENTERPRISES,
WZ Plot No. 3, Gujjar Market, Tihar Village, New Delhi - 110 018

Published by DEEP & DEEP PUBLICATIONS PVT. LTD.
F-159, Rajouri Garden, New Delhi-110027.
Phones: 25435369, 25440916
Sales Showroom: 2/13, Ansari Road, Daryaganj, New Delhi-110002
Phone/Fax: 23245122

IN THE SACRED MEMORY OF
MY GRAND PARENTS AND PARENTS
AAI RADHA BHATIA
and
Younger brother Devinder

Matapitror ahar ahah pujanam karyam anjasa

"Shantiparva of Mahabharata"
12(84) 126-128

DAY BY DAY ONE SHOULD DIRECTLY HONOUR ONE'S MOTHER AND FATHER

CONTENTS

R.C. Lahoti
Former Chief Justice of India

B-56, Sector-14,
R O. Noida (U.R) - 201 301
Telefax: 91 + 120+2516644
E-mail : lahotirc@gmail.com

FOREWORD

It is not only interesting but also satisfying to study the origin and development of Law in juxtaposition with most ancient and yet ever evolving concepts of ethics and morality which are essentially founded on the bedrock of *Dharma*, i.e. religion.

Dharma, though universal and timeless, has always been shrouded in mystery and shadow of mysticism has ever been following the moving *Dharma*. Law in its broadest sense is an order that rules all human activities and relationships in any organized, disciplined and civilized society. Law is invariably backed by some pressure enforcing its abidance, be it by the force of the society or of people or of an institution endowed with authority given to it by the people. According to a thought (though called orthodox), *Dharma* is the basic source of all laws. The modern thinking does not necessarily support that concept; rather it is divided—in the sense that it claims that law and *dharma* may not always go hand in hand; at times, they may be so diversified in their approach as to appear facing each other as opponents. It is in this backdrop that Prof. Dr. K.L. Bhatia's originality of thinking, nurtured by research and developed by deliberations, presented in the form of book, assumes significance.

According to Roscoe Pound,[1] there are 'two ideas running through definitions of law: one an imperative idea, an idea of a rule laid down by the law making organ of a politically organized society, deriving its force from the authority of the sovereign: and the other a rationale or ethical idea, an idea of a rule of right and justice deriving its authority from its intrinsic reasonableness or conformity of ideals of right and merely recognised, not made by the sovereign'.

1. 'More About the Nature of Law' in *Legal Essays in Tribute to Orrin Kip McMurray*, pp. 513, 515(1935).

Dharma and Law, both are of utter relevance and immense significance to the human beings and the society. The common characteristic of both is to enable distinction being drawn between what is right and what is wrong though the qualitative features of the touchstone and its mode of applicability may differ. All the jurists unanimously uphold tracing of the origin of law to historical source as one of the sources. And, once the jurist begins his journey into the domain of history somewhere he does come across religion as one of the moulds of history; the shape, location and impact may vary. The ultimate aim of law is to establish peace and order in society. The same goal, rather beyond, is what *Dharma* too seeks to achieve. Necessarily *dharma* does find itself as major contributor of the ultimate principles wherefrom the law owes its descent.

A man to groom into a full human being must necessarily have freedom or free will to move, live, act, and do whatever he chooses to do consistently with the ethical and moral standards acceptable to the community in which he has chosen to live and belong, free from coercion. *Dharma* dictates the man to do only what is good by time tested rules of ethics and morality. Those mandates would govern him even if he is alone, far removed from any community or society. In *dharma*, the process of determining what is good is self-oriented; it does not involve any coercion or external force which law does wield. In this sense law and *dharma* are not prevented from moving parallel to each other. They have the liberty of joining hands too. They are not necessarily antagonistic to each other. N.E. Simmonds[2] states—'even when legal theories do not give pride of place to the concept of a right in their accounts of legal reasoning, they tend to give considerable importance to the concept in the realm of moral argument.'

"The Hindu Jurisprudence or the legal system (*Vyavahara Dharmasastra*) is embedded in *Dharma* as propounded in the Vedas, Puranas, Smritis and other works on the topic. *Dharma* is a Sanskrit expression of widest import. . . . It would be futile to attempt to give any definition to that word. It can only be explained." Justice M. Ramajois[3] beautifully and authoritatively sums up various manifested aspects of *dharma*. He says—"though

2. *The Foundation of Rights, Central Issues in Jurisprudence*, p. 141.
3. *Legal and Constitutional History of India*, pp. 3, 9.

the word *Dharma* has such wide meaning as to cover rules concerning all matters, such as spiritual, moral, and personal as also civil, criminal and constitutional law, it gives the precise meaning depending upon the context in which it is used. For instance, when the word *'Dharma'* is used to indicate the giving of one's wealth for a public purpose, it means charity; when it is referred to the giving of *Dharma* to a beggar, it means giving of alms; when it is said that in a given case *Dharma* is in favour of the plaintiff, it means law or justice is in his favour; when it is said that it is the *Dharma* of the sons to look after their aged parents, it means duty; when it is said that it is the *Dharma* of a debtor to repay the debt to the creditor, it means a legal as well as pious obligation. Similarly when the word *Dharma* is used in the context of civil rights (civil law), it means that is enforceable by the State; in the case of criminal offence (in criminal law) it means breach of a duty which is punishable by the State; and when *'Dharma'* is used in the context of duties and powers of the king, it means constitutional law *(Rajadharma)*. Likewise, when it is said that *Dharmarajya* is necessary for the peace and prosperity of the people and for establishing an egalitarian society, *the word Dharma in the context of the word Rajya only means law, and Dharmarajya means Rule of Law and not rule of religion or a theocratic State.*

"*Dharma* in the context of legal and constitutional history only means *Vyavahara-dharma and Rajadharma* evolved by the society through the ages which is binding both on the king (the ruler) and the people (the ruled). . . . *Rajadharma* conferred power on the king to enforce obedience to *Vyavaharadharma* through the might of the State."

Dr. Bhatia's work 'Concept of Dharma . . .' would quench the thirst of intelligent seekers of truth who wish to study the inter-relationship (and conflict too) between *vidhi* and *dharma* from the point of view of their relevance to the humanity and its organizations (voluntary or involuntary).

20.04.09

Vijayadashmi (Sept. 28), 2009

(Justice R.C. Lahoti)
Fr. Chief Justice of India

PREFACE

Dharma is ubiquitous in Indian *Vedic/Indic*/Hindu philosophy. *Dharma* is "law", or "moral law", or "law and morality," or "natural law" by acceptance—*jus receptum*—which is believed to have been ordained by Divine Author; it is not a law as we understand it today.

I have *trimurti/triumvirate* visions while working on "Concept of *Dharma*: *Corpus Juris* of Law and Morality: A comparative Study of Legal Cosmology". First, "His Vision"—that is beyond description—Who blessed me with His Bliss. "*Dharma* is the law conceptually the relationship of Law, Life and Morality. The copyright of *Dharma* belongs to the Creator God Who Himself disseminated to the human beings to assimilate it for follow-up actions with reasons and rationality". Second, "Lead me from darkness to gleaming wings of light where new vistas of knowledge await to ring the bell". Third, "Open my eyes, so that I may behold wondrous things out of your law". (Psalms, 119:18).

I chose to do research on this unique area because we have so far believed the truth in the lie that the Western legal thought the only saviour for Indian legal perception forgetting that those Western scholars have had conceived their legal concepts as per their own systems requirement. They did so conscientiously as well as obediently as a duty and an obligation. We must acknowledge their scholarship. Our *Vedic/Indic/Sastric* ideas are hidden treasures of legal knowledge and provide deep as well as ample insights in a perfectly clear manner to unfold it and develop Indian Legal Theory on the legal cosmology for the futurology of legal concept conscientiously, obediently as a duty and an obligation. This is a modest attempt in this perspective. I aspire as well as wish that many more legal scholars of our country should peep deep into the legal cosmology of legal literature and develop Indian legal visions, perceptions and conceptions for a clear roadmap for Indian legal system. There is nothing pretentious, ostentatious and abstentious about it.

There are many approaches to *Dharma*. *Dharma* in legal science cosmology is innermost treasures as "law" and "law and morality" or "natural law" that is a truth. *Dharma* includes Law and Natural Law, Morals and Ethics as it is the manifestation of natural attributes of man in pursuit of justice that is his desire for his welfare. *Dharma* is ingrained in *Smritis* that are *Dharmasastras* which include the law codes dealing with some main subjects: law of constitution, law of administration, law of diplomacy, law of nations, codes of conduct, civil and criminal law, and punishment and atonement. All actions, thoughts, vibrations of any sort, behaviour, attitudes and aptitudes are governed by a law known *Karma* that demands perfect rebound. *Karma* is a law of the phenomenal cosmos that is part and parcel of living within the dimensions of time and space. Flexibility is the dynamic aspect of *Dharma*—the legal system—and the rigidity could easily dry up the entire legal system. *Dharma* and law and morality are inasmuch as impregnated as *Bhagavad Gita* and *Mahabharata* are rooted with each other. Therefore, *Dharma* is indeed *école de verité*—the school of truth. One who refuses to fulfil this obligation when lawfully requested may be forced to comply by the edict of *danda*. *Dharma* as law and morals is regarded as a universal morality, accessible to all rational persons. It is the combine of duty, right, and wrong, viz., to right the wrong is the duty and not the *vice versa*. Succession over the entire patrimony is wrong and as such questionable morality. *Dharma* enjoins duty to right such wrong. Though law of levirate (pregnancy or fathering a child by the brother of the deceased husband or through other sources other than the legal spouse) used to be right, but subsequently its practice became a questionable morality.

Dharma as *Vidhi* (law), *Nayaya* (justice), and *Yukti* (natural reason, logic and equity), *Vidya* (knowledge) sits supreme that binds human beings and all manifestations of Law, Life and Morality (LLM). It is a great intellectual concept of farsightedness, and unveils itself only to the most passionate, intense, sincere, and full of truth inquisitor *in propria persona.*

Dharma is infallible as it is solicitous of noble birth origins invented by the Great Creator—God—realized in three stages of *Vedic/Indic*/Hindu philosophy: *Brahaman, Paramatma and Bhagwan—Trimurti*—three manifestations—*Satyam, Shivam, Sundram*—of one God (*Ekam svadipra bahuda vadanti)*—disseminated and assimilated by the great sages, saints, seers, and mystics through millennia after millennia Therefore, *Dharma* as law and morals is entrenched and as such immutable since it is a heritage stronger than governments and kings, and rulers and kings of modern elected democracy.

With such pedigree of law, yet the idea of law figures seldom or at the remotest margins of Indian studies as a field of law, law and morality, and law and nature. The reasons are not far to seek. It may be nothing pretentious to say that with the entry of common law in India, the soup and sauce of this rich heritage evaporates. The British administrators did not accord recognition to *Vedic* concept of *Dharma* law and law and morality, because they had intended to introduce their own common law in India to advance their own interests in India. British judges in India needed access to the original legal texts of India to implement the British policy of "administering native law to the natives as personal laws of the natives", and so were born a "well intentioned, well conceived and well calculated misunderstanding as well as misconception".

The critics assert that *Dharma* as an idea of law has been conceded as too much idealistic as well as mythology and without any practical utility and relevance; it lacks universality; it is without any conscience reasoning and rationality; it is without any legal reasoning; it is a closed-minded system; it is only religious, and, therefore, in the realm of law it is only formalistic, pedantic, and simply non-adjustable.

Dharma in all modesty and assertion is not distinct from legal as well as moral values. *Dharma* is beyond the scope of any "ism". Even if per chance or mistake or misconception or misunderstanding, it is correlated to Hinduism or *Vedic (ism)*, which is the constant or perpetual pursuit of *Dharma*, that does not, in conscience, make any distinction between law and religion. In this sense, *Dharma* is faith; it is *Bhakti*; it is belief; it is conscience; it is worship; it is practice; it is propagation; it is professed; and, therefore, it is universal. *Dharme sarvam prathishtham; satyam sarve prathishtham; sarva dharma sambhav; sarve bhavantu sukhina, sarve santu niramaya . . . ;* Law is the foundation of the universe; truth and justice is the foundation of the universe; the whole universe is one family, it is universal order, and as such its universality is ubiquitous; the universality of *Dharma* law is impregnated aspiring the human good, human happiness, human dignity, and human flourishing for the whole mankind universally. *Dharma* as law is law of mankind universally, because conscientiously it is not confined only to a particular sect of a particular society. This is the inbuilt concept of universality of *Dharma*.

The inventors of the word *Dharma* have had farsightedness to develop the societal orderliness in accordance with laws of *Dharma*. Therefore, laws of *Dharma* were practically preaching cultural and jurisprudential harmony inasmuch as developing the concepts of law, morals, ethics, *danda* (punishment, sanction, force), person, *prakriti and vyavahāra* (law of civility, viz., conduct and behaviour, and also the manifestations of civil law), *Rajdharma* (law of constitution), *Rajayadharma* (law of administration), *Rajsasana* (law of good as well as sustainable governance/ management with inbuilt accountability and transparency), human dignity, democracy. If *Dharma* is said to be natural law or conceptual relationship of law and morality of Divinity of God that is having foundation on *yukti*, viz., reasoning, logic, and rationality to convince arrayed human beings like *Arjuna*, what more verisimilitude of *Dharma* one may imagine.

Dharma is *memoria technica* of Law + Morals + Ethics + Action + Justice and taken together constitute Natural Law, viz., Law and Morality, and Law and Nature. It is entrenched as Memory (*smriti* that follows to hold and support *sruti* from extinction), *Shabad* (the script, the language, the expression, the pedagogy) that supports perceptual knowledge (*Praman and anuman*) for posterity (*Parampara*), dissemination and assimilation of knowledge (*Vidyya:* deriving from Memory that is a form of perception) in search of knowledge (*Hetu*: Goal: aim: Inquisitiveness) to reserving and preserving it (*Sanskara*), and *Mimansa* (the law of interpretation with *Yukti* as well as *Tarka*, i.e., reason, logic, rationality, and equity). It is Rule of Law to serve Rule of Life.

Dharma is derived from the root *Dhri*: *Dharma dharayati dhartam; ato dharmani dharayam; dharne; dharayate iti dharma*, viz., to hold, to uphold, to support, to sustain (sustainability), to retain (values), to conserve (soil conservation against erosion and protecting from environmental erosion, global warming), to preserve (cultural heritage and values), to observe and to promote (human good, human happiness, human dignity, human rights), to develop (relationship between Law and Morality, and Law and Nature). This is the *Corpus Juris* of the immutable concept of *Dharma* and its legal cosmology.

Besides, comparative analyses of Western approaches to Law and Morality have in depth been made. A succinct analysis of the literature shows that law and morality or natural law are the older, which live not yesterday nor yet today, but stand for ever that has protean concept with a compendium term. Natural law or law and morality have had a chequered history of periods of frozen turbulences either acceptance of the existence of conceptual relationship between law and morality or rejection or neglect of law and morality. This appears to be the suspicion of the thinkers about the expression natural law that has changed from one age to the next presenting varying or different profiles of ideas about natural law thus confounding it with confusions of incongruent theorems making it a riddle wrapped in mystery inside an enigma. A succinct scanning of the literature shows that natural law has had been the scorn of bitter circumstances and has had several deaths. This has occurred in the hands of those who have worked against natural law in favour of positive law by declaring the death of natural law wishing that it would "never rise again from its [grave] ashes. Yet natural law survives and still calls for discussion, because the "funeral orations for the natural law have been premature". Thus, natural law could neither be defaced nor defiled irrespective of the endeavourers to perceive the complete divorce of law from morals. It survives and sustains because of new enlightenment in perceptions that have been highlighted in this write up. Therefore, it is imperative to have the comprehension of new enlightenment in perceptions to a revival or reawakening or modernization of natural law or law and morality concept rather than spiteful about the controversies of doctrinal issues that now lay far behind, for *de novo* future where we may sing a song with afresh melody, instead of melancholy, lead me from darkness to gleaming wings of light where new vistas of knowledge await to ring the bell. The new approach has to be without the quagmire of past tense, present imperfect and future indefinite. Who is the angel or sage to save it from the quicksand of legislative and executive quagmire? In the backdrop of the emergence of new constitutional and legal culture, the battle about law and morality is being fought in a new way on a new battleground. The concepts enshrined in constitutional vocabulary like 'legality', 'due process', 'procedure established by law', 'life and liberty', 'reasonableness', 'equality before the law and equal protection of the law', 'human dignity', appear to be very near or like or actually assimilable to law and morality or *Dharma* expression. Besides, in the question of law and sociology coordination, the expressions 'the rule of law', 'the rule of law to serve the rule of life', 'the legal order', 'judicial activism', 'judicial creativity', 'judicial innovation', 'judicial craftsmanship', 'justice, access to justice and distributive justice', 'disadvantaged groups of the society', 'neglected segments of the society', 'marginalized groups of the society', 'aboriginals', 'minority', seem to be value terms/expressions and rarely as well as insufficiently investigated by socio-legal eagles heuristically and empirically with social science research methodologies nevertheless do not lay far away from the eternal as well as internal morality, and in this area law and morality of *Dharma* can play its part. It is here that we see the relevance of law and morality of *Dharma* in the domain of law and sociology, which progressively aims at reducing/minimizing the degree of arbitrariness in the positive law.

Law and morality or *Dharma* places limits upon the arbitrary exercise of political, legislative and executive powers. In the backdrop of this, it is imperative that we the thinkers have to detach ourselves from the cobweb of positivists' illusion about eternal stability for harmonious sustainable governance. This insight may help to erase the misconceptions, misunderstandings and the misleading approaches to 'is' and 'ought', and conceivably assist to derive 'ought' from 'is' convincingly. In the conclusion of this preface, it may be submitted that *Dharma* is the epitome of whole legal matter entailing all aspects of law that sensitizes the relationship of law and morality which in legal cosmology is the conceptual relationship between law and morality. I can only submit that positive law, in fact, cannot survive without a "therapy" of *Dharma* Law and Morality.

In the successful culmination of this research work I have been nourished by the sound patronage of many visionaries. I wish to express my deep gratitude to them neither as a ritual nor as a fashion, because either of these expressions are expressions of formality as well as artificiality. I express my warm feelings to them since they are close to my heart. I express my deep gratitude to a noble soul who had been a source of encouragement to me. His divine blessings enabled me to understand and encapsulate the meaning of intricacies of *Sanskrit* expressions. It is he who encouraged me to take up this venture which I do as a mere act of infancy. And, for all wrongs and mistakes I am alone accountable. My sincere apology for the occurrence of the mistakes is because of my comprehension of *Sanskrit* expressions in the right perspectives. I am indeed immensely beholden to Him. I am beholden to Dr. Ashok K. Chauhan, the Founder President of Ritnand Balved Education Foundation (RBEF), who facilitated my visit to Max-Planck Institute for Comparative Public and International Law, Heidelberg, Germany, as a Guest Research Professor. He encouraged me to execute the present research work, because he could spark a willing spirit in me to pursue it. My profoundest gratitude to Dr. Ashok K. Chauhan for his solicitous help to take up this venture where even angels would afraid to tread. I also want to offer special thanks to Professor J.K. Mittal, Chairman, Amity Institute of Global Legal Education and Research (AIGLER), who encouraged me to get established on the path of knowledge and gain sufficient experience while pursuing this kind of research work at Max-Planck Institute. I owe a very special thanks to Professor Dr. Rudiger Wolfrum, Director, Max-

Planck Institute for Comparative Public and International Law, Heidelberg, Germany, and a scholar of the highest caliber and a dedicated researcher as well as a dedicated teacher, who enabled me to have deep insights into the secrets of legal cosmology of *Dharma* as law and morality while pursuing this research work at MPI. I am personally indebted to him for his encouragement, help, and his decision to facilitate my sojourn at MPI. I also owe acknowledgement to Professor Dr. Armin von Bogdandy, Director, MPI, for giving heart as a devout researcher as well as teacher to a teacher and his clear impetus on me by providing me a neat and clean environ at the institute to have scholastic interactions with the scholars at the institute. I unhesitatingly acknowledge the helping and supportive attitude of the library staff of MPI but for whom this research work would have not seen the light of the day. My special gratitude to Justice Shri R.L. Lahoti, Former Chief Justice of India, who acceded to my request to record his impressions by way of a critique foreword to this book that enhances the value of thought on "*Dharma* and Law and Morality". I feel much obliged to him. Finally, I very warmly express appreciation to my wife, Veenal Bhatia, son Sumeet Bhatia, an Advocate, daughter Manu and her husband Sandeep Sharma, a law scholar and an Advocate, for their support and understanding for what I selected to do at the cost of their sociological time. I unhesitatingly acknowledge with thanks to Shri G.S. Bhatia, Deep & Deep Publications Pvt. Ltd., New Delhi, to bring this book in neat time.

Professor Dr. K.L. Bhatia
Emeritus Professor of Law
College of Legal Studies
University of Petroleum and Energy Studies
and
Guest Research Professor
Max-Planck Institute for Comparative Public and
International Law, Heidelberg, Germany.

1

INTRODUCTION

Dharma and Natural Law theories as well as theorists have been frequently scorned by scholastic-jurists for a mixture of methodological, psychological, sociological and philosophical reasons. The paradigm of the wrath is the distinct entities of law and morals; God and Divinity; law and ethics; law and nature. There seems to be commonality in the critiques in three areas of criticism of natural law, viz., first, the method used to derive rules of natural law appears to make an illogical jump from questions of fact (what is) to questions of obligation (what ought); second, natural law theories have frequently been employed to justify the *status quo* and to validate what would seem to be unjust regimes; and third, natural law lawyers have failed to explain what effect the difference between natural law and human law has.[1] The critics perceive the origins of natural

1. See Michael Doherty, Jurisprudence: The Philosophy of Law, 2005, pp. 147-48; Erik Angner, Hayek and Natural Law, 2007; Charles Covell, The Defence of Natural Law, 1992, p. 29; Tony Burns, Natural Law and Political Ideology in the Philosophy of Hegel, 1996, pp. 1-41; Walter Farrell, The Natural Moral Law, 1930; Charles P. Curtis, Law As Large As Life A Natural Law For Today And the Supreme Court As Its Prophet, 1959; Michael Bertram Crow, The Changing Profile of the Natural Law, 1977; Roger T. Simonds, *The "Natural Law" Controversy:*

law are obscure, for the reasons that such concepts have originated without conscience and conscientious reasoning having closed-minded systems of legal reasoning and leading these people to say that law is formalistic, pedantic or simply unjust and non-practical.[2] Such invasions may be the whims that are not based on heuristic foundations because minimal insights into *Dharma* and Law and Morality. It is niche to submit that there is a seamless web between law and morality either in *Dharma* in the Indian perspectives or natural law in the Western perspectives. Therefore, it may be possible for the maximalists to evaporate the soup and sauce of irritants heralding of Law, Society and Development. *Dharma* and natural law traditions should not be construed as mere museums of different tools, instruments and mechanisms. Tools, instruments and mechanisms of *Dharma* and natural law are far from theoretical speculations; rather those have rationale humane approach to human good, human happiness, societal utility, national relevance and international co-existence. To have broader insights into the perceptions and visions of *Dharma* and natural law, one must have humane vibrations, rather than an old tired machine. *Dharma* and natural law are in constant pursuit of "life" that is not bare material existence, but is a matter of quality

---

Three Basic Logical Issues, Journal of Norte Dame Law School Natural Law Forum, (5) 1960, 132-138; see also Oliver O'Donovan, *John Finnis on Moral Absolutes*, in Nigel Biggar and Rufus Black (eds.), *op. cit*, 111-128; David Braybrooke, Natural Law Modernized, 2001; Rufus Black, *Introduction: The New Natural Law Theory*, in Nigel Biggar and Rufus Black (eds.), The Revival of Natural Law, 2000, 1-25 at p. 22: "Ultimately, the new natural law theory assures us that ethics is about the enhancement of human life"; Thomas Chappel, *Natural Law Revived: Natural Law Theory and Contemporary Moral Philosophy*, in Nigel Biggar and Rufus Black (edsa.), *op. cit.*, pp. 29-52.

2. See Patrick Olivelle, Manu's Code of Law A Critical Edition and Translation of the *Manava-Dharmasastra*, 2005, pp. 62-66. It is equally unwise to consider *Dharmasastras* as purely panditic commentaries with no relation to law or real life, just as it is silly to consider Panini as having no relationship to spoken Sanskrit or the *Carakasamhita* as having no connection to the practice of medicine or the *Natyasastra* as having nothing to do with the production of plays. The relationship of *Sastra* to practice in all these areas is more nuanced than envisaged by either of these extremes.

of mental as well as physical health living; it is a quest for truth as a manifest of human good and human happiness as human goal; it encompasses an aesthetic experience, viz., linked to life and knowledge; its spirit of beauty is equally a universal self-evident human good; it has bonds of human community, sociability and as such of practical/rational/objective, and not subjective, reasonableness; and, it is embedded with searching questions concerned to know how things came to exist and whether is not something greater and more powerful than human intellect, to which humans are subject. In the backdrop of this, the significance, importance, utility and relevance of law and morality as comprehensions of *Dharma* and natural law may concisely be presented as follows:

> The history of natural law is a tale of the search of mankind for absolute justice and of its failure. Again and again, in the course of the last 2,500 years, the idea of natural law has appeared, in some form or the other, as an expression of the search for an ideal higher than positive law after having been rejected and derided in the interval. With changing social and political conditions the notions about natural law have changed.
>
> The only thing that has remained constant is the appeal to something higher than positive law. The object of that has been as often the justification of existing authority as a revolt against it.
>
> Natural law has fulfilled many functions. It has been the principal instrument in the transformation of the old civil law of the Romans into a broad and cosmopolitan system; it has been a weapon used by both sides in the fight between the medieval Church and the German emperors; in its name the validity of International law has been asserted, and the appeal for freedom of the individual against absolutism launched. Again it was by appeal to principles of natural law that American judges, professing to interpret the Constitution, resisted the attempt of state legislation to modify and restrict the unfettered economic freedom of the individual.

> It would be simple to dismiss the whole idea of natural law as a hypocritical disguise for concrete political aspirations and no doubt it has sometimes exercised little more than this function. But there is infinitely more in it.
>
> Natural law has been the chief though not the only way to formulate ideals and aspirations of various peoples and generations with reference to the principal moving forces of the time. When the social structure itself becomes rigid and absolute, as at the time of the Schoolmen, the ideal too take a static and absolute content. At other times, as with most modern natural law theories, natural law ideals become relative or merely formal, expressing little more than the yearning of a generation which is dissatisfied with itself and the world, which seeks something higher, but is conscious of the relativity of values. It is as easy to deride natural law as it is to deride the futility of mankind's social and political life in general, in its unceasing but hitherto vain search for a way out of the injustice and imperfection for which Western civilization has found no other solution but to move from one extreme to another.
>
> The appeal to some absolute ideal finds a response in men, powerful political and legal developments, particularly at a time of disillusionment and doubt, and in times of simmering revolt. Therefore, natural law theories, far from being theoretical speculations, have often heralded powerful political and legal developments.[3]

It may thus seem that there is not only unceasing yearning of a generation that is dissatisfied with itself, the world and the new technocrat globalization as well as economic liberalization, which seeks solace—life, mental and health—in something higher, that is natural law, as a refuge, but there is a generation that seeks solutions of law, society and development only in the seamless web of natural law in crisis of legal systems at a time of disillusionment as well as doubts confounded by new developments of brutality of war, terrorism; internally displaced

3. W. Freidmann, Legal Theory, 1967, pp. 95-96.

persons; invasions on the human dignity of children, girl child, disabled persons, and women; threat to sustainability caused by global warming, environment pollution, soil erosion, bio-diversity; universality of peace and human happiness, etc.

Be that as it may, the concept of natural law is the magnum opus of Indian and German legal thoughts. The concept of natural law in the thoughtronics of Indian and German legal perceptions needs relook as well as reiteration. The jurisprudence of natural law from Indian and German perspectives has moral precepts, which are not *ipse dixit* but have an educative value of developing relationship between Nature and Law on the one hand and Morals and Law on the other hand. These precepts, indeed, are inner morality of Indian and German legal thoughtronics. Any scholastic silence may perpetuate the inanimate influence of Anglo-Saxon legal thoughts over Indian and German legal regime that is full of mine of knowledge. The scholastic endeavors have been to unfold the mists of *quo-animo* (with what spirit or intention) and *quo-jure* (by what right) of the concept of natural law in Indian and German legal languages that contain a significant element of history of law. *Dharma* in *Sanskrit language* manifests legal language of natural law or law and morality or law and nature in much more prominent as well as broader perceptibility than what it has been presented (as religion) in the narrowest way by narrow mindedness. Similarly, the German concepts of *Ordnung, Eigengesetzlichkeit* (coined by Professor Dr. Conrad) have much more prominent place in German legal language as "natural order" and near to the language of *Dharma*.[4] Grotius's legal

4. See in particular Erik Angner, *op. cit.*, pp. 29-30; Werner Menski, *From Dharma to Law and Back? Postmodern Hindu Law in a Global World*, Heidelberg Papers in South Asian and Comparative Politics, 2004, p. 10; concept of Ordnung, as per dictionary of economics, means "natural order" reading as "natural law"; German concept Ordnung has different connotations than the English version. Ordnung as per Cassell's German Dictionary means several things, namely, arrangements, classification, order, system, array, tidiness, orderliness, class, rank, order, succession, series, rules, regulations. Order or natural order refers not only to a state of orderliness, but to rules and

language of natural law is enjoined in his *De Jure Belli ac Pacis*, and Samuel Pufendorf's natural law language of 'sociality' is engrained in his abbreviations *DJN: De Jurae Naturae et Gentium Libri Octo*: On the Law of Nature and Nations, *DOH: De Officio Hominis et Civis Juxta Legem Naturalem Libri Duo*: On the duty of Man and Citizen according to Natural Law, and *Statu: De Statu Hominum Naturali*: On the Natural state of Men, that is imperative to the fundamental law of nature not as ethical egoism but to exoticise a modest return to limelight the modern law and morality philosophy "that the fundamental principle of human conduct was the desire for self-preservation."[5]

The evolution of Jurisprudence is nothing but reflects the rationalization of Natural Law. The concept of natural law has varied perceptions, visions, comprehensions, disseminations and assimilations in the, not static but dynamic, language of law. And, Legal Language is:

> Legal Language
> is
> interplay of words,
> a
> stream of expressions,
> a
> deluge of vocabulary,
> an
> inexhaustible repository of words,
> a quest for
> the knowledge and science of words.
> It is a snare of semantics,
> a syntactic rigmarole,
> the wonder of words.
> ....

---

norms regulating behavior of individuals who are required to follow prescribed rules and regulations as per moral and ethics norms.

5. See in particular Robert Shaver, *Grotius on Scepticism and Self-Interest*, *in* Knud Haakonssen (Ed.), Grotius, Pufendorf and Modern Natural Law, 1999, pp. 63-83; Craig L. Carr and Michael J. Seiler, *Pufendorf, Sociality and the Modern State*, in Knud Haakonssen (Ed.), *op. cit.*, pp. 133-57.

....
Legal language is the heritage
a heritage which enjoins
that
dispensation of justice
is
the moral dictum
It is a tale
of
the intricacies of Jurisprudence.[6]

Thus, it may be apt to submit that the history of natural law is a tale of quiet turbulences of the search of mankind for absolute justice and its failure, and there is nothing exaggeration as well as pretentious about it, because

> . . . Every war and every fair brings forth a new natural law.[7]

And, history affords testimony to it; to the love as well as care of sage and saint, and to the hatred as well as scorn of devout thinkers and men of letters. In the Western system, it has been a progressive movement from Stoics, Sophists, *ius naturale, ius gentium, ius civile, justum acquum et bonum natura, de jure naturali et gentium juxta disciplinam ebraeorum,* Church (Canon Law), to Individualism, Liberty, Natural Rights (as a consequence of fight against feudalism, fiefdom and monarchy) to Positivism to Modern Constitutions of the world. It may seem that it is a progressive movement from individual aristocracy to constitutional aristocracy, viz., constitutional morality and constitutional culture. This movement has never been static but a continuous evolution of thought process that inspired the unceasing search or quest or inquisitiveness during different turmoil of socio-economic-political periods pilgrimage progress of Ancient/Classical Age (Natural Law and Justice, Reason and Enlightenment), Silence (Dark) Age, Medieval Age, Renaissance

---

6. See K.L. Bhatia, Legal Language, a poem written by the author and published in his book of poems titled "*Main aur meri anubhooti*", 2008.
7. Michael Bertram Crowe, *An Eccentric Seventeenth-Century Witness to the Natural Law*, in Knud Haakonssen (ed.), *op. cit.*, pp. 184-188, at p. 111.

Age, Social Contract (from Status to Contract) Age and Revivalism, and quintessence of Rehabilitation. It may discern that conception of natural law, on the whole, as an order, which commands human respect and human dignity, becomes possible only when man becomes conscious as well as conscientious of his position in the universe, when law is no longer just a part of magic or rituals or religious rites, but emerges as a distinct concept devoid of inconsistencies of "positive law culture" and "positive law morality". From this summation, many distinctions of natural law theories are possible, depending on the criterion adopted.[8] They may be divided into authoritarian and individualistic, into progressive and conservative, into religious and rationalistic, into absolute and relativist theories. For a justice consideration the most important distinction would appear to be that between Natural Law and Higher Law, which invalidates any inconsistent positive law, and Natural Law as an ideal to which positive law ought to conform without its legal validity being affected. Broadly speaking, ancient and medieval law theories are of the first type, renaissance and social contract law theories of the second, and revivalism and modern natural law theories of the third. This change coincides on the whole with the rise of the modern State in democracy and its claim to absolute sovereignty.

In the backdrop of the above, it may thus seem that natural law have undoubtedly been inspired by the two ideas, viz., first, of a universal order governing all men, and, second, of the inalienable rights of the individual. This way natural law when used in the service of either of these ideas, natural law has formed an organic and essential part in the hierarchy of legal values. As the basis of an international order, it has, in a continuous line of development, inspired the Stoics, Sophists, Roman Jurisprudence and philosophy, the Fathers of the Church, the legal order of medieval Western society and Grotius' system of International Law. Through the theories of Locke and Pine, it has provided the foundations for the individualists of the American and other modern Constitutions of the global democracies.

---

8. *Cf.* Analysis by Erik Wolf, *Das Problem der Naturiechtslehre*, 1955.

Be that as it may, notions of conceptions of natural law from Indian perspectives are entrenched in immutable *Dharma* having its roots in *Sanskrit Lirit Dhri* that signifies to hold, to support (moral values in the construction of law), to sustain (sustainability), to retain (values), to conserve (against erosion of soil, environment, global warming, natural habitat), to preserve (cultural heritage and values), to observe and to promote (human good, human happiness, human dignity, human rights), to develop (relationship between Law and Nature and law and Morality). This is the foundation of ancient era that continued in the medieval age and continues with the vigorous force *a proprio vigore* in the modern age of constitutionalism that has Constitutional Morality and Constitutional Culture. It is embedded in *Rajdharma* (Law of Constitution), *Rajayadharma* (Law of Administration), *Rajsasana* (the law of good/sustainable governance with transparency and accountability), *Rajayashastra* (Science of the Nation State and Statecraft), *Dandaniti* (Sanctions, force and punishment), *Dharmashastra and Nitishastra* (Law and Legal Order of the State: *Vidhi-Vidhan*), and *Arthashastra* (Code of Conduct for the ruler and the ruled).

The sublime concept of Natural Law enjoins the philosophy of welfares'/welfarism (Welfare State) that sustained ancient administration, and, perhaps, if revisited may be a guideline for transparency, accountability, good/sustainable governance, and neat/clean administration for the present as well as future of democracy in India, at least. One example of eternal value of the concept of Natural Law is sustained in the depth of expression *Dharma*,[9] the beacon light, which shows the right path to the rulers of democracy (may be called the wonderland of bureaucracy) under any set-up of government of a welfare State has been summed by *Kautilya/Channakayya:*

> In the happiness of his subjects lies the King's happiness; in their welfare, whatever pleases himself the King shall not consider as good, whatever pleases his subjects, the King

9. *Dharma* includes Law and Natural Law, Morals and Ethics as it is the manifestation of natural attributes of man in pursuit of justice that is his desire for his social welfare.

shall consider as good. The King shall ever be active and discharge his duties.[10]

In nut shell the concept of natural law conveys "Preach each of the rules of law and/or morals not merely by speech but by observing each", and that is the message of Justice from ancient case as quoted by *Kalhana*.[11] The fundamental tenet of natural law is "an affirmation of the role of human reason in the design and operation of legal institutions. It asserts that there are principles of sound social architecture, objectively given, and these principles, like those of physical architecture, do not change with every shift in the details of the design toward which they are directed."[12] The *Vedas*, the *Smritis*, the *Nitis*, the *Mimansas*, good conduct or approved custom/usage, what is agreeable to conscience proceeding from good intention are the sources of Natural Law, and enjoin varied forms of natural law such as *Vidhi* (positive command), *Nishedha* (negative command), *Na Himsayet* (don't injure living beings), *Satyam Vada* (tell the truth), *Satyam Shivam Sundram* (only in truth and welfare lie the beauty of the system), *Yato Dharamsatato Jaya* (where there is righteousness there is the victory and that is the concept of Justice).

It seems that State or Social Control through Law is the conscientious gist of Natural Law and milestones for the establishment of *Rajdharma, Rajayadharma, Rajyasasana, and Rajayasastra*. Ensuring the welfare of the people is the quintessence of *Rajdharma*. It can be achieved only by having laws regulating the conduct of individuals and their enforcement through the State and her officials.

---

10. *Kautilya's Arthashastra* (English), p. 39; *Kautilyeeyatha Sastram (Sanskrit)*, Mysore University, 4th Ed., 1960, p. 42; Cicero as quoted by Edward S. Corwin: "Law is the highest reason, implanted in nature, which commands those things which ought to be done and prohibits the reverse. The highest Law was born in all the ages before any Law was written or State was formed. We are by Nature inclined to love mankind, which is the foundation of law", *Dharme Sarwam Prathishtam*: Natural Law is the foundation of the Universe.
11. *Kalhana's Rajatarangini*, translated by R.S. Pandit with a foreword by Pt. Jawaharlal Nehru.
12. Fuller, Anatomy of the Law, p. 117; Fuller, L., The Morality of Law.

In the ultimate analysis, concepts of natural law, have not only role to play in the enacting of laws in the most modern democratic systems but also throw light and guide the interpretation and enforcement of the laws enacted in order to secure justice to the individuals concerned. Ultimately, the concepts of natural law have pre-state origin and are of eternal value. They are also available to help the shaping and development of the *Supreme Lex* (the Constitution of India) to the Judiciary by supplanting the law. In the backdrop of this, the Apex Court (the Supreme Court of India) has been interpreting Preamble (Justice, Equality, Liberty, Fraternity, Human Dignity), Article 14 (Right to Equality), and Article 21 (Right to Life and Personal Liberty) in the light of law and morality or natural law. The case of *Sunil Batra v. Delhi Admn*[13] indicates how natural law that commands humane treatment to those in prison, convicted or undergoing trials or under trials, was regarded as included in Article 21, viz., right to life and personal liberty. In the case of *Air India v. Nergesh Meerza*[14] natural law unequivocally prevailed and shaped the interpretation of Article 14, viz., right to equality. *M.C. Mehta v. Kamalnath*[15] has developed the concept of "Public Trust" in relation to Environmental Laws and Sustainability that are close to natural law. The "Public Trust" Doctrine primarily rests on the principle that certain resources like air, sea, waters and the forests have such a great importance to the people as a whole and it would be wholly unjustified to make them subject of private ownership. The doctrine enjoins upon the Government to protect the resources for the enjoyment of the general public rather than to permit their use for private ownership or commercial purposes. The concept of "Public Trust" in relation to clean and pure environment as well as sustainability stands recognized in the ancient Indian literature engrained in *Puranas*, viz., he who destroys environment by contaminating it by his/her arduous refuge or otherwise commits sin (wrong) (violator of environmental law and negation of duty) and is a sinner (wrongdoer) (responsible for the breach of duty/obligation) and, therefore, responsible for *Dand*, viz.,

13. A.I.R. 1980 S.C. 1579.
14. A.I.R 1981 S.C. 1850.
15. (1997) 1 SCC 388.

punishment/sanction. *Vishakha v. State of Rajasthan,*[16] a case concerning sexual harassment at working place, *a multo fortiorari* speaks volumes about natural law or law and morality or *Dharma* to be humane to the sustainability of the dignity of women. The Basic Law of Germany, too, speaks about human dignity, equality, life and liberty, which are not distanced from natural law.[17] According to the Constitutional Court of Federal republic of Germany dignity of man requires the attribution of rights to the individual which enable him or her to defend his or her own design of life inasmuch as human dignity is a 'right of rights'.[18] The Federal Constitutional Court has coined the phrase that 'the dignity of man shall be inviolable as a legal right' as everybody has the right to his or her inviolable dignity;[19] human dignity constitutes an order of values that radiate to the whole body of law;[20] human dignity may be violated but not taken;[21] a waiver of dignity is not acceptable and, therefore, dignity is not at the disposal of the individual;[22] human dignity has an absolute effect.[23]

Seldom has there been any significant comparative research study of the concept of natural law or law and morality *vis-à-vis Dharma* in Indian and Western legal musings. A modest attempt, in this tiny write up, has been made through an exploratory research into gold mines of Indian and Western legal literature broodings. Research is to see what every body else has seen, and to think what no body else has thought. Be that as it may, the endeavors of the researcher have been addressed to the analysis of natural law *vis-à-vis Dharma* broodings comparatively with the axiom that this modest write up on the legal cosmology of

---

16. A.I.R. 1997 S.C.
17. Articles 1 (Basic Right to protection of human dignity), 2 (Right to liberty), 3 (Equality before the law), of the Basic Law of Germany.
18. See Donald P. Kommers, The Constitutional Jurisprudence of the Federal Republic of Germany, 2nd. Ed., 1997, Ch. 7, Human Dignity and Personhood, pp. 298 *et. al. see also David Kretzmer and Eckart Klien (Eds), The Concept of Human Dignity in Human Rights Discourse,* 2002.
19. BVerfGE 61, 126, 137 (1982).
20. *Luth Case,* BVerfGE 7, 198, 204 et. seq. (1958).
21. BVerfGE 87, 209, 228 (1992).
22. BVerfGE 45, 187, 229 (1977).
23. BVerfGE 75, 369, 380 (1987) 93, 266, 293 (1995).

Dharma and natural law is not to exoticism either India for the West or the West for India, because both have had their own perceptions, visions, conceptions, methodologies and techniques —sociologically, psychologically—as "neither The East is in the East nor The West is in The West", but

The East as East
And the West as West
Cradle the mind as mere concepts
Simply because
The human soul knows no compass
No geographical encapsulations
The present and the future
Hold the key
We know the reality is the thought
Discovery of the thought is a challenge
Present and future becomes a probe
Delving into the mind-brain linkage
As, Law and Nature and Law and Morality
It helps flow of thought and flow of information
In the colloquy —
Who are well informed?
Those whose actions are sound
Then whose actions are sound?
Of those who are well informed
This leaves us where we were
This leads us where we are
This tells us where we ought to be![24]

The results, on the whole, in the long-run, shall be to assess the utility and relevance of the concept of *Dharma vis-à-vis* natural law in the Indian and Western conjecture pondering in the present and the future, because thought is a reality and discovery of the thought is a challenge. It is time to probe into mind-brain linkages of Law and nature and law and Morality comparatively. This shall, indeed, help flow of thoughts, flow of

24. *Supra* note 6.

information and information sharing in the following colloquy, as I perceive, concept of natural law:

> "*Dharma* as Law and Morality or Natural law is a law and a set of such rules that regulate human conduct and human conduct depends upon human behavior, which is controlled by psychogenic and sociogenic influences."

The essence of *Dharma* and Natural Law or Law and Morality, further, I, therefore, conceive as follows:

> "*Dharma* is the law conceptually the relationship of Law, Life and Morality (LLM). The copyright of *Dharma* belongs to the Creator God Who Himself disseminated to the human beings to assimilate it for follow-up action with *Nyaya* (Justice) and *Yukti* (natural reason, logic, rationality and equity)."

2

FESTSCHRIFT OF THE DISTINGUISHING IDEAS OF NATURAL LAW

Natural Law means a tradition in morals. Tradition is an important part of culture, and especially the legal culture. 'Tradition as a myth' or the 'sentimental tradition' must have a contrast with the 'experienced tradition', and this 'experienced tradition' is a substantive and continuing body of attitudes and activities which is not only handed on, but is lived out and serves a basis for renewal as well as development.[1] Perceptibly, the proponents of Natural Law have perceived natural law from this point of view and that is the unique character of natural law. Positivists define law as any law which satisfies the appropriate technical criteria of enactment counts as law.[2] For anti-positivists this concept of law is problematic because of the absence of reference to its moral quality from the domain of law.[3] But, for

1. See particularly J. Bell, French Legal Cultures, 2001, pp. 6-7, 11-12, 14-17; Carl F. Stychin and Linda Mulcahy, Legal Method, 2003, pp. 23-25.
2. See reference to Fletcher as given in Carl F. Stychin and Linda Mulcahy, *op. cit.* at p. 6.
3. *Ibid.*

the positivists, the validity of law is determined simply by reference to the question whether it has been enacted in accordance with the formal requirements set down by the legal system.[4] Whereas a proponent of natural law shall argue that in order to count as valid law, positive law must be measured successfully against some standard found outside of the legal system, as under natural law there must exist some moral code of principles which exist irrespective of positive law, and against which it can be judged.[5] Be that as it may, natural law is the legal heritage of traditions in morals. How these traditions have evolved? Where from these traditions come? Who is the inventor of these traditions? For whom such traditions were evolved? Who says what to whom for what purpose and under what circumstances? These basic questions relating to natural law or law and morality have grappled the minds of thinkers from antiquity to date. Thinkers have devised the transcendental of natural law into natural (nature, God, Divinity, man, reason) and artificial and contrived paradigms. Be it be a jealousy or paradox, critics through their scholastic critiques have, mindfully or unmindfully, created controversies about natural law and have made natural law a riddle wrapped in mystery inside an enigma.

Natural law is immutable because it is as old as the antiquity, and it is as modern as its revivalism. Ideas about natural law have emanated as per the ideas of thinkers of different nations and different times. As each nation and era has had its own unique character so is true with the perceptions and visions of the thinkers. Each thinker grows and develops in accordance with the socio-economic-political conditions of his society. Be that as it may, the first and foremost question should be addressed to know in depth whether there is any correlation or association between law and morality. Unequivocally, there has been long correlation between law and morality. Believers' faith is that law has association with religion, customs, God and Divinity or Divinity of God, God and Divinity are inseparable and there can be only Divinity of God. As revealed laws of God in the form of Bible have dominated legal concepts in the West,

4. *Ibid.*
5. *Ibid.*

similarly, the revealed laws of God and His Divinity through the magnitude of *Dharma* vide *Vedas, Ritis, Nitis, Smiritis, Dharmshastras, Mimansas, etc.* have dominated legal concepts in India till their soup and sauce evaporated with the entry of common law. Succinctly, the relationship between law and morality may be attributed to the origin of law to the spiritual rather that the rational, as per western thought. In contrast to this, it has been argued that natural law has an immanent rationality that enables the man to reach the right conclusion.

> All human justice consists in conformity to the will of God. … This is the ultimate norm (eternal law) and basic rule for man's moral behaviour. …Because of its conformity with this eternal law, natural law is right: and all other righteousness in man's laws is derived from this eternal law. …Natural law … has an immanent rationality which enables man in principle to reach the right conclusion as to his temporal felicity. …[6]

Though the inclusion of morality in the domain of law helps to solve many problems,[7] such as disobeying immoral law, but jurisprudentially how far the problems which are the problems of law and moral both such as abortion, homosexuality, lesbianism, fair sex exploitation, girl child abuse, immoral human trafficking, begging, internally displaced persons, terrorism, can be minimized or eradicated with the moral or legal knowledge and moral or legal justification alone. This remains a million dollar question. The second question is concerning the concepts of morality. Morality is related to moral and ethical values. The legal thinkers have been grappling with the basic question whether morality is the product of law, or law the ultimate product of morality. This happened with the origin

6. H.A. Oberman, The Harvest of Medieval Theology, p. 100; M.B. Crowe, *The "Impious Hypothesis": A Paradox In Hugo Grotius,* in Knud Haakonssen (Ed.), Grotius, Pufendorf and Modern Natural Law, 1999, pp. 379-410 at pp. 404-405.
7. Alexy, R., *The Nature of Arguments about the Nature of Law,* in Meyer L, Paulson, S. and Pogge, T. (Eds.), 2003; Alexy, R., *The Nature of Legal Philosophy,* 17 (2004) *Ratio Juris,* 156.

and birth of conflicting opinions rejecting the presence of morals in the domain of law. But, natural law theses gave a rational theoretical frame to the modern state for the first time in the seventeenth century.[8] Should the end of law be confused with this riddle? Should this riddle be confounded with the proverb that it is wrapped in mystery inside an enigma? Since the issues of morality are decided by human conscience and instinct, therefore, the expression morality in relation to law/legal science may mean different things with different variables to different thinkers/scholars. May morality be the decisive guiding star for the legislators? If it be so shall there be occasions to further question whether law has to be morally valid in order to be legally valid. Olivecrona, however, calls the *'imperantum' and 'ideatum'* (behavior), viz., "the impression that the behavior in question shall be observed, and suggests that morality is the product of law and certainly developed social morality would probably be impossible if it were not for legal enforcement.[9] He further exerts that the law is, in fact, somewhat idiosyncratic, the progenitor of many of our moral standards.[10] In reaction to Olivecrona's assertion few illustrations are imperative. For example, we are, in our childhood age, conditioned into accepting that certain conduct say stealing is unlawful or wrong or unethical or immoral, and stamp of illegality lends these wrongs, moral/ethical wrongs a particular power. We internalize these rules to be our standards of morality. Further, the aspirations for the reforms of laws or revision of obsolete laws surely spring from a genuine, unselfish desire to improve the lot of society; morality is affecting law rather than the

8. See Merio Scattola, *Before and After Natural Law Models of Natural Law in Ancient and Modern Times*, in T.J. Hochstrasser and P. Schroder (eds.), Early Modern Law Theories Context and Strategies in the Early Enlightenment, 2003, pp. 1-30.
9. Olivecrona, Karl, Law as Fact, 2nd Ed., 1971; Olivecrona, Karl, *The Imperative Element in Law*, (1964) Rutgers Law Review, 794; George C. Christie and Patrick H. Martin, Jurisprudence, 2nd Ed., 1995, 925-930; Stephen E. Gottieb, *et. al.*, Jurisprudence Cases and Materials, 2nd. Ed., 2006.
10. *Ibid.*

reverse.[11] To this Olivecrona seems to assert that law reformers are moved by "enlightened self-interest", and law reformers are themselves subjected to some psychological probable or variables.[12] Psychology is internalized in people's minds that are the causation of human behaviour. Therefore, to laws reforms, the human mind responds to various forms of social pressure.[13] It may be submitted that psychological and sociological factors certainly condition psychogenic and sociogenic behavior patterns of human beings in general and of lawyers, Judges, jurists, officials, and legislators in particular 'induced to act in particular ways'.[14] As a result, on this summation, there may be infinite disagreements.

However, for Bentham and Austin there are distinct distinctions between 'positive' and 'critical' morality. Positive morality relates to such social conventions those are created by man, and critical morality being the standards by which those social conventions could be judged. Whatever the critical distinction between positive morality and critical morality may be, but matters of slavery, prostitution, call girls, abortion, victims of domestic violence, victims of sexual exploitation, victims of internal displacement—like migration of one particular segment of the society within the same sovereign Nation State—thus bringing demographic imbalances, victims of terrorism and militancy, victims of dictatorship, victims of democracy where accountability as well as transparency succumb to the recidivists of corrupt, politics of criminals and criminalization of politics seem to be matters of moral values, social values, social mores of obligation and duty, and political morality. Interactions of morality and legality may be the solicitations to such searching inquisitives. Finnis, a revivalist, perceives in it a riddle or puzzle of legal language, and exerts *a multo fortiorari* that the language of ethics and the language of law are similar and centre upon questions of obligation and

11. See Raymond Wacks, Understanding Jurisprudence: An Introduction to Legal Theory, 2005, pp. 189-190.
12. *Supra* note 1.
13. *Ibid.*
14. *Supra* note 4; see author's Conceptualization of Natural Law *supra* Introduction.

duty.[15] It may be that Finnis seems to be inspired by ethical studies, and it may be conceded that ethics change according to improvements in practical reasoning. What is ethical practical reasoning for those favouring imposition of Martial Law—a state of emergency—in a country, certainly may not be ethical practical reasoning for those who oppose it. Therefore, morality does not depend on a marriage of convenience between objectivity, subjectivity and rationality.

Be that as it may, the riddles of the language of 'Natural' and 'Morality' call for the understanding of different models of Natural Law that posit an interesting insight into the study of Law and Nature, and Law and Morality. It was a model of wisdom of antiquity, may be of reason and common sense that law was immutable as it was a heritage stronger than governments and kings, because the king was subject to law and not the reverse as the law made him the king. This practice was before the intrusion of 'king can do no wrong', viz., law was subject to king and not the reverse. It was a model of the Church (Catholic) that was responsible for the enforcement of law through its Canon Law as enforcement of law was scarcely in the hands of the government and the king, because it was more dependent on the practice and teaching of the Church and its Canon Law. It is the study of the model that originated with the decline of the authority of the Church, and the resurgence of kings and Parliaments that became wealthier and usurped the powers of the Church for the enforcement of laws through the authority of the governments. The origin of the Protestants seems to be another model in this perspective. The science and scientific inventions have strived to extinct superstitions and challenged the authority of the conjecture or interaction of morality, religion and law of the Church, because of the belief that science alone was the architect to change the destiny, because the Church was a big cipher for efficient government as it riddled with moral corruption. History affords testimony to it. It is a study of the model presented by the positivists who interpret the law-moral combine in altogether a different perception thus compounding the interstices. This model, in

15. John Finnis, Natural Law and Natural Rights, 1980; John Finnis (ed.), Natural Law, 1991.

most probability, seems to be the beginning of the jurisprudential developments of separation of law and morality that urged the minds of thinkers (legal and political), jurists, lawyers and legislators to part company with law and morality, and as such a new perception was conceived that law was what the sovereign willed law to be. Herein is the birth and origin of a new model of secularization of morality and its application to law. It is a study of the model of revivalism, and an in depth understanding of the modern model that presents the duty-obligation of those institutions of the government to have the continuum of law-moral interaction in the developed legal language of the present as a guide for the future innovations. In the backdrop of this development, it seems imperative to revisit to the debate of Natural Law as a *Festschrift* to find searching and perpetual answers to some of the baffling questions in a stifling situation, which asserts past perfect (in the unison of law and nature and law and morality), present imperfect (in the separation of law and morality as well as secularization of morality), and future indefinite (oscillation between the riddles of theses of positivists' and moralists' reasoning, rationality, scientific, common sense). This movement of natural law and its pilgrimage progress has to be revisited for some ends to meet.

What is natural law? The simple way to answer this ticklish question seems to be that natural law is a law that it provides a name for the point of intersection between law and morals.[16] In essence, the expression natural law or *jus naturale* was largely used in philosophical speculations of the Roman jurists of the Antonine age, and was intended to denote a system of rules and principles for the guidance of human conduct which, independently of enacted law or of the systems peculiar to any one people, might be discovered by the rational intelligence of man, and would be found to grow out of and conform to his nature, meaning by that word his whole mental, moral, and physical constitution. The point of departure for this conception was the Stoic doctrine of a life ordered "according to nature", which in its turn rested upon the purely supposititious existence, in primitive times, of a "state of nature"; that is, a condition of

16. A. Passerin D'Entreves, Natural Law, p. 116.

society in which men universally were governed solely by a rational and consistent obedience to the needs, impulses, and promptings of their true nature, such nature being as yet undefaced by dishonesty, falsehood, or indulgence of the baser passions. In ethics, it consists in practical universal judgments which man himself elicits. These express necessary and obligatory rules of human conduct which have been established by the author of human nature as essential to the divine purposes in the universe and have been promulgated by God solely through human reason. The inconclusive debate between 'is' and 'ought' has been extremely misunderstood, misconceived, misinterpreted and misconceptualised. But, *this tension of 'is' and 'ought' could have been prognostic had it been conceded that what naturally 'is', 'ought' to be, and this proposition may dispel many misgivings about natural law as a knot of law and nature, and law and morality.* Be that as it may, natural law has a chequered history; it is a history of natural turbulences. The history of natural law is the history of ancient and modern traditions of law as well as political theories of about four centuries. It is the history of antiquity, ancient past starting from Roman concept of natural law, middle age, and a constitutive part of the modern state and its notions beginning with the works of great modern philosophers as Thomas Hobbes, John Locke, Immanuel Kant, etc. who gave a rational theoretical frame for the state or nation-state. The models of natural law may succinctly be presented as follows.

1. Ancient Idea of Natural Law: Antiquity Idea of Innate

(a) This in brevity gives an account how natural law/law and morality traditions arose. The first general feature of natural law in the late antiquity was conceived as a set of innate rules, which the God engraved upon the heart of the human beings when He created mankind. Greek stoic philosophers had the speculation that a man who lived naturally was a man who lived by reason. This was natural order contrary to contrived order (artificial or man made). There was obviously superiority of natural order over contrived/artificial/man-made order. Natural order was indeed inherent and actual or potential. This speculation was the conjecture of nature, moral and human reasoning. *Epistle to the Romans* acknowledges the existence of a "written law in their Gentile hearts, which contains the same commandments as the revealed law.[17] Cicero's formulation of natural law philosophy *a proprio vigore* states natural law's three aspects, viz., universality and immutability, standing as a higher law, and discoverability by reason, that is enjoined in *De Re Publica*[18]:

> True law is right reason in agreement with Nature; it is of universal application, unchanging and everlasting. . . . It is not a sin to try to alter this law, nor is it allowable to attempt to repeal any part of it, and it is impossible to abolish it entirely. ...God is the author of this law, its promulgator, and its enforcing judge.

The Stoic view adopted by the Romans expressed by Cicero who recognized that laws which failed to conform to morals and reasons, might be regarded as invalid. It may be equated with the modern legal language of constitutional culture and constitutional morality, that is, any law that is incompatible with morals and reasons—constitutional culture and constitutional morality—is invalid. In this sense natural law seems to be a sort of first covenant between God and the mankind that promised salvation if the mankind worked in accordance with His Law, that is correct action and correct choice of mankind according to the morality and moral theory prescribed by His Will. Could it be conceived that natural law is a mode of thinking systematically about the connection between the cosmic order, morality and law. Epistemologically this offers to the correct and proper understanding of moral knowledge of law as well as the evolution of law and legal institutions. Early natural law

---

17. *Romans*, 2, pp. 14-15; for a critical analysis see Merio Scattoola, *op. cit.*, pp. 1-3; George C. Christie and Stephen E. Gottieb, *op. cit.*, note 33.
18. Book 3, Chapter 22, section 33; Stoicism or the foundation of the Stoic school of philosophy was named as such because it met in the Stoa of Athens (C. 320-250 B.C.); see also Brian Bix, A Dictionary of Legal Theory, 2004, pp. 142-144; Jean Porter, Nature as Reason a Thomistic Theory of the Natural Law, 2005; see also *Supra note 33*.

thinking—Sophists—can be seen in the legal language of those times *La loi naturelle, Das Naturrecht der Scholastik,, ius civile (*law of Romans for Romans*), ius gentium (*law of all people, i.e. law in relation to Romans and Non-Romans—people of other countries as well as nationality, e.g. slaves)*, ius naturale, justum acquumet bonum natura, de jure naturali et gentium juxta disciplinam ebraeorum.* It discerns that these were the important aspects of natural law in the early stages, and were further developed systematically by Plato (c. 429-347 B.C.); Aristotle (384-322 B.C.) [conceded that nature manifests a law or design by designing reasons. The natural order is associated with reason. They were grappled with a question whether law governed human behavior. Unequivocally, such a law governed in human nature. For them idea of justice is eternal and must be found in natural law.], and Cicero (106-43 B.C.).[19] It may further discern that in Stoic view 'natural law meant in accordance with reason'. The Romans adopted the approach as expressed by Cicero that laws which were incompatible with reason might be regarded as invalid. The Catholic Church Fathers also emphasized on the innate ideas of natural law. St. Augustine presented his view on natural law: "What are States without justice, but robber bands enlarged"?[20] His work begins: "*Lex scripta in cordibus hominum, quam nec ulla quidem delet iniquitas*" is well known to human beings and cannot be deleted at all from the human, viz., Mankind is governed by two laws: the law of nature and custom. The law of nature is contained in the scriptures and the gospel. Natural law overrides customs and constitutions. That which has been recognized by usage, or recorded in writing, if it contradicts natural law, is void and of no effect.[21]

(b) St. Thomas Aquinas (1225-74), a philosopher as well as theologian, was a leading exponent of natural law of thirteenth century who made a most rationally justification of natural law. It is believed that his rational justification of natural law

19. See Jean Porter, Nature as Reasons, *op. cit., George C. Christie and Stephen E. Gottieb, op. cit.*
20. City Of God, Book 4, iv.
21. See Merio Scattola, *op. cit.* p. 3; Raymond Wacks, *op. cit.*, p. 7; George C. Christie and Stephen E. Gottieb, *op. cit.*

influenced his followers in the medieval era—middle ages—who came to be known as Scholastics or Thomists; and it is also the belief that Aquinas still carries an influence on the modern thinkers of natural law known as revivalists or modernists. Aquinas in his distinguished work *Summa Theologiae* gives four distinct as well as distinguishing features of natural law as follows:

1. *Lex aeterna* (eternal law): Divine reason—known only to God. God's plan for the Universe. Man needs this law without which he would totally lack direction.
2. *Lex naturalis* (natural law): Participation of the eternal law in rational creatures discoverable by reason.
3. *Lex divina* (divine law): Revealed in the scriptures, viz., and God's positive law for mankind.
4. *Lex humana* (humanly posited law): Supported by reason; enacted for the common good of human beings; necessary because the *lex naturalis* cannot solve many day-to-day problems; and, people are selfish by nature; compulsion is required to force them to act reasonably.[22]

This seems to be the most comprehensive exposition of Aquinas' natural law that in unequivocal terms states that human posited law draws its power to bind from natural law, viz., participation of eternal law in rational creatures. In brevity, it appears Aquinas follows the models of Plato and Aristotle, and as such postulates 'a separate intellect that causes in us our own power of insight. Humans participate in natural law in the sense that as human beings we are able to grasp the essential principles of natural law, viz., and human nature's Creator's intelligent and intelligible plan for human flourishing. Man does not grasp it by any kind of direct knowledge of the divine mind, rather all those things to which man has a natural inclination, as a selfish man, one's reason naturally understands as good that to

22. *Summa Theologiae*, Part 2, 1st Part, questions 94, 96, articles 2, 4; see also Anthony J. Lisska, Aquinas's Theory of Natural Law: An Analytic Reconstruction, 1996; see also George C. Christie (pp. 127-187) and Stephen E. Gottieb (pp. 183-188), *op. cit.*

be pursued and their contraries as bad that to be avoided.[23] Thus, for Aquinas this postulate of law is binding on people's actions. Since people act according to their reason, therefore, their action must be regulated by reason when it commands. Aquinas' emphasis is on the good of the society as a whole and individuals' good must be subjugating to the societies good or community good. It seems to me that the seeds of this assertion may be seen in the *Vedic Rita* culture: *Sarve Bhawantu Sukhina Sarvey Santu Niramayya... We aspire for the good, happiness, prosperity as well as flourishing of the entire creatures of the Great Creator that include human beings, animals, natural habitat, whole environment, and above all the sustainability of the entire universe.* In the backdrop of this, it appears that Aquinas postulate of natural law is like this: Eternal law is the reason of the creator of all things and is revealed in the scriptures as Divine law; natural law represents the attributes of humans that allows them to make choices and follow their inclinations towards good; a man may use his reason to help himself progress, prosper as well as flourish; as a result people seek to reason practically as to how to attain individual good, community good, and society good. In sum and substance practical reasoning is human law. Besides, the end of natural law that is specific to human beings only is the social nature of man and his perpetual urge for the search of truth. And as such, as per Aquinas, human laws that are incompatible to natural law are corruptions of law that, as a consequence, is because of the imperfections of individual reason. Therefore, revelation is that such is the characteristics of human laws that lack the character of law that binds moral conscience. In the backdrop of this, one may look to his major contribution in natural law perspective is that Aquinas attributes to humans the ability to determine truth from falsehood by speculating reasoning; there are absolute moral values that we may not always see them does not, however, eliminate their truth; natural law precepts are inclinations, rather than the result of practical reasoning. The seeds of this assertion, to me, seem to be entrenched in *Vedic hymn: Tamso Maa Jyotirgamaya, Tamso Maa Sadgamaya : Lead me from darkness to light and from falsehood to*

23. *Ibid.*

ultimate truth. This conjecture of law and nature and law and morality needs *de novo* comprehension for the development of adapting fair means to reach fair ends in corruption ridden societies to bringing absolute transparency, accountability, and innovative political morality and political culture. However, there are difficulties and limitations of natural law to aspire to achieve such ends when invoked in an unjust society where human beings appear to convince us about the falsehood of their being intelligent as well as enlightened.

(c) Ten Commandments and Natural Law

This is the unique characteristic of natural law that corresponds to Ten Commandments engraved in Old Testament, which is the identity between Old Testament, Gospel and natural law, and nevertheless is a canonical tradition.[24] It has been exerted that the moral precepts of Ten Commandments are inherent in the Old Testament Law which concern good actions should accord with reason. It may seem that every rule of human reason derives from natural reason and this is in turn expressed by natural law. And as such, natural law and the Ten Commandments enjoin the contents of *lex naturae.*[25] Consequently, natural law is good because it alone is valid for the whole mankind. With this revelation, it may be asserted that human knowledge is insufficient to achieve salvation, and natural law alone can help to achieve the salvation, and as such natural law has to be revisited *de novo* with the Ten Commandments in order to recognize the true and the good with natural reason or natural will.[26] However, the darkness and the pride of the wicked minds of the wicked people fail to convince the convinced about the Law and Morality of the Ten Commandments Law which God revealed to Moses to follow to seek for a virtuous life, because the Old Testament Law was handed down between the law of nature and the law of grace.[27]

---

24. For critical analysis see Merio Scattola, *Before and After Natural Law, op. cit.*, pp. 4-5.
25. *Ibid.*
26. *Ibid.*
27. *Ibid.*

(d) Peculiarity of Plurality

Aquinas asks a searching question with utmost inquisitiveness whether the natural law contains just one precept or many precepts. The answer to this searching question seems hard because "everything searches for the good,"[28] and there is nothing pretentious about it. It depends upon the mores of time. All beings in the world aim at the good, prosperity, flourishing, happiness of self and of others, but how will human beings in the globe of the twenty first century would seek this that depends or suits the particular nature of the seeker. It cannot be concluded with a least stretch of imagination that the human beings of some part of the world only seek pleasure and no pain; human beings of some other part of the same world seek virtuous life; and human beings of some part of the same world seek to suffer from perpetual pains caused by man made strives as a consequence of global warming, environment degradation, militancy and terrorism, dictatorship and nepotism, corruptions, maladministration, bad governance, etc., rather human beings need to live in a society that search for their good, happiness, social harmony, virtuous life, prosperity, flourishing as well as nourishing, of course, with some soup and sauce. Without it is a solitary life and solitary life is nevertheless a solitary confinement.

(e) Universality and Universal Order

This model refers to the fact that ancient natural law is part of the universal order of the justice that governs the whole creation. However, the Scholastics and the Thomistics express different ideas inasmuch as that natural law partakes of eternal law that is of divine reason, which comprehends as well as prescribes the Universality and Universal Order. The Scholastics have made a distinction between God and Divine law, which also speaks about a distinction between God and the Divinity. How there could be a distinction between a God law and a

28. *Ibid;* see Thomas Aquinas, *op. cit.*

Divine law? Divinity seems to be the Grace of God, and Divine law emanates because of the Divinity of God, and the Cosmos—a world order or say Universal Order—is the creation with the Grace of His Divinity. For instance,

> *Sarva Dharma Sambhav or Vasudev Kutumbakam: signifies that the whole world is one or the whole world is with His Universal Order.* The distinction may be true from the Western point of view because of Catholic, Protestants, and German Calvinists perspectives, but, in the Indian perspectives the Law of God and the Divine Law there is distinguishing identification. How far the Western distinction between *lex naturae, humana and divina, lex Die, and lex aeterna* would achieve the ends of universality or universal order, rather which would defeat the basis of common heritage of mankind. Agreeing with the Scholastics point of view that good implies evil, virtue implies vice, command carries prohibition, order implies disorder, peace contains war and justice needs struggle, but the existence of a universal order or universality therefore makes possible the difference between good and bad governments.[29] Be that as it may, the ends of universality or universal order seem to be pursuit of justice where innocent person would not be condemned by an unjust judge.

In conclusion, it may be submitted that the precepts of natural law are with the same force and validity as all other rules of divine and human laws. It has also been argued that the failure of human law does not imply the disappearance of natural law.[30]

2. Medieval period and through the Renaissance

(a) Grotius and subsequent developments

Huig de Groot, or Hugo Grotius (1538-1645) as he is renowned, being a Dutch Protestant thinker is generally

29. *Ibid.*
30. *Ibid.*

associated with secularization of natural law. He advocates logical independence of natural law from Divine will. In his renowned work *De Jure Belli et Pacis* (1625) he *a multo fortiorari* states that even if God does not exist—*etiamsi daremus non esse Deum*—natural law would have the same content. His assertion is that irrespective of the existence of God, natural law holds good. For this, Grotius has been acclaimed a propounder of a purely secular philosophy of law, viz., dissociates natural law from its theological roots.[31] The assertion of Grotius is that man could reason, he could discover principles that are absolutely proper for all people. *De Jure Belli et Pacis*, asserts Grotius, is the proper or strict meaning of *jus or ius*, which is a moral quality found in the person that enables the person to have or to undertake something justly.[32] Vide this Grotius argues that a right is essentially something which a person has, and this quality becomes a power or a liberty, and as such relates exclusively to the beneficiary of just relationship.[33] Though this assertion carries the impetus of perplexity, but he has created a theory of law of nations that is built upon the principle of co-existence between sovereign nations. His former part of the assertion shows the impetus of developing Protestant thinking, and the later part of the assertion is a significant one developing the mutual inclusiveness amongst the sovereign nations, which seems to be the workable empirical hypothesis in the present scenario of the world where powerful inclines to overpower the non-declared powerful thereby creating a wedge between the sermon of co-existence and the practice of co-existence.

---

31. See Michael Bertram Crowe, The Changing Profile of the Natural Law, 1977, p. 223. Whether Grotius himself has the intension to be a secular philosopher or not rather an interpretation seems to have been fostered by his successors is not easily decided; Michael Bertram Crow, *The Impious Hypothesis: a Paradox in Hugo Grotius*, in Knud Haakonssen, (ed.), *op. cit.*, 3 *et al.; Grorgr C. Christie and Stephen E. Gottieb, op. cit.*
32. See Anthony J. Lisska, Aquinas's Theory of Natural Law an Analytic Reconstruction, 1996, pp. 231-232.
33. *Ibid.*

(b) Natural Law in Political Philosophy: Hobbes, Locke, Rousseau and Kant

Their theories are not jurists' theses, but are political thoughts based on "social contractarian" theories, which conceive of political rights and obligations in terms of a "social contract". This contract is not an agreement in lieu of some consideration, but this thought of "social contract" contains the idea that only with his consent can a person be subjected to the political power of another. This liberal thought can be seen in the American Declaration of Independence of 1776 against British colonial rule, which is based on an appeal to the "natural rights" of all Americans and directed to "life, liberty and the pursuit of happiness". In the language of the Declaration: "We hold these truths to be self-evident, that all men are created equal, and that they are endowed by their Creator with certain unalienable rights". Unequivocally, the similar stirring sentiments about "natural rights" of mankind have been expressed in the French declaration and her constitution of 1779—*droits de l'homme et du citoyen*. The rights, basic rights, natural rights, fundamental rights are now the concern of these political thinkers who are called as "social contractarians" and carry impetus in the legal regime. These political thinkers are Hobbes, Locke, Rousseau and Kant who looked to the concept of natural law as a way of justifying minimum principles of rights in their social contract theories. Thomas Hobbes (1588-1679) said that natural law teaches us the need for self-preservation, viz., law and government are required if we are to protect order and security.[34] According to Hobbes' 'social contract' thesis an 'orderly society' is above natural rights of men, and, therefore, men may have to surrender their natural rights/freedoms in order to create an orderly society.[35] Hobbes' thesis has been labeled as an "authoritarian philosophy" that places order above justice, because this shows the undermining the legitimacy of revolutions against authoritarianism/nepotism/dictatorship/ authoritarian-democracy.[36] It may be conceded that every human

34. See Raymond Wacks, *op. cit.; Michael Doherty, op. cit.*
35. *Ibid.*
36. *Ibid.*

action is acknowledged with essential selfishness, which is the consequence of competition (for limited supply of material possessions), distrust, and glory (we remain hostile in order to preserve our powerful reputations), and as a consequence propensity towards disagreement minus the berth of morality and the cause for living in constant fear, violence, danger of violent death, and war, and as such the "life of people, solitary, poor, nasty, brutish, and short."[37] In order to overcome this horror state of affairs, Hobbes concludes that in the clash-reflection of self-interest and social contract "peace is the first law of nature."[38] Hobbes' second law of nature is that we mutually divest ourselves of certain rights in order to achieve peace and this mutual transferring of rights is a contract and is the basis of moral duty. Hobbes derives his law of nature deductively from a set of general rules, viz., that people pursue only their own self-interest; the equality of people; the causes of quarrel; the natural condition of war; and the motivations for peace. And, from the deduction of these general principles, Hobbes third law of nature is, without any illusion, that merely concluding agreements can secure peace. This assertion of Hobbes carries a weight in the modern developments in the international arena, could the peace be secured by merely concluding agreements there could be no war, no strife, no turbulence with which some parts of the globe are grappled with. This happens, as a consequence, because of the breach of mutual social contracts due to the self-interests or selfishness. Hobbes' fourth law of nature is that morality consists entirely of these three laws of nature which are arrived at through the social contacts, and which may have a message in the present turbulent world scenario.[39]

John Locke (1632-1704) is critical of Hobbes thesis of social contract and calls it a mere nightmare.[40] Locke sees no problem with the life of the people before the origin and birth of social contract thesis, because life before the social contract was a 'total bliss' except for one flaw concerning the adequate protection of

---

37. *Ibid.*
38. *Ibid.*
39. *Ibid.*
40. Two Treatises of Civil Government and for a critical comment see *Ibid.*

man's right to property. Otherwise, as a strong reminiscent of Aquinas's postulates, it was an 'idyllic natural state'. What did Hobbes see the reasons that man forfeited some of his freedom? It may be naïve to submit that Hobbes seemed to be a sycophant of the government and its authority that it did not allow a dissent either in the form of expression or agitation or revolution against its misrule. Misrule sees justification in its order of management/governance howsoever corrupt it might be. Therefore, Locke, as a strong inheritor of Aquinas, reiterates that man adequately enjoys his rights and obligations under God WHO has given the man to enjoy.[41] Social contract thesis, according to Locke, is complex and fairly fails to explain man's rights and obligations including the right to property.

Be that as it may, Locke's thesis contains two important precepts conveying the inner meaning. First precept relates to its revolutionary nature. When a government is unjust or authoritarian, the oppressed people have the right to resist tyranny and overthrow the government, because a 'tyrant has no authority' to continue to rule. Second precept relates to man's right to property. God owns the earth and has given it to us to enjoy; there can therefore be no right of property. But if a man by his labour/work acquires some material objects (*res*), the worker/labourer acquires the right to the thing/object (*res*) he has created by his labour. This right over the thing/object/*res* is called the right of private ownership—the framers of the American constitution and the Indian constitution recognized this. Locke is hailed as the source of the idea of 'private ownership' and vilified as the progenitor of 'modern capitalism'.[42]

Consequently, it discerns that the state exists to preserve the natural rights of its citizens, and certainly cannot subjugate or infringe or oppress their rights as an oppressor or tyrant or dictator. Therefore, for Locke, when governments fail in the task of preserving the natural rights of its citizens, citizens have the right, and even the duty as well as obligation, to withdraw their

41. *Ibid.*
42. *Ibid.*

support and rebel.[43] In the backdrop of this, Locke rejects Hobbes' nature of state as nasty, brutish, short, solitary, and poor. Whereas, Locke asserts that we should not harm each other in life, liberty, or possession (property, private ownership). It may be submitted that Locke's theory seems to be convincing to the conceivers as well as framers of constitutional culture and constitutional morality, Human Rights, and Humanitarian Law enjoining rights, fundamental rights, basic rights since the ultimate end is the pursuit of human happiness. In order to achieve these ends, Locke has espoused a limited form of government, which functions with checks and balances among branches of government having genuine representation in the legislature that would minimize government and maximize individual liberty.

Jean-Jacques Rousseau (1712-1778) is an originator of the idea of "general will". He is oscillating between Hobbes and Locke. His conception rests on the idea that *social contract* represents an agreement between the individual and the community by which he becomes part of the "general will", viz., there are certain natural rights that cannot be removed, but by investing the "general will" with the total legislative authority, the law could infringe/remove these rights.[44] This unequivocally conveys that so long the government represents the "general will" it may do anything in infringing upon man's rights. Rousseau's perception, in this way, contains two faces of the same coin. On the one hand, he believes in 'participatory democracy', and, on the other hand, he has no inhibitions to invest the legislature/government with 'untrammeled power' under the influence of the "general will" that is nothing but voluntary subjection of individual to the 'will of the elected government of democracy'. It may be trite to submit that he is contrite of contrived ideologue, a paradox, a hypocrite, viz., "a democrat and yet a totalitarian".[45]

Besides, the vocabulary of 'natural law ethics' has vehemently been used very widely by Immanuel Kant (1724-

43. *Ibid.*
44. *Ibid.*
45. *Ibid.*

1804), a German philosopher, whose innovations in ethics work out a truly revolutionary philosophical ethics. He makes the concept of moral law basic and defies other moral concepts in terms of it. He sees humans as desiring and needing one another's company and support yet at the same time resisting social control and tending to unlimited self-aggrandizement. Nature brings about the development of human capacities by means of mutual antagonism in society. Kant says that by "antagonism I mean the unsocial sociability of men, i.e., their propensity to enter into society, bound together with a mutual opposition which constantly threatens to break up the society. Man has an inclination to associate with others. ...But he also has a strong propensity to isolate himself from others, because he finds in himself...the unsocial characteristic of wishing to have everything to go according to his own wish." (Kant: Idea for a Universal History). This shows Kant's assertions about the empirical aspects of human nature rather than building notions in abstract science that is non-empirical. This understanding of Kant has been due to the obvious reasons: "When Kant came on the scene, it had become the ruling tendency in Germany to derive not only morality but religion and Christianity from the principle of happiness. Everyone started with the natural drive to happiness and found in it a guide to all duties and virtues." (Knud Haakonssen). Kant let his dissatisfaction known through a revolution in the philosophical investigation of morality, and as such found his innovative empirical inroad in the natural law ethics. Kant has developed a theory of knowledge, which seeks to replace metaphysics with an explanation of knowledge based upon the thinking about our experience, viz., our understanding of *a priori* knowledge is limited to things we can actually experience. Therefore, through *posteriori* we can prove the facts or refute the facts and show them to be false, and can draw some inferences empirically/heuristically. Kant's natural law ethics seems in a quite different way 'justice as a virtue':

> Justice is the charity of the wise.
> Charity is general benevolence.
> Benevolence is the habit of love.
> To love anyone is to delight in his happiness.

> Wisdom is the science of happiness.
> Happiness is durable joy.
> Joy is a state of pleasure.
> Pleasure . . . is a sense of perfection.
> (Gottfried Wilhelm Leibniz, Ethical Definitions)

3. The Fall and Decline of Natural Law: Legal Positivism and Non-Cognitivism in Ethics

The rise of "legal positivism" and "non-cognitivism in ethics" are the major causes for the decline and fall of natural law, which indeed may be considered an unfortunate development. This is a period of legal positivism that is understood as the conceptual separation of law and morality. Legal positivism is opposed to natural law or conceptual relationship between law and morality thesis that 'natural law theory, a tradition of thinking about morality which goes back many centuries, and in which there are established ways of considering the implications for how we should act morally as law-makers, or as citizens facing legal rules'. Contrived criticisms like fallacy, whim, convention, mere fiction and fashion of natural law seem to be considered views of legal positivists responsible for the natural decline and fall of natural law. These attacks have chiefly been made by Bentham, Austin, Kelsen, and Hart and host of others. The common denominator among these positivists is that there is no essential/necessary/significant connection between law and morals, viz., the law as laid down (*positum* is : expositorial in Bentham's language) should be kept separate from the law as it ought morally (censorial : in Bentham's language) to be.[46] In the opinion of the positivists there seems to be an identifiable distinction between "ought" (which is morally desirable) and "is" (this actually exists). However, it seems to be the fallacy and jealousy of the legal positivists who unnecessarily created a fiction of natural law. What we may have to concede is that a positive law is unjust if it is incompatible with morals—natural law. The legal positivists may have to acknowledge that "natural law seeks to

---

46. See Raymon Wacks, *op. cit.*, p. 43.

find a coherent theory that will purge us of unjust legal systems. Just as quack medicine lacks scientific justification, unjust law lacks moral justification. This does not mean necessarily that neither works".[47] Had it been so simple there ought to have been no conviviality between positivists and non-positivists?

Be that as it may, there seems to be a conceptual difference between law and morality connections, because the emergence of positivism has been as a contrived reaction to the naturalistic fallacy. Jeremy Bentham (1748-1832) with his combination of 'a fly's eye for detail, with an eagle's eye for illuminating generalization'[48] constructed a comprehensive theory of law, logic, politics and psychology found on the principle of utility.[49] He develops his comprehensions because of apprehensions about the manner in which the common law has been explained. Common law, according to Bentham, is the law of immemorial custom, Judge and Co., lawyers' language incomprehensible to the layman, perpetuated in the name of precedent, which is not the justified expression of community needs and interests.[50] Bentham's quest has been for determinacy, and in his search of determinacy, he regards both common law and natural law ideas as dangerous fallacies. He believes that determinacy in law is from practice perspectives, rather than theory, and as such appeal to the law of nature is nothing more than 'private opinion in disguise' or 'the mere opinion of men, self-constituted into legislatures', 'contrary to reasons', and 'the mask of legal fictions'.[51] He, therefore, asserts that 'codification of laws (civil and criminal)', and nothing short of that, can only bring

47. See in particular Michael Doherty, *op. cit.*, p. 155.
48. H.L.A. Hart, Essays on Bentham, pp. 4 and 29.
49. Bentham's works, Of Laws in General, 1782, and An Introduction to the Principles of Morals and Legislation.
50. *Ibid.* Bentham ridiculed precedent as "dog law, which is nothing but a superstitious respect for antiquity ensures that senseless decisions of the past are repeated in the future, whenever your dog does anything you want to break him, you wait till he does it, and then beat him for it. This is the way you make laws for your dog; and this is the way the judges make law for you and me". Quoted in Postema, Bentham and the Common Law Tradition, 270-278.
51. Postema, *op. cit.*, p. 277.

determinacy, and also cure the fallacies created by common law as well as law and morals.

> A man need but open the book in order to inform himself what the aspect borne by the law bears to every imaginable act that can come within the possible sphere of human agency: what acts it is his duty to perform for the sake of himself, his neighbour or the public: what acts he has a right to do, what other acts he has a right to have others perform for his advantage. ...In this one repository the whole system of the obligations which either he or any one else is subject to are recorded and displayed to view.[52]

Though, because of his codification of laws assertion, Bentham may have been termed as Luther of legal positivism,[53] but unfortunately his idea could not flourish in his realm of common law systems. He may have been perceived as an ideologue of fallacy or fashion or fiction!

John Austin (1790-1859), another legal positivist thinker, was the disciple of Bentham, a friend as well as follower of James Mill and John Stuart Mill, and a true subject of the political system of his times conceived as well as conceptualized on the idea of "commands or imperatives."[54] In his conception positive law—law of/by man for man—is the only concern of law, and this positive law is a command or imperative to which there has to be adherence as well as habitual obedience, and man has to subject to this command or imperative. In Austin's perception there is no place of morals in the domain of law; law and morals are separate. His positive morality is different because that does not address that there exists relationship between Laws of Man and Laws of God. Does it mean that Austin's perception of law could be perceived as control over human behaviour—deviant or recidivist! Austin's conception of law seems to be the explanation of law and power (political) relationship in the

52. Bentham, Of Laws in General, quoted in Postema, *op. cit.*, p. 423, and Raymond Wacks, *op. cit.*, pp. 49-50.
53. H.L.A. Hart, Essays on Bentham, *op. cit.*, p. 29.
54. John Austin, Province of Jurisprudence Determined, 1832; C.K. Allen, Law in the Making.

language of commands or imperatives. Be that as it may, Austin has strived to construct the science of law rather than the art of legislation as Bentham has done.[55] Austin perceives law as a command of the sovereign and if there is disobedience to such command there is the notion of sanctions, which works as a threat or punishment against those who are in the habit of disobeying the command. Austin's notion of law contains three key concepts "command", "sovereign", and "sanctions". This concept of Austin has been a cause of criticism: "Who issues command When for Whom with What Authority (Will) and for What Purpose? This riddle seems to be inasmuch as mysterious as riding while saddling the artificial horse. Therefore, law seems to be portrayed as an artificial creation of human society, which may be nothing but an abstract entity.

Hans Kelsen (1881-1973), another legal positivist, has to be comprehended with pain and suffering because of the use of difficult as well as abstract conceptual *lingua fauna—norms and Grundnorm*—of Continental systems that is not so congenial to common law followers. Nevertheless his thesis is a recipe for legal knowledge through anew legal language.[56] Kelsen is a legitimate legal positivist since he insists on the separation of law and morals, what 'is' (*sein*) and what 'ought to be' (*sollen*).[57] Kelsen argues that for the understanding of law we may have to conceive it to be a system of 'oughts' or 'norms'. He further espouses that the law consists not merely of norms, but is made up of legal norms and legal acts as determined by these norms.[58] Legal norms, he opines, when acted upon describe actual human conduct.[59] He acknowledges that to understand 'the law' we require the application of certain formal categories of time and space, in particular the *Grundnorm* or the basic norm which lies

55. W. Morison, John Austin, p. 47 quoted in Raymond Wack, *op. cit.*, and p. 55.
56. Tur and Twining, *infra*, pp. 149-183, at p. 157.
57. Hans Kelsen, Pure Theory of Law; General Theory of Law and State.
58. *Ibid;* General Theory of Law and State, p. 39.
59. *Ibid;* see also Tur and Twining (eds.), Essays on Kelsen, pp. 23-24. Because of the use of the expression human conduct, Kelsen has been criticized as 'sterile', that is, his work is having no productive results.

at the heart of the legal system.[60] He perceives an unadulterated positive law by excluding the impurities of morality, history, politics, sociology, etc. He *a multo fortiorari* states that in order to arrive at a scientific theory of law, we need to restrict our analysis to the 'norms' of positive law only. He rules out the probabilities of all that cannot help to understanding the law objectively, viz., social purpose of law, its political function, because law has only one function, that is the monopolization of force. In Kelsen's words law can be disinfected from the elements of psychology, sociology, ethics, and political:

> This adulteration is understandable, because (these) disciplines deal with subject-matters that are closely connected with law. The pure theory of law undertakes to delimit the cognition of law against these disciplines, not because it ignores or denies the connection, but because it wishes to avoid the uncritical mixture of methodologically different disciplines . . . which obscures the essence of the science of law and obliterates the limits imposed upon it by the nature of its subject-matter.[61]

Kelsen also unhesitatingly explains his concept of 'norms', which means that 'something', 'ought to be' or 'ought to happen', especially that a human being ought to behave in a specific way. A norm, in order to be valid, that is, binding, must be authorized by another norm which, in turn, is authorized by a higher norm in the system, viz., *Grundnorm*.'[62] He unequivocally states that the separation between law and morality means that the validity of legal norms can flow only from another legal, as opposed to a moral norm.[63] Kelsen represents that there is a hierarchy of legal norms that forms a legal system, which is ultimately traced back to the basic norm called as *Grundnorm* of the legal system. By hierarchy of norms he means a complex

60. *Supra* 73. Kelsen uses the phrase 'application of certain formal categories of time and space' as a follower of the eighteenth century great philosopher Immanuel Kant
61. Pure Theory of Law, *op. cit.*, pp. 1, 4, 47.
62. *Ibid.*
63. *Ibid.*

series of interlocking norms which progress from the most general 'oughts' to the most particular or the concrete or higher norm: *Grundnorm*, viz., sanctions ought to be effectuated in accordance with the constitution. Be that as it may, Kelsen's definition of positive law through his model of 'norms' and '*Grundnorm*' may be acceptable to his continental system of conceptual framework, but, because of the complexity of norms and *Grundnorm* interlocking his theory inevitably fails to have convincing acceptability of the new legal order. Norms and *Grundnorm* may have beautiful landscape, but hardly any persuasive acceptability because Kelsen does not appear to have developed the positivism of positivists like Bentham and Austin.[64]

H.L.A. Hart (1907-92), a legal positivist, is a blend of analytical and linguistic conjecture philosophy to the study of law. Hart as a legal positivist, in his work *The Concept of Law* (1961 and revised ed. 1994), gives his clear *seriatim* as well as illuminated meanings to the "understanding of law, coercion, and morality as different but related social phenomena".[65] As a legal positivist, he denies any conceptual relationship between law and morality.[66] Though Hart recognizes the 'minimum content of natural law' or the 'core of indisputable truth' in the 'doctrines of natural law' by acknowledging that law is a social phenomenon; it can only be understood and explained by reference to the actual social practices of a community; there is a necessity for rules (moral/ethical) which protect persons and property; and in order to survive and sustain as a community certain rules (moral/ethics) must exist as a consequence of the human condition, but he is certainly not accepting any conceptual relationship between law and morality, or saying that law is derived from morals.[67] He only acknowledges the penumbrae of meanings in 'minimum content of natural law'. Hart unequivocally severs positivism from utilitarianism

---

64. See Joseph Raz critique, The Concept of a Legal System, and The Authority of Law; J.W. Harris, Law and Legal Science.
65. The Concept of Law, Preface; H.L.A. Hart, *Legal Positivism and the Separation of Law and Morals*, 71, Harv. L. Rev., 593 (1958).
66. *Ibid.*, p. 112.
67. *Ibid.*, pp. 55-56, 80, 89, 255, 105-106, 110, 112, 94, 34.

(Bentham) and command (Austin). He opines that law is more than the decree of a 'gunman', a command backed by a sanction. His 'Rule of recognition' is the 'fundamental constitutional rule of a legal system, acknowledged by those officials who administer the law as specifying conditions or criteria of validity which certify whether or not a rule is indeed a rule.'[68] Five different meanings may discern from Hart's positivism.[69]

1. Positivists view valid laws as the expression of the wills of human people, as opposed to the manifestation of any greater purpose, such as Divine will.
2. There is, for positivists, no necessary link between law and morality. This does not mean that positivism denies that law should be moral.
3. The analysis of legal concepts is deemed by positivism as distinct from other disciplines such as sociology, anthropology and history. The identification of legally valid laws is thus perfectly possible without reference to morality.
4. As a result, positivists' law is a closed system of logic and therefore all legal decisions are deducible from posited legal rules and require no external justifications of a moral or social nature.
5. Positivism, of a different sort, 'moral positivism', claims that moral judgments cannot be objectively verified by indicating demonstrable facts. Legal positivists deny that there are objective moral values.

In the backdrop of the above postulates, it may clearly discern that the distinguishing distinction between positivism and natural law is that positivism expresses that the concept of law is simply what the legal system in a given society recognizes as law, whereas naturalism considers law to be an ideal, commonly shared by human societies irrespective of the variance of moral values. The critics assert that positivism though cannot ignore the normative nature of law, but certainly

---

68. *Ibid.*
69. H.L.A. Hart, *Positivism and the Separation of Law and Morality*, Harvard Law Review, 1958, 593; see George C. Christie and Patrick H. Martin, *op. cit.*, pp. 690-707.

do not regard this as a moral premise, rather this can be a mere social technique.[70] Therefore, Hart's 'minimum content of natural law' seems to be an acknowledgement in silence of conceptual relationship between law and morality.

In concluding discussion on the decline and fall of natural law some basic assumptions still remain perplex because no convincing answers could be presented by non-naturalists. The positivists could have been happy with an ostensible smile on their faces seeing the death knell of natural law or complete evaporation of conceptual relationship between law and morality. Can man survive or sustain without morals? Are arguments of positivists convincing by withering law and nature, and law and morals linkage? Has natural law absolutely been eclipsed? It may be with modesty submitted that positivists' transience approach could not transgress natural law from the domain of law. Had it been so, why a wave of transformation with innovative metamorphosis thinking could have revived natural law not as a love for a sage or a specific intellectual spiritual exercise, but a transcendental as well as civil consciousness for renewed civility in law to the survival and sustainability of human beings facing the hostility of challenges.

4. Revivalism and Modernization of Natural Law—renewed renaissance and enlightenment

Natural law could neither be defaced nor defiled irrespective of the endeavourers to perceive the complete divorce of law from morals. Had it been so there could have been absolute chaos. It survives and sustains because of new enlightenment in perceptions. Therefore, it is imperative to have the comprehension of 'new enlightenment in perceptions' to a revival or reawakening or modernization of natural law concept. The under mentioned factors may seem to be the responsible factors for this wondrous evolution.

70. See Kramer, In Defence of Legal Positivism, 1999; Capps, Being Positive about Positivism, 2000; Guest, Why the Law is Just, 2000; Dyzenhaus, Positivism's Stagnant Research Programme, 2000.

- The natural law theory of Fuller, Finnis, and a German scholar Samuel Pufendroff, and justice in the sense of 'delinquent state', that is Gustav Radbruch as a staunch legal positivist during the era 'horrors of the Nazi regime' and his emergence as a 'naturalist moralist' associated in the drafting of the Basic Law of Germany.
- The post-world war recognition of new ways of looking at human rights where human rights obligations attach both to state and non-state actors. Human rights and their innovative expressions—'imperatives of rule of law to serve rule of life'—in the Charter of the United Nations, Universal Declaration of Human Rights, International Covenants, CEDAW, Delhi Declaration of 1959, emergence of new constitutional culture and constitutional morality as a common standard of achievement of human dignity as well as human rights working as a yardstick to measure the validity of positive law affecting rights, human rights, basic rights, fundamental rights or freedoms.
- The impetus of International Military Tribunal known as Nuremberg war trials which established the principle that certain acts constituted crimes against humanity. The judges in these trials 'crimes against humanity' have not explicitly appealed to natural law theory, but their judgments nevertheless represent the recognition of the principle that the law is not necessarily the sole determinant of what is right, but what it ought to be.
- The horrors of militancy or terrorism and its impact on internally displaced persons as to their human dignity, human rights to survive and sustain.
- Human right to 'fair trial' and impact of International Criminal Tribunal for the Former Yugoslavia.
- The developments of new constitutional culture safeguarding the human or civil or fundamental or basic rights in various jurisdictions of the globe with innovative judiciary as well as judges particularly the United States of America's Supreme Court, Supreme Court of India, and the Constitutional Court of Germany.

- Impact of new international culture such as liberalization, globalization, WTO.
- Impact of International Administrative Law against the recidivist of administrative deviant behavior; information technology; transparency, accountability, and sustainable governance where no one is stranger in the world and law operates 'law as just means to reach just ends'.
- Natural law is natural and as such infallible as well as inextricable.

Lon L. Fuller (1902-1978) is known for his 'inner morality of law' what is sometimes called a 'procedural natural law theory'—a view that focuses on the morality implicit in governance through legal rules. He asserts that there is a necessary conceptual connection between law and morality. He urges that law has an 'inner morality, and that a legal system is the purposive enterprise of subjecting human conduct to the governance of rules'.[71] Fuller espouses this as a sharp reaction to Hart arising out of a decision of a post-war West German Court known as The Nazi Informer case.[72] Under the Third Reich the wife of a German in 1944, desiring to be rid of her husband, denounced him to the Gestapo for insulting remarks he had made about Hitler's conduct of the war. He was tried and sentenced to death, but his sentence was converted to service as a soldier on the Russian front. After the ceasing of the hostilities of the war and the restoration of democracy in Germany with a new blend of Basic Rights, the wife was prosecuted in 1949 for procuring her husband's loss of liberty. She failed to sustain her defence that her husband was convicted for the offence that he had committed under the Nazi statute of 1934. The West German Court nevertheless convicted her on the ground that the statute under which the husband had been punished offended the sound conscience and sense of justice of all decent human

71. Lon L. Fuller, The Morality of Law, p. 39; see George C. Christie and Patrick H. Martin, *op. cit.*, pp. 214-222.
72. (1959) 71 Harvard Law Review, 593, and 630.

beings.[73] The moral of this citation is that Fuller refuses to regard the law of the Third Reich as a law, and Hart refutes Fuller urging that Nazi law of 1934 was a valid law as it fulfilled the requirements of the 'rule of recognition'. However, Fuller contends that Nazi law was a drifted law, the drift of the recidivist deviant, since far from morality and, therefore, failed to qualify as law, and as such the decision of the West German court was in right perspective of 'sound conscience and sense of justice of all decent human beings'. Fuller identifies eight kinds of legal excellence towards which a system of rules may strive to comprehend since they are the 'inner morality of law', viz., (1) Generality, (2) Promulgation, (3) Non-retroactivity, (4) Clarity, (5) Non-contradiction, (6) Possibility of compliance, (7) Constancy, and (8) Congruence between declared rule and official action. It discerns that Fuller concedes a 'procedural natural law approach' instead of a 'substantive natural law' approach. How far unjust laws of dictatorship regime or apartheid practices be treated? Would *Lex injusta non est lex* (an unjust law is not law) be essentially a sufficient answer to be satisfied?

Be that as it may, Radbruch, a German jurist, asserts that a law could not be legally valid unless it has passed the tests contained in the formal criteria of legal validity of the system, and it does not contravene basic principles of morality.[74] For Radbruch, there seems conceptual relationship between law and morality. Therefore, according to Radbruch, every lawyer and judge must denounce statutes that contravene 'basic principles of morality' not just as immoral, but as 'not having any legal

---

73. See 1934 Act that amended the Constitution of the German Reich permitting Hitler to issue decrees inconsistent with the Constitution. Hart supports it as a positive law and Fuller opposes it as opposed to all canons of morality, and as opines that what was wrong then could not be conceded a wrong now. A wrong decision of then cannot be conceded morally as well as legally right now. This is the contentious bane between Hart and Fuller. For an account of this case see Raymond Wacks, *op. cit.*, 153-155; Michael Doherty, *op. cit.*, pp. 159-161.

74. Radbruch, G., Introduction to Legal Philosophy, 1947. As quoted in Michael Doherty, *op. cit.*, pp. 159-161.

character'.[75] Radbruch's conception of law is born out of the sad experiences he encountered during Nazi regime and he encapsulates that Nazi laws were deemed to be void because those were contrary to morality.[76] Though Radbruch's concept has been criticized as 'too crude a way with delicate and complex moral issues',[77] and defended on the principle of *nulla poena sine lege* (no punishment without law, that is, if you are acting within the law at any given time then it should not be later declared that what you were doing was against the law), but shall be a matter of many more perplexities if Nuremberg or Tokyo or Yugoslavia trials are put to question. Evil, whether lesser or bigger, is an evil, and there can't be a choice amongst the evils.

John Finnis (1940-) is a scholar of 'restatement of natural law'. He revisits classical natural law with seven 'basic goods or forms of human flourishing' combined with nine 'basic requirements of practical reasonableness', and together these encapsulate the universal entrenched and immutable 'principles of natural law'.[78] His seven postulates of 'basic forms of human flourishing' are life, knowledge, play, aesthetic experience, sociability (friendship), practical reasonableness, and religion; his nine postulates of 'basic requirements of practical reasonableness' are the active pursuit of goods, a coherent plan of life, no arbitrary preference among persons, detachment and commitment, the limited relevance of consequences: efficiency within reason, respect for every basic value in every act, the requirements of the common good, and following one's conscience. Finnis strives to rebuild the edifice of natural law on these foundations. Finnis suggests that the moral success or failure of a law should not be at the mercy of lawyers' test language whether it is law, because

75. *Ibid.*
76. *Ibid.*
77. *Ibid.*
78. John Finnis, Natural Law and Natural Rights, 1980; John Finnis, Natural Law, Vols. I and II, 1991; see George C. Christie and Patrick H. Martin, *op. cit.*, pp. 193-214.

Lawyer's Law Language
Is the comprehension
Of
Apprehensions
Of
Law
Judge and Co.
Lawyer's language
Perpetuates in the name of precedent
Incomprehensible to a layman
Not the justified
Expression
Of
Community needs and interests.

What Finnis is suggesting is to understand as well as comprehend 'what is really good for human persons'; what expectations there are of law; what moral expectations are made of it.[79] Finnis urges that the legal system must satisfy, if not fully but to some extent, the common requirements of human good.[80] There are no precise yardsticks for assessing 'the common requirements of human good', because that varies from society to society and from time to time.[81] What Finnis is striving to convey is that these cannot be aspired to achieve in vacuum, but to achieve the purpose of these ends we require a 'community', and as such he urges that 'unjust laws are not simply nullities, but—because they militate against the common good—lose their direct moral authority to bind'.[82] His recipe is, therefore, integration of several absolute obligations with correlative absolute natural rights aiming at preventing any form of injustice, and has the following seamless web.

> There is, I think, no alternative but to hold in one's mind's eye some pattern, or range of patterns, of human character, conduct, and interaction in community, and then to choose such specification of rights as tends to favor the pattern, or

---

'd.

'.

> range of patterns. In other words, one needs some conception of human good, of individual flourishing in a form (or range of forms) of communal life that fosters rather than hinders such flourishing. One attends not merely to character types desirable in the abstract or in isolation, but also to the quality of interaction among persons; and one should not seek to realize some patterned 'end-state' imagined in abstraction from the processes of individual initiative and interaction, processes which are integral to human good and which make the future, let alone its evaluation, incalculable.[83]

This is the essence of Finnis's conceptualization of natural law and natural rights that, *inter alia,* also encapsulates the right not be tortured, not to have one's life taken as a means to any further end to achieve, not to be tried unfairly, not to be lied to, not to be condemned on fallacious or fictitious charges, not to be deprived of one's capacity to procreate, and the right to be taken into respectful consideration in any assessment of what the common good requires.[84] Finnis's restatement of natural law may precisely be presented that these principles are not deducible or inferred from mere speculations about human nature or about the nature of good and evil, or from a teleological conception of nature, rather they are inherent or inbuilt, viz., (1) Natural law posits that the act of positing law should be guided by moral principles in order to have coherent standards of legislation; (2) moral principles are derived, with practical reasonableness, from objective principles and not from subjective whim or fancy or custom; and (3) Law itself, its structure and its institutions is justified by moral norms.[85] Be that as it may, Finnis's revisit to natural law is that law conceptually cannot and should not be separated from morality, and moral evaluation seems to be central to understanding law. Succinctly, a valuable insight into Finnis's work unfolds the significance of moral issues, which sufficiently as well as articulately reveal the sterility and aridity

83. *Id.*, pp. 219-220.
84. *Id.*, p. 225.
85. See Michael Doherty, *op. cit.*, pp. 174-176; Raymond Wacks, *op. cit.*, pp. 29-31.

of minds of positivists who unreasonably endeavoured to marginalize the importance of moral issues in relation to law. Morals and law are integral part of each other inasmuch as an integral part of living a good life. Bix, a modern natural law scholar, articulates the importance of moral issues in positing law as follows:

> Law plays a role within Finnis's moral theory, in that there are certain common goods that are best obtained through the specific kind of social coordination that law offers., and there is a sense in which participation in the community and in the common good of building a (political) community is an integral part of living a good life. ... One cannot fully understand a reason-giving activity like law without the (moral) evaluation of what it would mean for the official statements and enactments to give citizens a good reason for action.[86]

This unequivocally shows that there is an internal connection between law and morality, which carries decisive reasons for action, viz., law is backed by decisive reasons for action or compliance, and that also makes law binding for its assertive role with respect to the common good of the community.[87] If one does not have decisive reason to comply with the dictate of law, then it entails that the dictate of such law is not law, for it is either immoral or unjust or unethical.

There seems some perceptible change in the perception of scholars and thinkers for the conceptual continuity of law and morals relationship. This move of continuity seems to create some sort of rapprochement between naturalists and legal positivists, because the legal positivists have almost rejected natural law, that is, rejection of conceptual relationship between law and morals. This model of continuity is not for the sake of ostentatious or pretentious rapprochement because of arid

---

86. Bix, Natural Law: The Modern Tradition, 2002, pp. 88-89; Bix, *On the Dividing Line between Natural Law Theory and Legal Positivism*, 75 (2000) Notre Dame Law Review, 1613.
87. See Mark C. Murphy, Natural Law in Jurisprudence and Politics, 2006, pp. 1-24, p. 1, 9.

behaviour and the scant regard the legal positivists have shown towards naturalists. This movement is with some basic assumptions that natural law has given the modern state a rational framework. It is not a question of love for antiquity and obscure as well as skeptics about the progress of modern state scientifically and technologically. It is a question of continuity of modernity with the scales or variables of morality which are the basic foundations of the frame of the Nation-State where the 'lowly and the lost' and the 'affluent' have the natural right to living with the right to equality of human dignity, liberty, freedom, distributive justice, access to justice, viz., to enjoy equally the fruits of the State. In this process, a German scholar Samuel Pufendorf (1632-1694), who was offered the chair of *ius gentium* in 1661 in Heidelberg University and who through his academic teachings as well as writings, rescued the natural law from oblivion and has given a masterfully comprehensive and powerfully rule-centered view of morality.[88] He is a key-figure in the modern shaping of natural law. His place in the history of legal science is unequivocal since he perceives conceptually obligation is central to morality and law thought, and this obligation indicates a social relation—'sociality'—in which one person directs the actions of another.[89] For the creation of this *lingua fauna* in law-morality relationship, Pufendorf occupies an unparallel place in the domain of law-morality relationship conceptually. Pufendorf derives duties (obligations) from laws. And for this wondrous contribution he has been criticized that he has no idea of the depth of natural law,[90] criticism seems to be oblivion. Pufendorf in *DJN (De jure naturae et gentium libri octo: On the law of nature and nations), EJU (Elementorum jurisprudentiae universalis libri duo: Elements of universal jurisprudence), DOH (De officio hominis et civis juxta legem naturalem libri duo: On the duty of*

88. J.B. Schneewind, *Pufenorf's Place in the History of Ethics*, in Knud Haakonssen, (Ed.), Grotius, Pufendorf and Modern Natural Law, 199, 123; Samuel Pufendorf, The Present State of Germany, Translated and edited by Michael J. Seidler, 2007.
89. *Id.*, p. 219.
90. Ian Hunter, *The Love of a Sage or the Command of a Superior*, in T.J. Hochstrasser and P. Schroder (eds.), Early Modern Natural Law Theories, 2003, 169.

man and citizen according to natural law), and De statu hominum naturali: On the natural state of men) presents the fundamental law of nature as an imperative inasmuch as that 'any man must, inasmuch as he can, cultivate and maintain toward others a peaceable sociality that is consistent with the native character and end of humankind in general.'[91] It unequivocally seems the emergence of the ideal of a genuine scientific knowledge of morality, which in Samuel Pufendorf's words "rests entirely upon grounds so secure which are capable of producing a solid science. So certainly can its conclusions be derived from distinct principles that no further ground is left for doubt."[92] There seems a conceivable argument in Pufendorf's key assertion where he draws a distinction between physical and moral entities. He opines that 'physical entities are created, and their properties flow from the substances subtending them. Moral entities, however, arise through imposition (*impositionis*), and their properties (moral duties) flow not from the essential moral nature (form, entelechy, soul), but from the purposes for which they have been superadded to physical beings'.[93] He asserts, "We seem able, accordingly, to define moral entities most conveniently as certain modes, added to physical things or motions, by intelligent beings, primarily to direct and temper the freedom of the voluntary acts of man, and thereby secure a certain orderliness and decorum in civilized life."[94] It emerges that the main aim of Pufendorf's construction of moral entities is

---

91. Craig L. Carr and Michael J. Seidler, *Pufendorf, Sociality and the Modern State,* in Knud Haakonssen, *op. cit.*, p. 133.
92. Samuel Pufendorf, The Law of Nature and Nations, 1672, *DJN,* excerpts quoted in Jean Porter, Nature As Reason a Theomistic Theory of the Natural Law, 2005, pp. 227-28; Craig L. Carr and Michael J. Seidler, *Pufendorf, Sociality and the Modern State,* pp. 133-157; Thomas Mautner, *Pufendorf and the Correlativity Theory of Rights',* pp. 159-182; Michael Nutkiewicz, *Samuel Pufendorf: Obligation as the Basis of the State,* pp. 183-198; J.B. Schneewind, *Pufendorf's Place in the History of Ethics,* pp. 199-234, in Knud Haakonssen, Grotius, Pufendorf and Modern Natural Law, 1999.
93. *Ibid.*
94. *Ibid;* see in particular, Ian Hunter, *the Love of a Sage or the Command of a Superior,* in T.J. Hochstrasser and P. Schroder (Eds.), Early Modern Natural Law Theories, 2003, pp. 175-177.

to break the metaphysical nexus between physical and moral nature contained in the notions of substantial form, viz., Pufendorf's moral conception of moral entities is intended to locate morality in the ends—of tempering and civilizing.[95] It emanates that there is a complete departure from earlier notions of natural law, which purport to derive morality from transcendent rational entities or laws common to God and man, whereas in Pufendorf's conception there is an absolute transformation of natural law in *de novo* enlightenment.[96] In the backdrop of this, it seems unequivocally that Pufendorf is emphasizing the anthropological underpinnings of his natural law in the striking desubstantialisation of morality in his *DJN De Jure Naturae et Gentium:The Law Of Nature and of Nations* by destroying the whole program of deriving moral duties from a moral nature embedded in the person and acceded to through reflection on divine or transcendent reasons.[97] Pufendorf in his *DJN* ably argues that a single individual may be the bearer of several moral *personae* civil as well as ecclesiastical, commercial and familial, public and private—each with its own duties arising from the purposes from which it was instituted.[98] In his *DJN* he advances his able argument that many human beings may be represented a single moral person, as in the case of civil associations and States, where individual subordinate their individual wills to the will of a 'composite moral person' (*persona moralis composite*) for the achievement of certain purpose/ aim/object, viz., social peace and security.[99] Pufendorf denies the transcendent moral personality anchored in the nature of man, say the figure of the priest, and he assign historical circumstances/reasons for this anti-metaphysical anthropology in his *DJN* as follows:

> Also we should not forget, that, just as one person may at the same time be in different states [*pluribus statibus*], provided only that the obligations accompanying those

95. *Ibid.*
96. *Ibid.*
97. *Ibid.*
98. *Ibid.*
99. *Ibid.*

> states do not conflict, so the obligations attached to any one state may in their parts be derived from different principles. Hence he who gathers the obligations flowing from any one principle, and omits all others, does by no means immediately form a state [*status*] to which no obligations can or should adhere, save those which he himself recollects [*meminit*]. So he who has gathered from the Sacred Scriptures alone the parts of the duty of priests [*partes officit sacerdotum*], assuredly cannot deny that those priests are also obligated to perform such duties as are required by any constitutions of individual governments [*civitatum*]. And so we also who are here treating merely of the duties of man [*hominis official*], which can be shown to be necessary by the light of reason, do by no means maintain that any such state of man, which includes such obligations alone [i.e., those 'recollected' from a single principle or source IH], ever did exist, can exist, or should exist.[100]

This *a proprio vigore* reveals that all persons including the priests have duties to perform which may arise from a plurality of principles such as 'inner-self reflection', and 'external civil determinants'. This may have been developed because of the aridity of catholic conservatism which did not attach any significance to 'external civil determinant' in the exercise of their [priests] 'inner-self reflection' since priests might have been behaving as superhuman than ordinary humans. As such, this chaos must have been fountainhead of regression in the civil society and telling upon the progressive development of the civil society. This also reflects upon the selfish aspect of the figure of the priests who might be irritants to the moral persona of ordinary civilians. Be that as it may, Pufendorf's anti-metaphysical anthropology should be seen in this perspective because of specific religious and political circumstances operating in Germany. *Therefore, his frontal scorning on metaphysical anthropology seems to be the groundwork for the separation of religious and civil governance that lay at the heart of his*

100. *Ibid.*

natural law concept (emphasis supplied).[101] For Pufendorf it is not a question of love or hate of a sage, rather assimilation of duties imposed by historically existing governments to which all mortal persons belong. This in brevity may be the language of Pufendorf's "Sociality" that reiterates as well as makes the serviceable notion of natural law to the achievement of peace and stability in the society of frozen turbulences of the age and time. Some have strived to criticize Pufendorf as an unoriginal thinker who merely reiterated his illustrious predecessors Grotius and Hobbes, but such voices seem to be of pedantic style and full of aridity, absurdity, obscurity.[102] It must not be forgotten that because of the absence of good translations of his works in English that he has been frequented with attacks and language should not be the cause of jealousy as well as aridity.[103] It seems unnatural as well as immoral to charge him of plagiarism of Grotius and Hobbes because he has been a stirring challenge to religious orthodoxy of those who might have behaved above laws of civil governance. Pufendorf has worked in league with both Grotius and Hobbes for bringing transformation in the society.[104] Criticism must not be for the sake of criticism, and, therefore, who criticize or neglect Pufendorf they fail to see and appreciate Pufendorf's distinctive contributions to the evolution of modern moral and political thought. The under mentioned thought from his *DJN* is evident to have insights into Pufendorf's concern for moral matters:[105]

> But those who have heretofore undertaken to cultivate this discipline, and who seem to have accomplished its task so well in the class of natural entities, have—the matter speaks for itself—not given moral entities the attention they deserve. Many people have not even thought about these things; others have dealt with them, but only lightly, as if

101. *Ibid.*
102. See Craig L. Carr and Michael J. Seidler, *Pufendorf, Sociality and the Modern state, op. cit.*, pp. 133-134.
103. See Thomas Mautner, *Pufendorf and the Correlativity Theory of Rights*, in Knud Haakonssen (ed.), *op. cit.*, pp. 159-181.
104. *Ibid.*
105. *Id.*, pp. 135-136.

they were worthless or unimportant fictions. This despite the fact that it greatly behooves man to know the nature of such entities, which he has received the faculty to produce, and whose power deeply suffuses itself throughout his life.

Pufendorf does not undermine the idea of God as divine law giver, rather it underlies his entire argument. He begins to examine the nature and origin of those moral entities that are the source of moral distinctions and obligations among human beings, and as such he explains the relation between moral entities and natural law; he discusses why humankind needs natural law, that is, moral norms to govern and order itself; he examines in depth how it is possible for human beings to govern themselves and order their relations according to that law. In the backdrop of this, he explains his principle of 'sociality' is binding upon humankind as the foundation of natural law, and to secure 'sociality' the civil society is required by obligation to promote it.[106] From this it emerges that Pufendorf has deep conviction in traditional jurisprudential belief that 'law is essentially the command of a superior which bends the will of a subject with obligatory force.'[107] He in his *DJN* describes God's legislative role as well as man's positive law making role thus:[108]

> With respect to its origin, law is most conveniently divided into *divine* and *human*, the former having God as its author and the latter man. But if law is considered according to the necessary agreement it has with its subjects, it is divided by a different rationale into *natural* and *positive*. The former is so attuned to the rational and social nature of man that there can be no moral and peaceful society for humankind without it; or—if you prefer—it has a sort of natural goodness, that is, a utility which from its own native orderliness affects humankind in general. Although there is yet another reason for that denomination, in that natural law can be discovered and known from men's own innate

---

106. *Ibid.*
107. *Id.*, p. 137.
108. *Ibid.*

> mental powers and from a consideration of human nature in general.

For Pufendorf, natural law is divine because it is legislated by God—not as a positive law—, and it is natural in the dual sense of fitting humankind's nature as well as its well being and accessible through the exercise of reason.[109] He thus explains two features of the moral character of natural law: first, it obligates the will; and, second, it promotes the good of humankind, which is required to be restricted by laws to conduce to man's welfare.[110] He opines that dignity and nobility are humankind's special attributes that God has bestowed on humankind, viz.[111]

> The dignity of human nature and its preeminence over other living things required that men's actions conform to a certain norm, one apart from which their order, decorum, or beauty is surely inconceivable. Man owes his supreme rank to the fact he has an immoral soul endowed with the light of understanding and a faculty of judging. Choosing and, as well, becoming highly skilled in many arts.

According to Pufendorf, moral status of natural law and humankind's obligation to obey it can only be accomplished by establishing the principle/concept/notion of "sociality" that is the fundamental law of nature from which more specific legal requirements are derived.[112] This is possible by an appeal to 'observation' rather than to 'metaphysics', and that is the heuristic/empiricism of Pufendorf:[113]

> There is no more direct and appropriate way of discovering the natural law than to contemplate carefully man's nature, condition, and inclinations, though this consideration must necessarily include as well a reflection

109. *Id.*, p. 138.
110. *Id.*, p. 140.
111. *Ibid.*
112. *Id.*, p. 143.
113. *Ibid.*

on other things external to man, especially those capable of befitting or harming him in some way.

It may thus seem that Pufendorf advances two claims to 'sociality'. First, there is a law of nature which binds all humankinds to cultivate society, that is, sociable, apart from personal expediency or prudence; second, there are natural inclinations that give additional support to this law.[114] It, therefore, discerns that Pufendorf clearly distinguishes morality (propriety) from expediency (prudence).[115]

Be that as it may, it is apparent that this novel as well as innovative model of natural law propounded by Samuel Pufendorf has a flare of renaissance because it has facilitated the growing interest of the State in scientific method that has as well shaped the vision of the State by an anthropomorphic thought process, viz., "inclinations of human character" that "is a discipline, not a nature, that leads to civil society".[116] In Pufendorf's natural law language this is the 'only alternative in the brutish life of the state of nature,'[117] and as such this seems to be the conceivable convincing argument that man is born brutish, he behaves like brutish, and he acts like brutish. Pufendorf clearly shows that 'a working legal system clearly allows, and even requires, that certain nonphysical relationships and consequences be found within its process. God has given men a sociable attitude that is not Aristotle's "political animal" but is characterized by the logic of the intellect: "That right against all men and to all things, which according to Hobbes accompanies the state of nature, is to be extended no farther than sane reason admits" . . .'.[118] He asserts that it is the intellect that determines just what "flows, as it were, from the very nature of the thing itself", and that can/cannot be asserting in making

114. *Id.*, p. 145.
115. *Ibid.*
116. See critical assessment of Pufendorf's *DJN* by Michael Nutkiewicz, *Samuel Pufendorf: Obligation as the Basis of the State,* in Knud Haakonssen, *op. cit.*, pp. 183-197 at pp. 183-185.
117. *Ibid.*
118. *Ibid.*

legal and moral claims.[119] He does not ignore the eternality of natural law that is due to its origin in God who is the author of natural law, but he, nevertheless, argues that origin is irrelevant for analyzing the true nature of law and its accompanying idea of obligation.[120] He expresses his concern with the ontological status of the natural laws rather than with their genesis, and as such he expresses:[121]

> And although it be probable that the important principles of natural law were given to the first men by God, to be passed on to others afterwards by instruction and custom, yet the knowledge of that law can none the less be called natural, inasmuch as its necessary truth can be gathered by mental processes or the use of natural reason. And because the propositions which define natural law are suggested to the minds of men by a contemplation of the nature of things, they are referred back to the author of nature, even to God.

It unequivocally seems that Pufendorf defines the laws of nature simply as the "dictates of reason" that "most men agree on the one point that the Law of Nature should be deduced from the reason of man himself, and should flow from that source, provided it not be perverted."[122] It also seems that Pufendorf has been examining the view/perception/vision that the prototype of natural law is found in divine justice; it is only because of that God's intellect is just that "the world is not ruled by evil."[123] In the backdrop of this, Pufendorf eliminates the discussion on the issue of the origin and concentrates on the concept of law qua law.[124] Pufendorf assumes a moral realm where principles of natural science cannot be extended into political theory or legal science theory.[125] He inasmuch as recognizes the concepts of

---

119. *Ibid.*
120. *Id.*, p. 187.
121. *Ibid.*
122. *Ibid.*
123. *Id.* p. 189. This is similar to Aquinas's perception and view in "The Mind and Power of God".
124. *Id.*, p. 191.
125. *Ibid.*

obligation and of right as he acknowledges that to act morally means to act in accord with a rule; right is a power (*potestas*) that charges the will to act in accord with the stipulations of agreements (pacts and promises); the concepts of obligation and of agreements are closely linked and the condition for entering into agreements lies "in understanding the force of obligation."[126] Pufendorf is incongruous from other natural law theorists because he maintains that men have an *a priori* notion of obligation; he believes that he establishes the State on the basis of agreement and contract; he asserts that in the state of nature devoid of moral bonds, men could never formulate a social contract.[127] Pufendorf's moral realm is not located in space or vacuum; it is located in the context of society itself.[128] For Pufendorf the purpose of society—in the realm of social, moral, political—"is not the perfection of this world of nature ...but it is the perfection in a distinctive way of the life of man, in so far as it was capable of a certain beauty of order above that in the life of beasts, as also the production of a pleasing harmony in a thing so changeable as the human mind."[129] It shows that Pufendorf criticizes that theory of political society that denies the uniqueness of man and the political order.[130] And that is the methodological as well as pedagogical revolution of Pufendorf in legal science.

In the backdrop of the above, it may be worth to ask what place Pufendorf occupies in the realm of law and morality interaction. Pufendorf is neither unoriginal nor pedantic thinker rather he is a scientific, heuristic and empiricist in his approach because his conviction is that human society is almost entirely a human artifact, and social life arises from choices and agreements and not from impersonal or supernatural causes.[131] Pufendorf strongly makes out his point of view that "whether it can be said in any useful sense that *God set before Himself and man*

126. *Ibid.*
127. *Id.*, pp. 194-195.
128. *Ibid.*
129. *Id.*, pp. 196-197.
130. *Ibid.*
131. See J.B. Schneewind, *Pufendorf's Place in the History of Ethics, in Knud Haakonssen (ed.), op. cit.*, p. 200.

a common end, or that the order constituted for man, that is, the observance of the law of nature, produces the end of creation as set down by God."[132] Broadly speaking, obligation is key element in Pufendorf's thought about law and morality: "An obligation is that whereby one is required under moral necessity to do, or admit, or suffer something."[133] Be that as it may, this undoubtedly is Pufendorfian model of law and morality arising from the fruits of Protestantism and Enlightenment that helps to overcome puzzles of unrealistic, non-heuristic as well as non-empiricists.

Be that as it may, Pufendorfian model of law and morality has remained in oblivion because till half of the nineteenth century most German jurists have been accustomed to consider law as every command of the State that claimed to be law.[134] But, the horrible or terrible experiences of the Nazi regime naturally caused German jurists to raise again the question of the natural law that they have begun to reflect upon the reality, the function, and the essence of natural law, viz., law rests on eternal basic norms, founded either in reason or divine will.[135] The history of natural law, its eclipse, and its rebirth is the story of seesaw between these two basic views, besides Catholic and Protestant seesaw natural law. Be that as it may, Pufendorfian model is out of oblivion. This rebirth of natural law in Germany seems to be looking to the solutions of the seesaw problems in the perennial task of law; the principle of predictability (*Rechtssicherheit*) that is an appeal to the individualistic and dialectic conscience of the people that positive law has to give way to transpositive law.[136] In brevity, it seems that this notion of natural law is the key discussion of law and morality in Germany in the present scenario, and it is reportedly said that the federal Constitutional Court has translated natural law ideas in some of its decisions,

---

132. *Id.*, p. 208.
133. *Id.*, P. 219.
134. See Freiherr von DER Heydte, *Natural Law Tendencies in Contemporary German Jurisprudence*, (1) 1956 Notre Dame Law School Journal, Natural Law Forum, 115.
135. *Ibid.*
136. *Id.*, pp. 120-121.

one perceives that Rudolf Laun's prophecy of 1924—that natural law would be reborn in Germany—may seem to be fulfilled.[137]

5. Natural Law: Re-examined *De Novo*

In the backdrop of the above narration, it seems apparent that Natural Law or Law and Morality have had a chequered history of periods of frozen turbulences either acceptance of the existence of Law and Morality or rejection or neglect of Law and Morality. This appears to be the suspicion of the thinkers about the expression natural law that has changed from one age to the next presenting varying or different profiles of ideas about natural law thus confounding it with confusions of incongruent theorems. It also seems, from the above delineation, a tug of war between the expression natural law assigning the meaning or the meaning assigned to the conceptual framework of natural law. For example, I take a photograph in the lawns of my house and hang it in my drawing room with a caption on it: THIS IS THE EQUATOR OR THE UNIVERSE OR THE INFINITE OR MODERN ART OF CONFUSION. Its significance is known to me alone or may occur to the future generations that there is no reason to think at all that this is equator or universe or infinite or art of confusion. It is like Socrates telling to his judges that the unexamined life is not worth living; nor is an unexamined thought worth thinking.[138] It is not the debate of supremacy of whom; it is a question of accepting the heuristic, empiricist as well as socio-legal-anthropology of beauty of natural law or law and morality. If we set aside law and morality whether the superior courts—superior courts are right because they are superior; not superior because they are right—have the warrant of authority to hold a law of the legislature unconstitutional. This warrant of authority or grant of authority to the superior courts is not a lawless act, but is a necessary armour in their hands to keep the States, the policy conceivers and the policy-makers, the law-makers, the Houses of legislatures, and the Executive within their prescribed powers, otherwise the

137. *Ibid.*
138. As quoted in Charles P. Curtis, Law as Large as Life a Natural Law for Today and the Supreme Court as its Prophet, 1959, pp. 3-4.

governments could not proceed as cherished; "and indeed would certainly have foundered."[139] What is this articulation? It is certainly not a saint or sage pattern of law; it is natural natural law or natural element in our law. This is the way the serious thinkers, and not the flamboyant, seriously concerned with law—legislators, lawyers, judges, political scientists, politicians, policy planners, parties plaintiffs and parties defendants—shall think in a natural law or law and morality. Justice Holmes is neither ostentatious nor pretentious when he says, "Judges know how to decide a good deal sooner than they know why. [Because], judicial decisions depend on a judgment or institution more subtle than any articulate major premise."[140] It emanates that all human justice consists in conformity to the will of God as known through eternal law; this is the ultimate unchangeable as well as immutable truth for man's moral behaviour; it is because of this conformity that natural law is right, and all other righteousness in man's laws is derived from this eternal law; natural law has an immanent rationality which enables man in principle to reach the right conclusion as to his temporal felicity; and often repeated charges made against the ethics of natural law—despotism, decisionism, positivism, ethical relativism—are without foundation and exercise in artificiality as well as futility.[141]

Natural law or law and morality are the older, which live not yesterday nor yet today, but stand for ever.[142] It is on the similar hypothesis: "If, per impossible, law did not come from God, it would still bind under pain of fault; just as if, per impossible, there existed a man not created by God, he would still be rational."[143] Be that as it may, God is beyond human imagination or intelligence and He would have not imagined that men would create so much fuss about natural law or law and morality different from the way He could have decided in

139. *Ibid.*
140. *Id.*, p. 15; see also Michael H. Hoffheimer, Justice Holmes and the Natural Law, 1992.
141. *Infra 169*, p. 29.
142. *Ibid.*
143. See Michael B. Crowe, *The Impious Hypothesis: A paradox in Hugo Grotius*, in Knud Haakonssen, *op. cit.*, p. 12.

favour of natural law or law and morality.[144] Nevertheless, natural law should serve as a basis for positive law, which seems to be the foundation of the most perfect government, and the fundamental rule for all positive law, for many negative consequences of positive laws that conflict with the natural law support the claim that natural laws are advantageous for mankind.[145] Legal rights conceded outside the domain of natural rights endowed by law and morality convey the most microscopic view of such rights people experience pleasure and enjoyment. Therefore, Richard Stone, a modern thinker on natural law or law and morality, expresses his moral sentiments in support of conceptual relationship between law and morality in the modern sense of law, society and development in the most heuristic as well as empirical way:

> The first duty of the state is that of protecting the society from the violence and invasion of others. ...The second duty is that of protecting as far as possible every member of the society from injustice and oppression of other members, which means establishing an efficient administration of justice. The third is that of promoting work and institutions which facilitate commerce. The fourth is encouraging the education of the people. And the fifth is supporting the dignity of the sovereign [that is, people, Constitution and Parliament].[146]

Be that as it may, a succinct scanning of the literature shows that natural law has had been the scorn of bitter circumstances and has had several deaths. This has occurred in the hands of those who have worked against natural law in favour of positive law by declaring the death of natural law wishing that it would

---

144. *Id.*, pp. 28-29.
145. See Erik Angner, Hayek and Natural Law, *op. cit.*, p. 36.
146. *Id. p. 4;* Richard Stone, *Adam Smith on What the State and Other Public Institutions should and should not Do*, in M. Fry (ed.), Adam Smith's Legacy, His Place in the Development of Modern Economics, 1992; Rufus Black and Thomas Chappel in Nigel Biggar and Rufus Black (Eds.), *op. cit.*

"never rise again from its [grave] ashes."[147] Yet natural law survives and still calls for discussion, because the "funeral orations for the natural law have been premature."[148] This unequivocally seems to be a reviving study *de novo* of the contours of natural law taking account of its paradoxical role in the bitter-sweet or soup-sauce human history, traditions, and limitations, which has "served both as a stimulus to reform and bulwark against change."[149] In the backdrop of this, the relevance and utility of "universal and divine reason" reflect the universe of natural law.[150] This is due to the clash of laws between positive law and natural law. Positive laws vary in different countries of the globe and at different times; natural law does not vary.[151] This shows the infallible *locus classicus* of natural law which is "the unwritten and unfailing statutes of heaven ...whose life is not of today or yesterday but from all time, and no man knows when they were first put forth."[152] Natural law refers to "laws of range sublime whose parent was no race of mortal men,"[153] because "in nature is commandment; she does not ask for

---

147. See Michael Bertram Crows, The changing Profile of the Natural Law, 1977, ix. It is a belief in Hindu philosophy that he who is made to die survives a long life. Natural Law is made to die several deaths shall survive a long life.
148. *Ibid.*
149. See A.L. Harding, A Reviving Natural Law, in *Id.* x; see also Charles Covell, The Defence of Natural Law, 1992; Philip Anthony Harris, The Distinction Between Law and Ethics in Natural Law Theory, 2002; Hubert Rottleuthner, Foundations of Law, 2005; Robert P. George, Natural Law, 2003; Robert P. George, In Defense of Natural Law, 1999; Mark C. Murphy, Natural Law in Jurisprudence and Politics, 2006; Michael H. Hoffheimer, Justice Holmes And The Natural Law, 1992; R.W. Dyson, Natural Law and Political Realism in the History of Political Thought, Vols. I and II, 2005; T.J. Hochstrasser, Natural Law Theories in the Early Enlightenment, 2000; Mark E. Graham, Josef Fuchs on Natural Law, 2002; Robert P. George and Christopher Wolfe (eds.), Natural Law and Public Reason, 2000; Mark C. Murphy, Natural Law and Practical Rationality, 2001.
150. A.L. Harding, *Id.* at p. 4.
151. W. Jaeger, *Die Anfange der Rechtsphilosophie und die Griechen*, as quoted in Michael Bertram Crow, *op. cit.*, p. 6.
152. *Ibid.*
153. *Ibid.*

laws."[154] This undoubtedly speaks of the "whole life of man ... governed by nature and the law [and of a] law valid for all men given by nature."[155] This idea of natural law in the cosmological, moral as well as legal cosmology sense has had to keep pace with the social evolution for its consistent and constant quest for justice. This conception of natural law, which is unwritten but, of course, superior to and is the measure of man-made law, has not gained the day without a struggle.[156] Natural law has been an eye sore of the prejudices of word-spinners, conscious deceivers who present the appearance of truth by juggling with words seemingly jaundiced thought dealing in pseudo-science.[157] The march of struggle as well as survival has a long journey from *Sophists* (derived from *Sophos*: a wise man) to *Stoic* who are believed to be the first to have systematized the concept of natural law. The implications were seen by Socrates, Plato, and Aristotle. Socrates' life of "intellectual mid-wifery" has focused attention inescapably upon the problems of man and morals, rather than talking about philosophy in abstract. His search has been engaged for "goodness, justice, courage", and so on to give practical shape to ethical investigation inasmuch as "what is ethically right must be the object of objectively valid knowledge."[158] In support of his argument, Socrates has *a proprio vigore* expressed in the famous dictum that *"virtue is knowledge"* as against the *Sophists* for in his legislation.[159] And, he has urged that any attack on natural law could be regarded as attacks upon which communicable knowledge was a chimera.[160] Socrates' life mission has been for a kind of society that would give weight to the natural law and to demand for them the obedience we would give to our parents.[161] His visionary plan of justice has been human justice that must be referred to a superamundane justice,

---

154. *Ibid.*
155. *Id.*, p. 7.
156. *Ibid.*
157. *Ibid.*
158. *Id.*, p. 11.
159. *Id.*, p. 16.
160. *Id.*, p. 12.
161. *Ibid.*

an ideal justice, which the human lawgiver must try to see this justice in order to imitate it every principle of good governance.

Socratic perceptions of virtue, knowledge, natural law, justice, obedience, and good government has influenced Plato's emphasis upon reason and for Aristotle's doctrine of practical wisdom, and ultimately for the refined idea of natural law in the *Stoics* and their successors who have epitomized morality in the maxim: "Live according to nature."[162]

Corpus juris of above mentioned natural law has subsequently influenced the perceptions of Marcus Tullius Cicero (106-43 B.C.) and the *Roman Jurisconsults* enshrined in *ius civile, ius gentium, ius naturale, ius commercii,* rapproachement between *ius gentium and ius civile,* and the beginning of *Digest* and of the *Institutes of Justinian.*[163] *Ius civile* has been meant for the Roman citizens and *ius gentium* for non-Romans in their relation to Roman citizens, and, therefore, it may be opined that *ius gentium* and references to contract, commercial transactions as the consequences of war, etc. in the *Institutes Justinian* moves closer to positive law, and makes it even resemble modern positive international law—*ius gentium* as the natural law proper to mankind.[164]

In the backdrop of the above, it is nevertheless significant to mention that this profile of natural law has been a boon of Christian Contribution to the growing insistence upon the natural law in the New Testament, and then in the Church Fathers and the ecclesiastical writers or Scholastics of the early Christian century who have identified the natural law with the divine law or division of laws into human and divine would make natural law the positive law of God or a pantheistic interpretation of natural law that identifies nature and God, viz., "nature that is God."[165] This may be classified as "Church governance and royal supremacy". Thereafter it has been a dead end—Dark Age—in the history of natural law till its revival in the medieval ages.

---

162. *Id.*, p. 31.
163. *Id.*, pp. 36-51.
164. *Ibid.*
165. *Id.*, pp. 52-71.

It may thus seem that the contours of natural law have had tradition in the past, and the achievements of the past indeed play a significant part in the formulation and subsequent development of a theory of natural law. This may be the contributions of Medieval Canonists and civilians of the Middle Age[166] who have identified natural law as natural law; the mosaic law; the law of the prophets; the law of the gospel; the apostolic law; and the canon law with one common denominator of precepts of moral laws, viz., conceptual relationship between law and morals or morality.[167] This has set the stage for the delineation of natural law by Scholastics and thinkers of theology that ultimately resulted in the works of Thomas Aquinas who has strived to "get as close as is humanly possible to the natural law" has hardly been improved upon by his successors.[168] Thomas Aquinas's natural law sketch, in brevity, seems to be, "if the natural law is to continue" it must be restored in "man's moral court of appeal."[169] This assumption may be due to the fact that Aquinas has had to face the frozen turbulences of Natural law traditions. Aquinas's description of law in his *Summa Theologiae* is "a certain rule and measure of action by which one is induced to act or restrained from acting", and as such in his perception *"Law is nothing other than an ordination of reason for the common good by him who has the charge of the community and promulgation."*[170] It seems that Aquinas has all along been working towards the identification of natural law with the principles of the practical reason, viz., he admirably accords place to reason in human action. It discerns that there are four qualities that unequivocally explain Aquinas's conception of law:

- It is a work of reason or mind;
- it is aimed at the common good;
- it proceeds from one having authority;
- it is promulgated.

166. *Id.*, pp. 72-110.
167. *Ibid.*
168. *Id.*, pp. 111-191.
169. *Id.*, p. 136.
170. *Id.*, pp. 166-167.

It undoubtedly shows the dependence of law on action, and reason is the principle of human action. It also shows the identification of law with a universal proposition of the practical reason, and practical reason is obviously rational, which is not merely speculative but practical intellect.[171] His precept of natural law can be reduced to a single fundamental precept: "Do good and avoid evil"[172] which is deduced from his celebrated axiom:

> Since the good has the nature of an end, and evil is its contrary, it follows that the objects towards which man has a natural inclination are naturally apprehended by reason as goods and, consequently, as things which ought to be done, and their contraries as evils and to be avoided. Thus the order of the precepts of the natural law follows that of the natural inclinations. In the first place there is in man an inclination to good following the nature which he shares with all substances, inasmuch as every substance the preservation of its being according to its nature. Following this inclination those things are of the natural law which preserve the life of man and hinder what is contrary to it. Secondly, there is in man a more particular inclination which follows the nature which he shares with other animals. According to this, those things are said to be of the natural law which "nature has taught all animals" such as the union of male and female, the education of offspring and so on. Thirdly, there is in man an inclination to good, which follows the rational nature which is proper to him. Thus man has a natural inclination to know the truth about God and to live in society. Following this, whatever regards such inclination belongs to the natural law, e.g. that man should avoid ignorance, that he should not injure those with whom he ought to have intercourse and so on. . . .[173]

This celebrated passage tells what good and evil imply, and rationality as well as reason helps to discover good and evil

171. *Ibid.*
172. *Id.*, p. 176.
173. *Id.*, p. 178.

independently. Aquinas regards it as a development of natural law that depends upon an analysis of the natural ends of action. He urges, "Everything that causes in an action a lack of proportion to the end is said to be against the law of nature."[174] Consequently, this is precisely the concept as well as perception of natural law on the exercise of reason. However, the measure of reason depends upon the diversity of sociological as well as psychological aspects that action and reason permeate variations due to differences of moral insights, moral intellects and morality. And, Aquinas also unhesitatingly acknowledges that the causes of actions or particular actions vary in infinite ways.[175] Certainly, what is good for us may be evil for others, and as such questions of good and evils have no fixity.

In the backdrop of the above, it appears that the profile of natural law is not final, because it painfully as well as painstakingly has been sketching between the *antiqui* and the *moderni* profiles of relationship between law and morality. However, it has strived to reach to the understanding of the enlightenment of oppositions between Catholic and Protestant thinkers from the time of the Reformation in the sixteenth century and the rise of "secular natural law". Succinctly, the range of inconclusiveness of the discussion leads to three propositions, viz., first, the natural law is not merely indicative or ostensive; it is a genuinely prescriptive law, expressing the will of God, second, precept and prohibition do not constitute the totality of goodness or malice in observance or transgression of the law; God's will presupposes an objective goodness or malice in the actions concerned and adds the special obligation of divine law, and third, the natural law is truly a law of moral laws and God is its Divine Author.

However, the above learned and judicious divine articulations have not been the cause of complacent, because the genesis of the above have not been conceivably convincing to the misconceived opponents who have been intriguingly rejoicing by the attacks upon reason. Consequently, Hugo Grotius in his epoch-making *De jure belli et pacis*, described as a watershed in

---

174. *Id.*, p. 180.

175. *Id.*, p. 190; *see also Tony Burns, Aquinas's Two Doctrines of Natural Law*, Political Studies: 2000, Vol. 48, 929-946.

the history of natural law ideas, ushering in the '*secularization of natural law*', has devised his 'impious hypothesis' to take the natural law out of the theological controversies of the time and age that has helped to remove the natural law from all theological contamination.[176] He, in his 'impious hypothesis', asserts:

> What we have been saying (viz. about the natural law) would have a degree of validity even if we should concede that which cannot be conceded without the utmost wickedness, that there is no God, or that the affairs of men are of no concern to him. . . . Herein, then, is another source of law besides the source in nature, that is, the free will of God, to which beyond all cavil our reason tells us we must render obedience. ...Natural law is the dictate of right reason indicating that an act, according as it conforms to or is in disagreement with nature, individual and social, is either morally wicked or morally necessary and in consequence such an act is commanded or forbidden by God, the author of nature.[177]

His reticence is revealing and more than a rhetorical flourish. It seems that natural law cannot be the work of an autonomous human reason; it is a work of divine reason, discovered and reiterated by human reason. Therefore, Samuel Pufendorf, the most influential follower of Grotius, in his versatility has asserted that natural law theory depended upon a notion of '*Socialitas*' that has special emphasis on the social nature of man, his *socialitas*.[178] It is the social nature of man that is the very heart of human nature, which could only develop its peculiarity and reach its completion in the social context.[179] According to Pufendorf, only human relations could give real

176. *Id.*, pp. 223-245, at pp. 224-225; *see also Michael B. Crowe, op. cit.* What a paradox in neo-natural law Western thought that is exclusive of Divine Authorship is conceived as secularism neo-natural law!
177. *Ibid.*
178. *Op. cit.*
179. *Ibid.* Pufendorf was laying the groundwork for the separation of religion and civil governance that lay at the heart of his natural law.

dignity to human beings: *dignatio nominis humani.*[180] It may be no exaggeration to submit that this has influenced the modern thinkers on law and morality giving more emphasis as well as priority to the elements of reason and ability to think. Pufendorf has also incorporated the concept of human dignity into his doctrine of natural law, viz., the idea of natural equality of all human beings.[181] Man has human dignity because of his 'immortal soul' and because he has been "indu'd with the Light of Understanding."[182] He opines that every human being has been endowed with it since all human beings are equal by nature.[183]

In the backdrop of the above, it seems that another profile or face or side of natural law thinking has emerged, that is, the concept of human rights. Human rights or "rights of man" are as old as natural law or law and morality. References to human rights can be seen in ancient and medieval times because of ostentatious violation of Roman citizen-rights or citizen rights to slaves; the idea of the essential equality of all men or citizenship of the world or dignity and vocation of the human person or freedom and natural rights have been recognized.

Human rights or rights of man are appreciatively associated with the names of John Locke (1632-1704), Jean-Jacques Rousseau (1712-78) who asserted alarming concern about the recognition of the rights of man against the background or phenomena of fiefdom, feudalism, or violation of individual rights by unscrupulous princes/kings who have no love or concern for the freedom as well as liberty of man. History affords testimony to this. I may submit that Indian perception of natural law or law and morality embedded in *Dharma* gives preference to "duty of man" because right flows from duty.[184] This is the basic contrast between the Indian and Western thinking process. Be that as it may, human rights, indeed, are

---

180. *Ibid.* For critical analysis see David Kretzmer and Eckart Klein (Eds.), The Concept of Human Dignity in Human Rights Discourse, 2002, p. 44.
181. *Ibid.*
182. *Ibid.*
183. *Ibid.*
184. *Infra.*

incredible. Neglect of human rights has been indigestible. John Locke sees man's natural rights depend upon a "law of nature", a law whose writ ran already in the "state of nature", before men had contracted to found civil society.[185] Majesty of human rights or rights of man has been voiced because of struggle between rule of law and arbitrariness represented in the maxim: *Quod principi placuit legis habet vigorem*, i.e., the will of the emperor has the force of law. Locke presents this view because he has had the experiences of the 'Glorious Revolution' of 1688, and as such argues that man brings into civic society certain basic rights he already enjoyed in the condition of nature, the rights of life, liberty and estate, which the State cannot abolish but must protect and enforce.[186] This innovative approach towards human rights or rights of man makes Locke as an 'ideological father' of the American Revolution and has been reflected in the American Declaration of Independence (4th July, 1776) with an inroad in the Constitution of the United States of America (adopted on 17th September, 1787) with its nine Amendments (ratified on 15th December, 1791). Locke says, "The state of Nature has a Law of Nature to govern it, which obliges every one; and Reason, which is that Law, teaches all mankind, who will but consult it, that being all equal and independent, no one ought to harm another in his Life, Liberty or Possession."[187]

What Locke has been for American Revolution, Rousseau has been, as an ideological progenitor, of the French Revolution, not so dissimilar to Locke's perception inasmuch as—"Man is born free, and everywhere he is in chains" is his best remembered phrase in his *Social contract*.[188] This phrase has been a guiding spirit for the French revolutionaries who overthrew the *ancient regime*. This has been an inspiration source not for imprescriptible, but for absolute, and inalienable individual rights enshrined in the Declaration of the rights of Man and Citizen, 1789 adopted by the convention of 29th May, 1793, and inevitable part in the French Constitution of 22nd August, 1795.[189]

185. *Supra note 193*, p. 237.
186. *Id*. at p. 242.
187. *Ibid*.
188. *Id*., p. 243.
189. *Ibid*.

Similar things have happened elsewhere in the world to have had freedom from fiefdom, feudalism, imperialism, colonialism, absolutism, etc. in search of human happiness, human liberty, human freedom, human right to life, liberty, equality, justice, fraternity as epistolary to natural rights. Besides, these have been a source of inspiration for the development of political, social, economic rights by putting curbs upon the exercise of political authority/power, and setting of objective standards of good and evil for individual conduct. This programmed, embraced with enthusiasm, has been a recipe for the inclusion of natural rights in the march towards constitution-making during the eighteenth and nineteenth century. Though positivists of the nineteenth century, twentieth century as well, have been content with the rejection or refutation of natural law or conceptual relationship between law and morality at its face value, but the natural law has survived under another face, viz., natural rights. It is reborn from the ashes of World War II to gaining prophetic berth in the International Pronouncements of Human Rights which carry the piety of recognition with it universally, such as United Nations Charter, 1945; Universal Declaration of Human Rights, 1948; European convention on Human Rights, 1950; International Covenant on Civil and Political Rights, 1966; International Covenant on Economic, Social and Cultural rights, 1966. It is alive because of its intrinsic value, and as such having respectful berth in the new constitutional culture of India and Germany, and a host of other countries free from the Colonial uncultured. In the backdrop of this, it is imperative to make in depth probe, in the modern scenario, on the function of law and morality or natural law rather than spiteful about the controversies of doctrinal issues that now lay far behind, for *de novo* future where we may sing a song with afresh melody, instead of melancholy, *lead me from darkness to gleaming wings of light where new vistas of knowledge await to ring the bell.*

6. Law and Morality—New Perspectives

Natural law or law and morality have to be perceived from novel account of the historical roots that may be a distinguishing perspective of natural law or law and morality. It may not be, now, in a good taste to continue with the discussion on distinction between natural law and positivism or legal positivism. The above mentioned delineation on natural law is not complete, but it is the exposition of some of the scholastic views well circulated in the discussion, but others are equally important as well as significant. On the whole, the basic issues have been highlighted that speak sufficiently on the known controversies about natural law or law and morality. Be that as it may, controversy aside, in depth probing in new areas with innovative insights on law and morality may have to be exercised gleaming. Unnecessary prolonged or stretched discussions on some issues do not convince anyone, because that seems to be continuing with the wrong that otherwise is not a wrong and, therefore, 'it is better to suffer wrong than to do it'.[190] There seems some danger of unnecessary discussing also because that sometimes permeates unattractive tendencies, as has been observed by Professor Brian Bix: "One of the unattractive tendencies of contemporary legal and political philosophy [is where a commentator] does not discuss anyone's views, but a family of views. This allows one to construct one's target by selecting features from a variety of authors so that the combined picture is in fact no one's view, and all those cited as adhering to it would disagree with it."[191] Be that as it may, before we may discuss the imperatives of new perspectives in law and morality in the present scenario for some futuristic perceptions, it may, in brevity, be submitted that human law that violates natural law is, of course, not a law, for the safe conclusion that the argument 'whether an unjust law is really a law' is of less significance, and as such seems to be controvertible due to the contrived approach between naturalists and non-naturalists, i.e. positivists.[192] There is conceivable convincing argument that natural law is predominantly about human good and morality;

190. See Plato, Gorgias, 469c, as quoted in Joseph Raz, *On the Socratic Maxim*, Vol. 75:5. Notre Dame Law Review, 2000, p. 1797.
191. See Brian Bix, *On the Dividing Line Between Natural Law Theory and Legal Positivism*, Vol. 75:5, Notre Dame law Review, 2000, p. 1614.
192. See Kent Greenawalt, *How Persuasive is Natural Law Theory*, Vol. 75:5, Notre Dame Law Review, 2000, 1647 at 1649; Jeremy Waldron, *Lex Satis Iusta*, Vol. 75:5, Notre Dame Law Review, 2000, 1829.

Legal Positivists thesis about what makes a human law a law may be perceived from this point of view that legislators should take account of the truths of natural law, and judges interpreting statutes should be guided by the original meaning of law and morality.[193] Connection between natural law and God has created unconvincing debate. However, it is seen in modern times that there is a strong correlation between belief in natural law and belief in God.[194] Nevertheless, it has been seen, and rightly so, that Naturalists have *a proprio vigore* asserted that individuals may or can discover the natural law *de novo* independent of their religious beliefs or discover the natural law without invoking religious premises, and that shall be a robust natural law theory, undoubtedly.[195] Though there are differences between law and morality, but it is mostly agreed that law should be morally sound, that moral principles do underlie the law, and that law and morality combine âim at the implementation of justice: "Justice is the end of government. It is the end of civil society."[196] Justice is law and virtue to achieving equal freedom; justice is distributive justice because it takes care of human wants as well as needs; it is interactive justice because it is security to human beings.

Be that as it may, it is conceivable that natural law or law and morality have the following norms which have convincingly been accepted:[197]

---

193. See Kent Greenwalt, *op. cit.* at p. 1652.
194. See Rufus Black and Thomas Chappel, in Nigel Bigger and Rufus Black (Eds.), *op. cit*; see also *Supra note 173...*
195. *Supra 217.*
196. See Richard W. Wright, *The Principles of Justice*, Vol. 75:5, Notre Dame Law Review, 2000, 1859; Justice refers to the family of moral concepts connected particularly with law and politics, politics here being understood broadly in the sense of public decision-making regarding the distribution of goods. Justice is a subset of morality. Stephen G. Gottieb, *op. cit.* p. 247; Aristotle says: "When men are friends they have no need of justice", J. Barnes, Ed., Complete Works of Aristotle, 1984.
197. See David F. Forte, *The Natural Law Moment*, as quoted in Kent Greenawalt, *op. cit.*, pp. 1650-1651; see also Tony Burns, Natural Law and Political Ideology in the Philosophy of Hegel, 1997. Hegel says, "Natural law is distinct from positive law; but to prevent their difference into an opposition and a contradiction would be a gross misunderstanding."

1. Human life is integrally related to all of existence.
2. Human nature is universal.
3. The defining characteristic of human beings is their reason or rationality.
4. Human beings have inherent purposes or self-evident goods (the approach Finnis defends).
5. These purposes, or goods, are discoverable by reason, reason being understood in broad sense to include the light of experience.
6. Morality is objective, universal, and discoverable by reason.
7. People's moral obligations are consonant with their own true purposes, or their realization of self-evident goods, and with their true happiness.
8. At the deepest levels, no conflict arises between individual good and the common good.
9. Human laws appropriately reflect the natural law (though not every dictate of natural law should be subject to State correction). Human laws appropriately determine details left open by natural law, such as the precise punishments for various crimes, and they settle matters of indifference.
10. Human laws that are not in accord with natural law are not really law in some sense. A failure to accord with natural law may occur if a human law requires behavior that natural law forbids, or if a law forbids behavior that natural law values, or if the burdens and benefits of a law are highly unjust.

In the backdrop of what has been said, it seems that natural law is out of eclipse, for we seem to have reached a point of functional approach to law and morality interaction, which may be helpful for reshaping as well as rehabilitation of law and morality or natural law for the emerging millennia that encounters a number of challenges. Each and every challenge has genuine questions of morality—hidden or apparent—in search of genuine answers to such genuine moral questions. Sound and not arrayed human behavior shall help to develop a new natural law culture.

In view of what is said above, the issue concerning 'dignity of the human person' needs reiteration in the changing world scenario which seems to dominate in the revival of natural law of the twenty first century. This content has to be articulated from new reasons perspectives human approximate—human beings neither devils/sinners nor angels/saints—aspires to explore. This may be heuristic or empirical or practical or pragmatic approach to the natural law inasmuch as Roscoe Pound (1870-1964) has made considerable contribution to natural law: "The function of a philosophy of law is to discover how law may serve the needs of the community and it is the "social engineering" function through which law serves the human interests, social interests, and the national interests."[198]

Concept of human dignity is as old as concept of natural law. The concept of human dignity, therefore, plays a significant role in the universality of human rights that are inviolable. Man is born free and rational by nature, and it is the *ratio* (mind, reason) through which man excels in his potentialities which are hidden in every human being.[199] What is morally good and beautiful is derived from this faculty to develop perceptions, to formulate visions, to foresee, to plan, to think, to select, to decide, to urge, to steer to human action, to repress the irrational affects according to the rules of nature and reason. This is because of the dignity which is the most important characteristic of human person: "Dignity is someone's virtuous authority which makes him worthy to be honored with regard and respect".[200] Human dignity has international as well as constitutional value in new international and constitutional culture.[201] The Preamble of United Nations Charter of 26 June, 1945 provides:

198. See Roscoe Pound, Justice According to Law, 1951; *The Revival of Natural Law*, 17 (1942), Notre Dame Law Review, pp. 287-372.

199. *Supra note* 197 *at* pp. 22-25.

200. *Ibid.*

201. See Jochen Abr. Frowein, *Human Dignity in International Law*, in David Kretzmer and Eckart Klein (eds.), *op. cit.*, pp. 121-132.

> We the People of the United Nations determined ... to reaffirm faith in fundamental human rights, in the dignity and worth of the human person ...

Similarly, the preamble of the Universal Declaration of Human Rights of 10 December, 1948 provides:

> Whereas recognition of the inherent dignity and of the equal and inalienable rights of all members of the human family ...

Article 1 of the Universal Declaration of Human Rights reads:

> All human beings are born free and equal in dignity and rights. They are endowed with reason and conscience and should act towards one another in a spirit of brotherhood.

Preamble International Covenant on Civil and Political Rights, 1966, and Optional Protocol to the ICCPR, Aiming at the Abolition of Death Penalty, 1989 recognize the human dignity:

> ... That abolition of the death penalty contributes to enhancement of human dignity and progressive development of human rights.

International Covenant on Economic, Social and Cultural Rights, 1966, International Convention on the Elimination of all Forms of Racial Discrimination, 1966, Convention Against Torture and other Cruel, Inhuman or Degrading treatment or Punishment, 1984, Convention on the Elimination of all Forms of Discrimination Against Women (CEDAW), 1979, CONVENTION ON THE RIGHTS OF THE CHILD. 1989 read as follows:

> ... Recognition of the inherent dignity and of the equal and inalienable rights of all members of the human family is the foundation of freedom, justice and peace in the world.

Vienna Declaration and Programme of Action, 1993, United Nations Millennium Declaration, 2000 *a multo fortiorari* read:

> ... We have a collective responsibility to uphold the principles of human dignity, equality and equity at the global level.

Human dignity is the key concern of many modern constitutions of the world. Dignity of the individual is the magnum opus of the Supreme Lex of Germany and India. Human right to human dignity is immutable and entrenched as inalienable fundamental freedom as well as basic right enjoined in the Constitution of India and Basic Law of Germany and governed by the Supreme Court of India and the Constitutional Court of Germany. The Constitutions of India and Germany are influenced by the avowed faith ingrained in the Charter of the United Nations, and the Universal Declaration of Human Rights. The *Grundgestez* (Basic Law) of the Federal Republic of Germany of 23 May, 1949 enjoins in Article 1:

> The dignity of man is inviolable. To respect and protect it shall be the duty of all public authorities.
>
> The German people therefore uphold human rights as inviolable and inalienable, and as the basis of every community of peace and justice in the world.

The Constitution of India of 26 November, 1949, the date on which it has been adopted, and 26 January, 1950, the date from which it has been enforced, ordains in the vocabulary of the Preamble

> We the people of India having solemnly resolved to *constitute* India into Sovereign Socialist Secular Democratic Republic and to *secure*
> Justice, Social Economic and Political
> Equality, Status and Opportunity
> Liberty, Thought, Expression, Conscience, Belief, Faith, and Worship
> And *to promote*
> Fraternity
> *Assuring*

The Dignity of the Individual

. . . .

It is the spirit of brotherhood—fraternity—that the constitutional cultures of many modern countries of the globe reflect inasmuch as assuring the human dignity. Fraternity cannot, however, be installed unless the dignity of each of its members/citizens/individuals is sustained, maintained, retained, conserved, adopted, and promoted. The constitutions, therefore, say that the State-*Reich*, in India and Germany, and in any country of the world, will assure the dignity of the individual/human dignity. The constitutions seek to achieve this objective by guaranteeing equal fundamental rights/basic rights to each and every individual, so that he/she can enforce his minimal rights, if invaded by maximal authority of the State, in a court of law.

The expression human dignity does not have any definite meaning, because the concept is based on the essence of the individual personality, which is influenced by a variety of philosophical, theological, ideological, and natural law traditions, and as such it seems difficult to seize the meaning of the concept of human dignity. Be that as it may, it has multifaceted explanations that encompass the right to be treated with honor and respect within the domain of right to life and personal liberty. Human dignity shall mean right to be humane. Human dignity is assured contra to "man is born free but everywhere he is in chains". The concept of human dignity has inherent values because of its inalienable, universal and indivisible character. Human dignity is enhanced if liberty (of thought, expression, belief, faith, worship, and conscience), equality (of status and opportunity), justice (social, economic, and political), and unity in diversity (in a pluralistic society) are ensured to advance/grow/bloom/gleam. That shall groom, grill, as well as nourish the individual to excel his personality as well as dignity.

Human personality and human dignity, perhaps, seem to be offshoots or species of "life and personal liberty" and in the ultimate analysis life and personal liberty mean something more than survival or animal existence.[202] It would include the right to live with human dignity and shall encompass all those aspects of life that go to make a man's life meaningful, complete, and worth living with dignity must be declared to be an integral component of the right to live.[203] Besides, human dignity has a special relevance in the constitutional context because of pluralistic character of the modern societies.[204] Be that as it may, human dignity includes right to life and personal liberty that include the "finer graces of civility and human civilization". Life is lived at many levels. Life, liberty, and dignity make the whole concept of human right to human dignity. While the external mundane activities of life have their own place, they are the manifestations of an inner, unseen, unperceived activity—which, indeed, is the real "life" that a human being lives.

The right to live with human dignity is recognized as a repository of various human rights,[205] viz., right to healthy environment,[206] pollution free water and air,[207] protection against hazardous industries,[208] education of children at least up to 14 fourteen years of age in those jurisdictions where there is high rate of illiteracy (States' duty and parents'/guardians' duty vis-à-vis children's right),[209] emergency medical aid,[210] right to

---

202. See *State of Maharashtra* v. *Chandrabhan*, A.I.R. 1983 S.C. 803.
203. See *Olga Tellis* v. *Bombay Corp.*, A.I.R. 1986 S.C. 180; *Maneka Gandhi* v. *Union of India*, A.I.R. 1978 S.C. 597.
204. See *Indra Swahney* v. *Union of India*, A.I.R. 1993 S.C. 477; *T.M.A. Pai* v. *Educational Foundation* v. *State of Karnataka*, A.I.R. ; see also the case decided by the Grand Chamber of the European Court of Human Rights, Strasbourg, *D.H. and others* v. *The Czech Republic*, decided on 13 November, 2007 concerning the right to education and discrimination.
205. See *Francis Coralie Mullin* v. *Administrator, Union Territory, Delhi*, (1981) 1 SCC 608.
206. See *M.C. Mehta v. Union of India*, A.I.R. 1987 S.C. 1086.
207. See *B.L.Wadhera* v. *Union of India*, A.I.R. 1996 S.C. 1446.
208. See *Vellore Citizens Welfare Forum* v. *Union of India*, A.I.R. 1996 S.C. 2715.
209. See in particular Article 21-A and 51-A (k) of the Constitution of India; *J.P. Unnikrishanan* v. *State of Andhra Pradesh*, A.I.R. 1993 S.C. 2178.
210. See *Parmanand Katara* v. *Union of India*, A.I.R. 1989 S.C. 2039.

health,[211] privacy,[212] shelter,[213] livelihood,[214] timely medical aid/treatment in government hospitals,[215] right not to be driven out of a State,[216] right to fair trial,[217] etc. The dignity of man, as per the Basic law of the Federal Republic of Germany, requires the attribution of rights to the individual which enable him or her to defend his or her own design of life inasmuch as human dignity is a 'right of rights'.[218] To respect and to protect the dignity of man shall be the duty of all State authority—legislature, the executive and the judiciary—because the dignity of man is the corner stone or the constitutive principle in the system of basic rights.[219] The Federal Constitutional Court of Germany expressly qualifies the Basic Law phrase 'the dignity of man shall be inviolable' as a legal right as everybody has the right to his or her inviolable dignity.[220] In *Luth's case* the Federal Constitutional Court of Germany unequivocally has stated that human dignity constitute an order of values that radiate to the whole body of law.[221] It also expresses that human dignity may be violated but not taken.[222] A waiver of dignity is not acceptable as dignity is not at the disposal of the individual.[223] According to the

---

211. See *State of Punjab* v. *Mohinder Singh Chawala*, A.I.R. 1997 S.C. 1225.
212. See *People's Union of Civil Liberties* v. *Union of India*, A.I.R. 1997 S.C. 568.
213. See *U.P. Avas Avam Vikas Parishad* v. *Friends Co-operative Housing Society Ltd.*, A.I.R. 1996 S.C. 114.
214. See *Madhu Kishwar* v. *State of Bihar*, (1996) 5 SCC 125.
215. See *Paschim Bangal Khet Mazdoor Society* v. *State of West Bengal*, A.I.R. 1996 S.C. 2426.
216. See *National Human Rights Commission* v. *State of Arunachal Pradesh*, A.I.R. 1996 S.C. 1234.
217. See *Police Commissioner Delhi* v. *Registrar, Delhi High Court*, A.I.R. 1997 S.C. 95.
218. See Donald P. Kommers, The Constitutional Jurisprudence of the Federal Republic of Germany, 2nd Ed. 1997, Ch. 7, Human Dignity and Personhood, p. 298 *et. al.*; David Kretzmer and Eckart Klien, (Eds.), The Concept of Human Dignity in Human Rights Discourse, 2002.
219. BVerfGE (from the collection of decisions of the Federal Constitutional Court/FCC) 87, 209, 228, 1992.
220. BVerfGE 61, 126, 137 (1982).
221. BVerfGE 7, 198, 204 (1958).
222. BVerfGE 87, 209, 228 (1992).
223. BVerfGE 45, 187, 229 (1977).

jurisprudence of the Federal Constitutional Court of Germany human dignity has an absolute effect, and as such the principle of proportionality does not come into play as long as an intrusion upon human dignity has been established.[224] The Federal Constitutional Court of the Federal Republic of Germany in a famous tape judgment of 1970 (privacy of mail and telecommunication) has been called upon to formulate its opinion whether a person is a mere object in the State. The court has emphasized that it is contrary to human dignity to make persons the mere objects in the State or of the State; it means to treat a person in such a way that calls his quality as a person (a subject) principally into question, the treatment of the individual must be the expression of disdain, must be qualified as contemptuous treatment; the image of the man in the Basic Law is not that of an isolated, sovereign individual, rather, the Basic Law has decided in favor of a person's dependence on and commitment to the community, without infringing upon a person's individual value; restrictions and limitations to freedoms, as such, do not interfere with human dignity and do not make persons mere objects of the State.[225] From the decisions of the Federal Constitutional Court of the Federal Republic of Germany, it seems that the right to human dignity is the right not to be treated in specific ways; it is a modal right. The discussion on the cases of the Apex Courts of India and Germany unequivocally show the concern of the superior courts regarding the considerations of morality in law and law in morality as both are inescapable as well as inseparable from each other.

Besides, rights of disabled persons, internally displaced persons, refugees, migrants, children (particularly victims of sexual harassment and unnatural offences), girl child (girl child

---

224. BVerfGE 75, 369, 380 (1987); 93, 226, 293 (1995).
225. BVerfGE 30, 1, 25, 26,(1970); BVerfGE 45, 187, 228 (1977); BVerfGe 87, 209, 228 (1992); BVerfGE 27, 344, 351 (1970); see second abortion case where the court held that a pregnant woman who is obliged to take part in the counseling procedure with a view to avoid abortion does not suffer a violation of her dignity, because the law treats her as a partner, recognizing her autonomy and responsibility: BVerfGE 88, 203, 281 (1993).

as a domestic servant another kind of bonded labor), sexual harassment of women at working place, women as victims of domestic violence (CEDAW), rights of old aged parents/ persons, rights of disadvantaged groups of society, right of aboriginals, minority groups, etc. are within the domain of human right to human dignity inasmuch as law and morality domain. These perceptions of law and morality need to be addressed in the thoughtronicing in the present and the future, because thought is a reality and discovery of the thought is a challenge. Human dignity and freedom of expression are interwoven, because freedom of expression is the oxygen of writers' creativity to disseminate and assimilate information through any media is imperative in civilized governance.[226] Besides, freedom of expression and right to education are coordinated inasmuch as education shall be directed to the full development of the human personality; freedom of expression is empty phrase unless education equips every individual with freedom of the word, the ability to read and write.[227] Evil of despotic power of husbands over wives *vis-à-vis* human happiness needs *de novo* thinking in new world order in the realm of law and morality.[228] Perspectives of victims of crimes, victims, particularly children, of terrorism as well as militancy, children who have lived a war and fight to survive and their dreams to have rights of dignity, minorities and minority rights seem to be the challenges to law and morality in the present scenario unless the shadows of the evils are evaporated or completcly eclipsed or eradicated. Besides, new thinking in the liberalization as well as globalization, WTO and the challenges to copyright, trade, design, TRIPS, Corporations and international trade procedure and practices, new consumerism *vis-à-vis Caveat Venditor vis-à-vis Caveat Emptor*, implications and implementation of International Humanitarian Law in non-armed conflicts, that is terrorism/militancy and the victims of such conflicts (terrorism as a challenge to international

226. See Nadine Gordimer, *Reflections of Nobel Laureates*, in Yael Danieli, Elsa Stamatopoulou and Clarence Dias (Eds.), The universal Declaration of Human Rights: Fifty Years and Beyond, 1998, vii.
227. *Ibid*.
228. See M.F. Perutz, Nobel laureate in Chemistry, 1962, in *Id*. at p. ix.

humanitarian law), non-state actors—rebels, insurgents, belligerents, national liberation movements, rebel groups, armed opposition groups, parties to internal armed conflicts, mercenaries—rights, accountability, human rights and human dignity abuses, etc. open a flood gate for law and morality debate. Respect for human rights is of importance if protecting human dignity is a key.[229] For example, trouble with polygamy does not relate to patriarchal reasoning (despotic governance of husband) in modern natural law, but in the law and morality relationship as well as coordination it seems to be enhancing the piety of dignity of both men and women inasmuch as "...there can be little doubt that the main reason why polyandry is not more commonly practiced, is the natural desire in most men to be in exclusive possession of their wives."[230] These challenges are closely related to law and morality. Are problems of abortion, taking the innocent life of a child in the womb of the mother, fetus and its related problems, pregnancy of innocent girl child, gays, lesbianism, surrogate child, etc. in any way distinct from law and morality? Why positivists' laws could not resolve these problems which are challenge to civility? A novel as well as innovative and distinctive natural law or law and morality approach with a non-arrayed methodology to yield conceivably convincing results shall be sound and fruitful lest genuine law and morality relationship eclipses or evaporates or withers.

7. Quintessence of the quicksand of Law and Morality: A Remaking for Rehabilitation of Natural Law or Law and Morality

The debate on Law and Morality or Natural Law is illustrative of inconclusive discussion that leads to no result. It is a puzzle ordained in a riddle that is in quest of whom? Is Law in quest of Morality or Morality in quest of Law, or Law in quest of Law and Morality in quest of Morality? The discussion is oscillating between orthodoxy and modernity and in search of

---

229. See Andrew Clapham, Human Rights Obligations of Non-State Actors, 2006.

230. See E. Westermarck, The History of Human Marriage, 1921, Vol. III, p. 206 in Knud Haakonssen, *op. cit.*, pp. 559-581 at p. 559.

some prophet to rehabilitate it. The survey of Natural Law or Law and Morality conveys the mixed impressions of the insights of thinkers. However, looking at the insights of natural law thinkers, it may be safe to say that "like a harlot, the natural law is at the disposal of everyone."[231] This unequivocally shows the contradictions in the history of natural law, in brevity, from middle Ages to modernity. It is worth to submit that the pilgrimage of natural law has been transformed from tradition to theology and from theologically grounded interpretation of human morality into a philosophical framework for driving or testing and supplementing determinate moral norms. This transformation has left considerable room for disagreement at the level of theory, and consequently the emergence of many theories of natural law emanating in the period starting from the middle Ages to the scientific as well as technological Age of Modernity, and as such compounding confusions. Some theories give greater emphasis to prerational nature, others insist on the autonomous sufficiency of practical reason to general moral norms. Be that as it may, these theories are united in diversity by their insistence that the natural law can ideally be expressed in terms of a set of moral norms derived from one or two first principles, as given by nature in the wider sense, or by the exigencies of practical/empirical/heuristic reason itself.[232] What does this transformation convey? This conveys that take nature as nature or nature is reason or "the natural law is nothing other than the law of reason or obligation, insofar as nature is reason."[233] This is a process of remaking or reshaping of natural law. And, in this profile, the quintessence of the quicksand of natural law is to come out of the quagmire of past tense, present imperfect and future indefinite. Is there any prophet or angel to rehabilitate natural law? Is it Law itself? Is Judiciary the only angel to save it from the quicksand of legislative and executive quagmire? We need not involve ourselves in the complexities of *Vocabularies technique et critique de la philosophie* of 'nature' or 'natural', which conveys eleven meanings for 'nature' and

231. See A. Ross, On Law and Justice, pp. 1-9; B. Hamilton, *A Developing Concept of Natural Law*, in Michael Bertram Crowe, *op. cit.*, pp. 252-253.
232. See Jean Porter, Nature as Reason, *op. cit.*, at p. 28.
233. *Id. at* p. 53.

thirteen for 'natural'. We have to search for objective instead of abject, scientific, empirical and heuristic approach to law and morality for a lasting solution to the inconclusive debate otherwise we shall continue to beat around the bush. The fact of the matter is that the law cannot abdicate a moral responsibility. In the backdrop of the emergence of new constitutional and legal culture, the battle about law and morality is being fought in a new way on anew battleground as indicated above "New Perspectives of Law and Morality". One may refer to the Hart-Devlin and Hart-Fuller debates, particularly Devlin's *The Enforcement of Morals,* 1959, which may be taken as *a multo fortiorari* exposition of the view that the law cannot abdicate a moral responsibility. The concepts enshrined in constitutional vocabulary like 'legality', 'due process', 'procedure established by law', 'life and liberty', 'reasonableness', 'equality before the laws and equal protection of the laws', 'human dignity', appear to be very near or like or actually assimilable to law and morality or natural law expression. Besides, in the question of law and sociology coordination, the expressions 'the rule of law', 'the rule of law to serve rule of life', 'the legal order', 'judicial activism', 'judicial creativity', 'judicial innovation', 'judicial craftsmanship', 'justice, access to justice and distributive justice', 'disadvantaged groups of the society', 'marginalized groups of the society', 'neglected segments of the society', 'aboriginals', 'minority', seem to be value terms/expressions and rarely as well as insufficiently investigated by socio-legal eagles heuristically and empirically with social sciences research methodologies nevertheless do not lay far away from the eternal as well as internal morality, and in this area natural law or law and morality can play its part.[234] It is here that we see the relevance of law and morality in the domain of law and sociology, which progressively aims at reducing/minimizing the degree of arbitrariness in the positive law. Positive law does not welcome any check on the exercise of its arbitrariness, whereas natural law or law and morality places limits upon the arbitrary exercise of political, legislative and executive powers. In the

234. See also Selznick, P., *Natural Law and Sociology*, 6 (1961), Natural Law Forum, pp. 84-108.

backdrop of these perspectives, it is imperative that we the thinkers have to detach ourselves from the cobweb of positivists' illusion about eternal stability for harmonious sustainable governance. This insight may help to erase the misconceptions, misunderstandings and the misleading approaches to 'is' and 'ought', and conceivably assist to derive 'ought' from 'is' convincingly.

3

PRUDENTIA JURIS OF *DHARMA*

Dharma is ubiquitous in Indian *Vedic*/Hindu philosophy. *Dharma* is "law" or "moral law" by acceptance—*jus receptum*—which is believed to have been ordained by Divine Author; it is not a "law" as we understand it today. *Dharma* and its philosophies are pervaded moral and legal rules, moral and legal traditions as well as culture, moral and legal reasoning as well as rationality, and, therefore, *Corpus Juris* of scholastic moral and legal traditions as well as cultural ethos. Therefore, *Dharma* is magnum opus of *Vedas, Ritis, Nitis, Smritis, Dharamshastras, Mimansas, Upanishads, Ramayana, Mahabharata, Bhagvad Gita,* and scholastic writings who devoutedly not only vouch for but describe the gigantic aspects of practical law in several periods of *Indic (Vedic*/Hindu*)* history. Ancient Indian intellectual history enjoins the rudiments of *Dharma* that intend to serve as a comprehensive, *Vedic*—inspired basis for living a "good life in a good society in a good polity".

Dharma is solicitous of noble birth origins invented by the Great Creator—God—realized in three stages of *Vedic*/Hindu philosophy : *Brahaman, Paramatma and Bhagwan—Trimurti*—three manifestations—*Satyam, Shivam Sundram*—of one God (*Ekam svadipra Bahuda Vadanti*)—disseminated and assimilated by the great sages, saints and mystics through millennia after millennia.

Therefore, *Dharma* as Law and Morals and Law and Nature is entrenched and as such immutable since it is a heritage stronger than governments and kings, and rulers and kings of elected democracy.

With such pedigree of law, yet the idea of law figures seldom or at the remotest margins of Indian studies as a field of law, law and morality, and law and nature.[1] The reasons are not far to seek.[2] It may be nothing pretentious to say that with the entry of common law in India, the soup and sauce of this rich heritage evaporates. The critics assert that *Dharma* as an idea of law has been conceded as too much idealistic as well as mythology and without any practical utility and relevance; it lacks universality; it is without any conscience reasoning and rationality; it is without any legal reasoning; it is a closed-minded system; it is only religious, and, therefore, in the realm of law it is only formalistic, pedantic, and simply non-adjustable.[3]

Dharma, in all modesty and assertion, is not distinct from legal as well as moral values.[4] Philosophical developments only led to the contemporary debates that *Dharma* is religion alone

---

1. The British administrators did not accord recognition to *Vedic* concept of *Dharma* Law and law and morality, because they had intended to introduce their own common law in India to advance their own interests in India. British judges in India needed access to the original legal texts of India to implement the British policy of "administering native law to the natives", and so were born a "well-intentioned and well calculated misunderstanding". See Patrick Olivelle, *Supra note* 2 (Introduction), *op. cit.*, p. 62.
2. See in particular Donald R. Davis, Jr., *Hinduism as a Legal Tradition*, Journal of the American Academy of Religion, http://jaar:oxforjournals.org/cgi/content/full of 17.10,2007; see also Fali S. Nariman, India's Legal System: Can it be Saved?, 2006, pp. 1-10: Societies in ancient India that is Bharat were governed by 'moral law', *Dharma*, which was ordained by a Divine Author—law by acceptance: *Jus receptum*.
3. *Supra note* 2 (Introduction).
4. See in particular *Journal of Indian Philosophy*, volume 32, 2004, pp. 421-830; James L. Fitzgerald, The Mahabharata, Volume 7, 11. The Book of the Women, 12. The Book of Peace, Part One, 2004, General Introduction, p. xvii: Anchors the translation of the Sanskrit word *dharma* with "law", "rule", "norm", "duty", "obligation", and so on.

and not knit with legal and moral values. Varied views on *Dharma* are relevant inasmuch as varied views on natural law are relevant in varying ways to the comprehension of *Dharma* as laws and morals in practice. It has been comprehended that theory without practice is pointless and practice without theory is mindless. *Dharma* as legal science and moral/ethical science is not without reasoning as well as rationality; it is not without conscience and conscientious reasoning; it is not purely religious-cosmetic; it is not a closed-minded system of legal reasoning leading the people to say that *Dharma* as legal and moral science is formalistic, pedantic or simply non-workable. Had it been so, how it could be possible that five utmost foolish sons of a king could be made intelligent in law, ethics, values, diplomacy, kingdom management and good governance, developing sustainability, promoting human dignity for human good as well as human happiness.[5] This example and many other examples speak volumes about the practical utility and relevance of *Dharma* as legal and moral science that is full of convincing logic and reasons. Succinctly, it shall be submitted that *Dharma* as legal as well as moral science is objective and not subjective, and should not be conceived as a watertight compartment category of Hinduism or religion alone.

Dharma is the *Prudentia Juris* of law, law and morals, and, law and nature. *Dharma* is the primeval seed from which all manifestations of law—legal law, natural law, moral law, positive law—emanate and have into existence just like a great tree with all its roots, trunks, branches, twigs, leaves, flowers, and fruits which spring forth from the earth, which itself supports the tree, and in which it is rooted. Therefore, *Dharma* is the seed of every legal action—legality, morality, and natural. Nothing can exist without *Dharma*. Everything is *Dharma* nature; *Dharma* is the soul of every deed of law and its action.

Dharma as a study of Law and Nature, and Law and Morality is an in depth study on the history of laws and social organization of the ancient Indian society that has intellectual roots of the classical/ancient Indian Legal Thoughts in action. *Dharma* relates to the relationship between law and human

5. See the stories contained in *Panchtantra*.

beings, human conduct and human behaviour. What verisimilitude I may imagine, and there is nothing pretentious about it, that *Dharma* is the Legal Cosmology scientifically of Legal, Natural and Moral science. Its roots are engraved in ancient Indian classical literature—poetry in prose and prose in poetry—that is religious, ethical, moral, social, natural, cultural, and legal (may be termed as religious law, moral law, law of ethics, divine law, legal law as a guide to the law conceivers as well as law makers, *Vedic* law, Hindu law), and deal with all natural, legal, moral, and ethical duties and obligations, and rights, and purely part of *Dharma*. The legal rules are very much precepts of injunctions of purely moral obligations. *Dharma* is impregnated with *Nyaya* and *Yukti*, viz., according to the general precepts, *Dharma* be administered in accordance with *Nyaya* (Justice) and *Yukti* (natural reason, logic and equity). Therefore, *Dharma* is theoretically beautiful and heuristically practical method of societal ordering through the sanction or threat of *Dand* (punishment, sanction), ruler's or justice, dispenser's or *Nyaya Devta's or Dharam Devata's*, who is not blind folded, punishing rod. *Dharmo rakhshati rakhshita*: If you respect or protect *Dharma* (law, duty, obligation) *Dharma* (law) protects you; if you disrespect or disobey *Dharma* (law), *Dharma* (law) will not only scorn at you but destroy you, because its rod will not spare you.

Dharma is beyond the scope of any "ism". Even if per chance or mistake or misconception or misunderstanding, it is correlated to Hinduism or *Vedic (ism)*, which is the constant or perpetual pursuit of *Dharma*, that does not, in conscience, make any distinction between law and religion. In this sense, *Dharma* is faith; it is *Bhakti*; it is belief; it is conscience; it is worship; it is practice; it is propagation; it is professed, and, therefore, it is universal. *Dharme Sarvam Prathishthtam*: Law is the foundation of the universe. *Vasudev Kutuambkam* and *Sarva Dharam Sambhav*: The whole universe is one family; it is universal order, and as such its universality is ubiquitous. In the backdrop of this, *Dharma* as law is law of mankind universally, because conscientiously it is not confined only to a particular sect of a particular society. It aspires *Sarve Bhavantu Sukhina, Sarve Santu Niramaya...*: The universality of *Dharma* law is impregnated aspiring the human good, human happiness, human dignity and human flourishing of all creatures universally equally; it does not aspire for the good, happiness, dignity and flourishing of Hindus alone; its aspiration is for the whole mankind universally. This is the inbuilt concept of the universality of *Dharma*.

The inventors of the word *Dharma* have had farsightedness to develop the societal orderliness in accordance with laws of *Dharma*. Therefore, laws of *Dharma* were practically preaching cultural and jurisprudential harmony[6] inasmuch as developing

6. See J.D.M. Derret, Religion, Law and the State in India, 1968; see also J.A.B. van Buitenen, The Bhagavadgita in the Mahabharata, 1981, pp. 1-36, asserts that the expression Vedas ordain the expression *Dharma* which establishes that *Dharma* is a meaningful and beneficial action which Injunctions (*Vidhi*) urge a person to engage in for specific reasons for follow up action. *Sruta (that which is heard), Sruti (that which is knowledge by hearing), and Srotriya (that an expert in sruti, conveyed to a student)* are expressions assigned to *Vedas*. This teaching would ideally comprise the entire *Vedic corpus* from the oldest hymn to the *Upanisadis* texts, but practically limits were set upon it by the branch (*sakha*) of a particular *Veda* (e.g. *Rigveda, Atharvaveda, Samaveda, Yajurveda*) to which teacher and student belonged. *Veda* which was heard was without beginning, for it stretched backward through the uninterrupted succession of teachers and students to the beginning, when it was given along with creation and then discovered by the primordial seers. It was without an author, human or divine, since it was part of creation; moreover, were it authored it would necessarily be flawed by the author's imperfections, and its authority diminished. So has been the case with the expression *Dharma* which originates from *Vedic/Indic* sources. *Dharma* as law and morals thus validate itself insofar as it is the source of knowledge of law, morals, ethics, duty, obligation, virtue, the true nature of right action, ideally good behaviour, law of four social orders or law of four patterns of life, good deeds, meritorious deeds, rule, norm, custom, responsibility, a law, the laws, law, lawful deed, meritorious lawful deed, the good law, right (noun), and right (adjective), justice and just, virtuous, good character. *Dharma* therefore cannot be translated but only transcribed. *Dharma* is beginningless; *Dharmasastra* is invoked what Manu has recorded (*Manavadharmsastra*). *Dharma* is *Yoga*, and *Yoga* means self-yoking to a particular effort to win a goal. *Yoga denotes a broader concept than discipline or method. It implies the process of a difficult effort; a person committed to it; the instrument he uses; the course of action chosen; and the prospect of a goal.*

the concepts of law, *Danda* (punishment, sanction), person, *Prakriti and vyavahara* (Law of civility, viz., conduct and behaviour, and also the manifestations of civil law), *Rajdharma* (law of constitution), *Rajayadharma* (law of administration), human dignity, democracy, good governance, good management with inbuilt accountability as well as transparency. In the backdrop of this, if *Dharma* is said to be Natural Law of Divinity of God that is having foundation on reasoning, logic, and rationality to convince arrayed human beings like *Arjuna*, what more verisimilitude of *Dharma* one may imagine.

In the backdrop of the above, the expression *Dharma* has no parallel either in English vocabulary or any other vocabulary, though some scholars have endeavoured to its origin in Indo-Iranian or Indo-Germanic antiquity but failed to extract its impression, because it is a *Vedic* rather than an Indo-Iranian or Indo-Germanic word.[7] As observed earlier, the notions of the juris vicissitudes of natural law or law and morality from Indian perspectives are entrenched in immutable *Dharma* having its roots in *Sanskrit Lirit Dhri*—shall be discussed in detail later on—that signifies to hold, to support, to sustain (sustainability), to retain (values), to conserve (conservation of soil from soil erosion, deforestation, environmental pollution, global warming), to preserve (cultural heritage and values, cultural identity), to observe and to promote (human good and human happiness, human dignity, human rights, human flourishing), to develop (relationship between law and nature, and law and morality). This, in brevity, is the Natural Law or Law and Morality of *Dharma* that is the prophet and angel of classical ancient Indian Legal thought. Though there may have been its eclipse due to the stifling of time and tide, yet we have to strive extremely hard for its transformation for the present as well as future. Otherwise, we shall be wrestling with the proverbial phrase like perfect past, imperfect present and indefinite future. *Dharma* is neither religion nor religious thought nor conservative. It is a prognosis progressive movement, like

---

7. See Paul Horsch (Translated by Jarrod L. Whitaker), *From Creation Myth to World Law: the Early History of Dharma*, 32 (2004), *Journal of Indian Philosophy*, pp. 423-448; Joel P. Brereton, *Dharma in the Rigveda*, 32 (2004), *Journal of Indian Philosophy*, pp. 449-489.

progressive movements of societies, of Law and Morality—Natural Law—with intellectual roots of the classical ancient Indian thought in action. It is a movement of righteousness, virtues, and virtuous duty. Right is prognosis of duty and negation of duty never gives the occasion for the claiming of right. In *Dharma* duty predominates right. Therefore, it is a progressive movement of law, logic, and reasoning. Its manifestations constitute *Rajdharma, Rajayadharma, Rajsasana, and Rajayashastra* to secure, assure and promote law, liberty, equality, justice, fraternity, human dignity, humanity, universality of one global family as well as order *(Vasudev Kutumbkam and Sarva Dharma Sambhav)* as a principle of co-existence and as a common heritage of mankind, universality of sustainability, conservation, retention, observance, promotion, human dignity, human good, human happiness, human flourishing. *Dharma* is law, Rule of Law to serve the Rule of Life, *Rajdharma and Rajayadharma* and its strategies helping as imperative to reduce or minimize or eradicate or eliminate administrative deviant behaviour. Besides, it promotes free flow of information and knowledge in the most secular intellectual aspects (*AA No Bhadraa Kratvo Yantoo Vishvata: Let noble thoughts come to us from every side)* to bringing transparency, accountability for good governance/management. In sum and substance, it is a concept of cultural and equally legal culture, evolution.

Be that as it may, the teaching and learning of *Dharma* as a study of Law and Nature and Law and Morality has remained confined to philosophy and humanity disciplines, and has never been a part of legal studies in the Indian Universities. May be, due to the ubiquitous weightage the common law manifestations have in the Indian legal fraternity. Therefore, the study of the concept of *Dharma*, the *Corpus Juris* of Natural Law, in Indian perspectives has to be *proprio vigore* in the following manifestations.

(i) *Dharma* and the concept of *Vidhi* (Law) and *Danda* (Punishment).

(ii) Dharma and the concept of person/man/human being.

(iii) *Dharma* and the concept of State: Sovereignty, *Rajdharma, Rajayadharma, Rajyashastra, Rajasasana: Good/Sustainable Governance/management.*
(iv) *Dharma* and the concept of human dignity.
(v) *Dharma* and the concept of information and knowledge: A Roadmap for Good/Sustainable Governance/management—accountability and transparency.
(vi) *Dharma* and the concept of Democracy, Polity and Synergetic Comity.
(vii) *Dharma* and the concept of Justice—Social, Political, Economic, Distributive, Access to Justice.
(viii) *Dharma* and the concept of logic and reasoning—practicality and heuristic.

i. *Dharma* and the Concept of Law (*Vidhi*) and Punishment (*Danda*)

It has been seen that Western natural law theorists conceptually consider reason to be the fundamental element of human nature. It emphasizes that it can be used to discover the principles requisite for human accomplishment. It also emphasizes the derivation of principles of right action from the application of practical reasonableness to the pursuit of human good. It also says that the principles are inherent in human nature. It also tells that the principles are self-evident and are apprehended by reflecting on human nature.[8] It also asserts that natural law theories concede these principles to be the basis of ethical conduct and law in society. It *mutatis mutandis* says that there are basic human goods requisite for human fulfillment and that through the application of practical reason to their pursuit one can derive universal principles of right conduct, that is, natural law.[9] It may discern that Western natural law perceptions imperatively are contrived because they are subjective in their formulation of key or core issues such as the

8. Finnis, Natural Law and Natural Rights, 1980; Lisska, Aquinas's Theory of Natural Law, 1998.
9. Finnis, *op. cit.*

basic human goods and practical reasonableness in their application to life situations of human beings.[10] Not only surprisingly but paradoxically, men and women approach moral questions differently and that casts doubt on the universality of Western approach to natural law.[11]

In contrast, *Dharma* is the *Corpus Juris* of *Vedic Corpus* and is certainly not the key or core term in the religious vocabulary of the *Vedic corpus*. It is *memoria technica* of Law + Morals + Ethics + Action + Justice and taken together constitute Natural Law, viz., Law and Morality, and Law and Nature. This combines the knowledge and interpretation of different times and continued to flourish from millennia after millennia entrenched as Memory (*Smriti* that follows to hold and support *Sruti* from extinction), *Shabad* (the script, the language, the expression, the pedagogy) that supports perceptual knowledge (*Praman and anuman*) for posterity (*Parampara*), dissemination and assimilation of knowledge (*Vidyya:* deriving from Memory that is a form of perception) in search of true knowledge (*Hetu: sign:* Aim: Goal: Inquisitiveness) to reserving and preserving it (*Sanskara*). How? This what has been conceived by thinkers, scholars, *Risis, Sages, Seers* who have interpreted *Vedas, Puranas, Upanishads, Ramayana, Mahabharata, Bhagavad Gita,* which form as *Memoria Technica* (*Mimansas*: The Law of Interpretation) giving rise to different schools of thoughts, various *Sakhas and Charanas* supportive to the development of universal stages of law, that is, *Rajdharma* (Law of constitution), *Rajayadharma* (Law of Administration), *Rajsasana* and *Rajayasastra* (Law of Good/ Sustainable Governance/Management with accountability as well as transparency), and Rule of Law to become Rule of Life. Therefore, it is evident that *Dharma* is not religion, or Hindu Religion, or Hinduism. *Dharma* is the essence of Natural Law approach that is entrenched in *Vedic* knowledge. *Vedic* approach is universal—*Aarayya*—to all human beings to follow with

10. Henderson, Lynne, Whose Nature? 1990; King, Michael, Nature's Intelligence or Human Reason? Natural Law in Maharishi's Vedic Science, and in Legal and Ethical Thought, 1997.
11. Gilligan, Carol, In a Different Voice, 1982, as quoted in Michael S. King, *Natural Law and the Bhagavad-Gita: The Vedic Concept of Natural Law,* (15 &16) 2002 & 2003, *Ratio Juris*, pp. 399-415 at p. 400.

continuity as a duty as well as obligation for the full development of a universal aspect of human nature to promote right action with a 'developed intellect, clear mind, balanced emotions, and full perception'.[12] This alone holds and supports to fulfill his or her society's highest ideals of moral, ethical as well as lawful conduct. This is the unique ubiquitous universality of *Dharma*—Natural Law—and its right action (practicing technique) substantially helps to decrease or minimize substance of abuse and recidivism, and supports improved well-being. But for this, *Dharma*—Law and Natural Law—is immutable. The essence of *Dharma*, I, therefore, conceives as follows:

> "*Dharma* is the law conceptually the relationship of Law, Life and Morality (LLM). The copyright of *Dharma* belongs to the Creator God Who Himself disseminated to the human beings to assimilate it for follow up action with *Nyaya* (Justice) and *Yukti* (natural reason, logic, rationality and equity)".

Etymologically, *Dharma* is derived from the root *Dhri: Dharma, Dharayati Dhartam* and this infallible legal cosmology is indicated in *Rigveda: ato dharmani dharayam* that spells its value *Dharane*, viz., to uphold, to hold together, to support *Dharayate iti dharma*,[13] viz., to sustain (sustainability), to conserve (soil

---

12. Michael S. King, *Natural Law and the Bhaguvad-Gita, op. cit.*
13. See *Sharannagati, http://www.srivaishnava.org dated 17.10.2007;* Paul Horsch, *From Creation Myth To World Law: The Early History of Dharma*, Vol. 32, 2004, Journal of Indian Philosophy, 423; *Rigveda and Brahdaranyaka Upanishad* enjoin this universal *Vedic* law as quoted in Paul Horsch, *op. cit;* see also Joel P. Brereton, *Dharma in the Rigveda* Vol. 32, 2004, Journal of Indian Philosophy, 449; Patric Olivelle, *The Semantic History of Dharma*, Vol. 32, 2004, Journal of Indian Philosophy, 491; see also James L. Fitzgerald, The Mahabharata, 11 and 12 Books 'the Book on Women' and 'The Book of Peace", 2004, *Dharma* means preserving, maintaining; in the service of good law; men's meritorious lawful duty toward women, which is defence *raksana*, "keeping and preserving, protecting, defending, guarding profound responsibility. Men sacrificed life in a meritorious, lawful struggle (i.e. a *Yudha*-war

conservation against erosion and protecting from environmental erosion, global warming), to retain (values), to preserve (cultural heritage and values), to observe and to promote (human good, well-being of human beings, human happiness, human dignity, human rights), to develop (relationship between Law and Nature, and Law and Morality). This is the *Corpus Juris* of this immutable concept of *Dharma,* and as such supreme and infallible. It may be related to the nuances of *Latin* word *firmus* (firm) and *forma* (form) or *German Lingua fauna halten* (to hold), and *stutzen* (to support).[14] It is the creation of "the world order" (Cosmos) against chaotic disorder—insecure, unstable and shaky. This creative action is "law" both the 'eternal law' of nature/Creator/God as also the 'moral law' governing mankind. In the *Vedic lexicon* the term *Dharma* has been used 63 times in *Rigveda;* it occurs 13 times in *Atharvaveda;* it is found in 22 passages in *Yajurveda;* it invariably is used in 9 passages in *Upanishads.*[15] This Law and Morality conceptual relationship may be presented in the following theorem:

---

that conformed to enjoined duty, *dharma,* and produced merit, *dharma,* for all who so conformed their behaviour, hard it was) to protect the earth and all the life earth makes possible, to hold, to support, the text justifies the entire system of family and society grounded in this theme of *raksana.*

The expression *Dharma* cannot be translated, but can only be transcribed. In *Shantiparva of Mahabharata Dharma* has been transcribed as good deed; merit; meritorious deed; duty (and, in specific context, rule, norm, custom, obligation, responsibility; law, the laws, the law, law; lawful deed; meritorious lawful deed; the good law; right (noun) and right (adjective), justice and just; virtue, good character; virtuous; see James L. Fitzgerald, *The Mahabharata,* 11 and 12 Books, 2004, pp. 641-644.

14. Paul Horsch, *op. cit.*
15. Joel P. Brereton, *op. cit.*

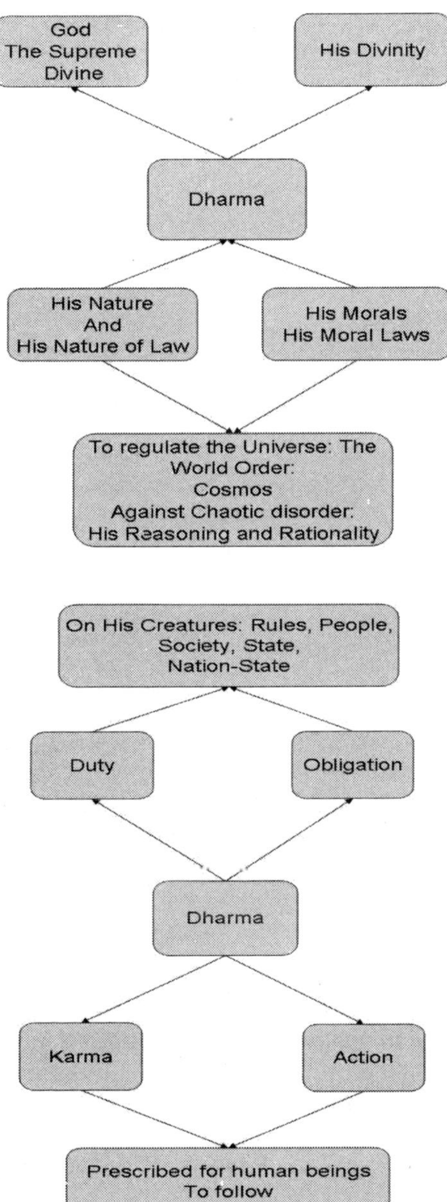
God
The Supreme
Divine
His Divinity
Dharma
His Nature
And
His Nature of Law
His Morals
His Moral Laws
To regulate the Universe: The
World Order:
Cosmos
Against Chaotic disorder:
His Reasoning and Rationality
On His Creatures: Rules, People,
Society, State,
Nation-State
Duty
Obligation
Dharma
Karma
Action
Prescribed for human beings
To follow

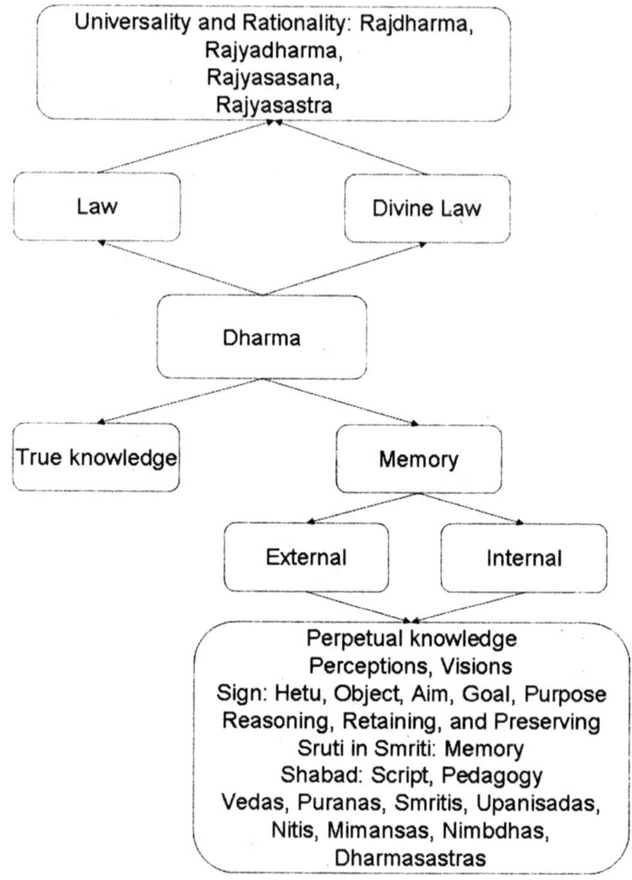

It unequivocally discerns that *Dharma* has a broader connotation and ordains law, religion, rectitude and morality regulating life and conduct of human beings so as to fit into the wider context of nature and the Cosmos—the world order.[16] It means the whole gamut of law, justice, morals, ethics, manners, and customs. It ordains an ordered social hierarchy with duties, obligations and responsibilities as first priority living

16. http://www.srivaishnava.org dated 17.10.2007.

harmoniously as well as happily with psychological and sociological state of affairs within the framework of *Dharma.*[17] This I have expressed above when I submit the concept of natural law: "*Dharma as Law and Morality or Natural Law is a law and a set of such rules that regulate human conduct, and human conduct depends upon human behaviour, which is controlled by psychogenic and sociogenic influences.*"[18]

Dharma may be conceived as a culture which ordains the essentials of social law and also the essentials of individual law. Humans have to observe the code of conduct as a duty, obligation, and responsibility—this is *Dharma.* The inevitable and inexorable vision of the concept of human dignity is inbuilt in *Dharma,* which provides the *modus Vivendi* as to how to live from cradle to grave/ashes gracefully as well as peacefully by means of action—*Karma.* This perception of *Dharma* has the facets of *Rita* (harmony), social *Dharma: Ashrams* (stages of life), Human *Dharma* and *Swadharma* (individual or one's personal or individualistic *Dharma*). Thus, adherence to *Dharma* is imperative for the reason that the human propensity to be good and do well is a natural characteristic. *Dharma* is infallible since its concern is for all living beings making life worth. Therefore, it unequivocally appears that *Dharma* relates to moral, nature and conduct than to religious.[19]

In the backdrop of the above, it seems that the root *Dhri* meaning is instrumental as the means by which an action is effected, and, therefore, the root meaning survives not as a cosmological myth but as a clear comprehension of the concept to its consistent seamless web of law+nature+morality meanings, such as law, order, duty, obligation, custom, quality, classification, adjudication, justice, truth, model, rule (*la, loi*).[20] This root meaning also sustains "to uphold (*halten*), or to support (*stutzen*) law and nature, and law and morals relationship so beautifully gained for humanity. It seems a conceivable seamless web as *Dharma* is understood in a dynamic functional sense

17. *Ibid.*
18. *Supra* Introduction.
19. *Supra* 122.
20. See Paul Horsch, *op. cit.*, pp. 426-427.

rather than a mere mythological parallel or cosmological myth or rituals controlled by the priests to the cultic level.[21]

Dharma in the ethical-moral-social sense is the foundation of order, stability and regularity, and as such "becomes a general law (*Gesetz*) to which human beings must conform."[22] In the perspective of this, it may be expedient to say that what *Rita* is to cosmic territory, *Dharma* to the moral, social sphere.[23] It seems that *Dharma* in its relation to humans at all levels in all places is conceptually used in the ethical/moral-juridical/law sense. As such, it is the etymological translation in precision of law, duty, obligation, and right seamless web. Nevertheless, in the realm of *Dharma*, the "social law" becomes the duty, obligation of the individual person.[24] Thus, from the ethical standpoint, *Dharma* also implies a "commandment", that is "an obligation."[25] For example, where the duty to reproduce is involved, viz., the procreation of male offspring from one's wife alone to continue or perpetuate progenitor: *Prajana sveshu daareshu shouchmadroh ev ca.*[26] This unequivocally demonstrates the origin and birth of custom as well as customary law that "bears people too many places, each according to its fixed domicile, with different languages and various laws (*nanadharmanam*)."[27] This is the universality of *Dharma* conveying the sense of universal order and plurality of customs. *Vedic* literature and its *lingua fauna* does not give the abstract meaning of the concept of law, rather it gives concrete meaning of the concept of law by separating *Dharma* from cosmic-rituals, and *a multo fortiorari* it is transformed into the ethical/moral-juridical/law seamless web.[28]

In the backdrop of the above, it may be safe to submit that despite its deep association with natural-cosmic phenomenon (world creation); *Dharma* conceptually is used in the ethical/ moral-juridical/law relationship conceptually (elevation to

21. *Ibid.*
22. Paul Horsch, *op. cit.*, p. 430.
23. *Id.*, p. 431.
24. *Id.*, pp. 432-433.
25. *Ibid.*
26. *Mahabharata, Shantiparva* 60, 7-8.
27. *Ibid.*
28. *Ibid.*

world law).[29] It is a transformation from the 'cosmos support, stability, permanence and regularity' to 'commandments, duties, obligations and customs of people' sustainable to the maintenance of the social order.[30] This 'social order' is broadly perceived as the 'world law' that comprises all realms of the globe—the cosmic-ritual, and ethical/moral-juridical/law. Such innovations of *Dharma* are ordained in *Vedas, Puranas, Upanishads, Samhitas, Nitis, Smritis, Dharmshastras, and Mimansas;* are accepted, 'even preserving its traces of cosmologic origin'.[31]

In sociological-legal perspectives the binding authority of *Dharma* as law has been acknowledged. It binds the king and the weaker or affluent and the lowly and the lost equally as *Dharma* is the King of Kings, and as such all are equally subject to *Dharma Law* and not the *vice versa*: *Tadait-kshatrasayya kshatram yadharma// tasamaadharmaratparam naasit// atho abllian balliyasamashansatai dharmen// yathaa raagayya evam: Law is the king of kings; nothing is superior to law; the law aided by the power of the king enables the weak to prevail over the strong.*[32] Dr. S. Radhakrishnan also observes, "even kings are subordinate to *Dharma*, to the Rule of Law'.[33] *Dharma* Law is truth. It is said that one who speaks the truth that he speaks in accordance with the law, and one who speaks in accordance with the law that he speaks the truth: *Satyam Vada Dharmam Cara: Speak the truth, conduct yourself according to the law.*[34] Therefore, *Dharma* in this perspective is supreme law, right virtue, and ethical/moral merit.[35] Be that as it may, the concept of *Dharma* is decisive in the sense of law, moral law, duty, obligation, right in all stages of life—*Varna*—and is indeed a significant "reason for the

29. *Id.*, pp. 434-435.
30. *Ibid.*
31. *Ibid.*
32. See Sarvadhikari, History of Hindu Law, Tagore Law Lectures, 1880, p. 10 as quoted in M. Rama Jois, legal and Constitutional History of India, Vol. I, p. 10.
33. Dr. S. Radhakrishnan, The Principal Upanishads, p. 170.
34. *Taittiriya Upanishad and Brahdaranyaka Upanishad*; see also Paul Horsch, *op. cit.*, p. 437; Joel P. Brereton, *op. cit.*, pp. 484-485; Patrick Olivelle, *op. cit.*, pp. 496-497.
35. *Ibid.*

formation of the immense *Dharmsastra* literature."[36] *Dharma* in the sense of moral law has been personified as the Judge—*Dharma Devta*—who is not blindfolded—for the dispensation of justice in accordance with his *Dharma Chakra*. Consequently, with the decrease of *Dharma*—Morality, *Adharma*—immorality—increases. It thus seems that, on the whole, the legal process and the world process is heavily as well as significantly determined with the development of the moral/ethical *Dharma*.

Dharma is thus perceived as a sustainable model for the development of Indian laws on the foundations of Law and Morals, and Law and nature. Therefore, *Dharma* expresses a variety of morals that are action-based,[37] that is, "that an individual will strive to do the right thing at the right time and will give his best. Appropriate action, following one's duty, is the aim of life (*Dharma, karma*), not just *Moksha*.[38] For example, *Varna* system in the Indian society has had been conceived, and rightly so, upon the concept of action and duties to society towards its welfare. Accordingly, the modern discrimination growth by castes is a perversion and shorn of *Dharma's* true meaning.[39] Another radiant illustration may be cited from Article 51-A (j) of the Constitution of India, 1950, which enjoins that "it shall be the duty of every citizen to strive towards excellence in

---

36. See P.V. Kane, History of *Dharmsastra*, Vols. I-V, Vols. I & III; see and *cf*. Paul Horsch, *op. cit*., p. 437.
37. See Hinduism, http://www.haryana-online.com dated 17.10.2007.
38. Werner Menski, From *Dharma* to Law and Back? Postmodern Hindu Law in a Global World, Heidelberg papers in South Asian and Comparative Politics, 2004.
39. *Bhagavad-Gita*, IV, Canto 13 *Chaaturvarnyam mayaa srishtam gunakarma vibhaagashah; Tasya kartaaram api maam viddhyakartaaram avyayam*: The four varnas were emanated by me, by the different distribution of qualities—*Gunas*—and actions; know Me to be the author of them, though the actionless and inexhaustible.; Annie Besant, The *Bhagvad Gita* Text and Translation, 2002 ed.; Hinduism, *op. cit; see Manu's Code of Law Manvadharmasastra, op. cit*., p. 40: Sudra for Manu is often a code of word; it identifies the enemy and it encompasses a wide cross-section of society, both past and present; see James L. Fitzgerald, The *Mahabharata, Shantiparva*, 11 and 12, 2004, p. 79, *Chaaturvarnah* laws relate to The Everlasting Good Law or Meritorious Laws of the four social orders and the four Patterns of Life.

all spheres of individual and collective activity so that the nation constantly rises to higher levels of endeavour and achievement".

In the backdrop of the above, it manifestly and undoubtedly appears that the concept of *Dharma* is the treasure house of values + ethics + morals + law + action + duties + obligations and together constitutes the "science of law", life and literature as well as the repositories of civil society that man seeks to have civility.[40] In other words, *Dharma* relates to law, morality, ethics, and moral as well as ethical life of humanity. It refers to the underlying order in nature, and also signifies 'the way things are'. Legally, morally, and ethically, *Dharma* means 'right way of living' and 'proper conduct'.[41]

Horizons of *Dharma* as law have been examined and re-examined in depth by many scholars. *Dharma* has long been recognized as a centerpiece of law, but, however, unfortunately as well as ironically, misunderstood because of the contrived and artificial comprehension of *Dharmsastra* by the colonial rule in India urging that it is only personal law applicable to Hindus.[42] Donald R. Davis argues that *Dharma* is ubiquitous in the all pervading scholastic traditions of India that is Bharat and beholds wondrous things about law as legal rules, legal categories, legal duties, legal obligations, morals, ethics and legal reasoning.[43] He, therefore, conceives that conceptually *Dharma* in *Dharmasastra* refers to law; there is close affiliation between *Dharma* and law, such as "the *Dharma* of rulers, *Dharma* of ruled, *Dharma* in familial as well as filial relationship, *Dharma* in society, and the *Dharma* of others.[44] In this perspective, understanding of *Dharma* as law shall necessitate the expansion

---

40. See Swami Vireshananda, The Ideal of Ethics in the Upanishad, Sri Ramakrishnan Math, http://www. Sriramakrishnanmath.org dated 17.10.2007.
41. *Sanatana dharma or Hinduism*, http://dharma.indviews.com dated 17.10.2007.
42. Donald R. Davis, Jr., *Hinduism as a Legal Tradition*, Journal of the American Academy of Religion, 30 May, 2007, http://jaar.oxfordjournals.org dated 17.10.2007.
43. *Ibid.*
44. See *Dharmsastra, Arthasastra, Shantiparva, Ramayana, Bhagvada-Gita, Mahabharata*; see in particular James L. Fitzgerald, *The Mahabharata*, *op. cit.*, p. xvii.

sense of law to include wider variety of binding rules that would reach every realm including morality, rather than conceiving it to its restrictive understanding that it is a law that refers to courts, contracts, crime, punishment, and administered by a state.[45] The problem with this restrictive thinking of law is that it is hopelessly conceived, limited historically to recent centuries and geographically by and large to European countries and their colonies.[46] *Dharma* as law is conceived to speak of justice and order with perpetual effects that produce results in both intermediate and ultimate goods for the performer and society.[47] Besides, *Dharma* as law expresses in the form of heuristically ascertainable rules (*Vidhi*) that is the cause of knowing *Dharma* realistically (*Jnapakahetu*), rather than confining to mere arm chair speculations.[48] In this view, though *Dharma* as law is morally intuited, but *Dharma* as law rather is discerned through an investigation of empirical sources, and this is the most scientific way of comprehending *Dharma* and law. This view also unfolds that just ends are reached by just means. This helps to better understanding of means and manners of legal acts (*kartavya, karma*), viz., to comprehend to differentiate ordinary acts from legal acts. This way *Dharma* as law provides for correct or proper procedure to take into account inevitability of mistakes, intentional or unintentional, for effective mode of action both punishment (*Danda*) and penances (*Prayascitta*) that ameliorate or rectify legal mistakes or transgressions.[49] For example, thieves begging rulers for punishment as a form of penance or judges pronouncing both a punishment and penance (*Prayascitta*) for adultery.[50] However, *Dharma* as law is also concerned with legal procedure (*Vyavahara*), the object of which is truth, how to eliminate doubts and adjudicate conflicts over

---

45. *Supra* note 147.
46. *Ibid;* see also Berman Harold J., Law and Revolution: The Foundation of the Western Legal Tradition, 1983; Fitzgerald James, *Dharma* and its Translation in the *Mahabharata,* (32) 2004, Journal of Indian Philosophy, pp. 671-685.
47. *Supra* note 147.
48. *Ibid.*
49. *Ibid.*
50. *Ibid;* see also Jolly Julius, Hindu Law and Custom, 1928, pp. 263-267.

differing claims to be right or just or the cause of making judgments in cases of doubts about *Dharma* (*Samadehanir, Nyayahetu*).[51]

Unfortunately, this rich as well as significant legal side of *Dharma* was caused to eclipse. The reasons are not far to seek. *Dharma* as law and *Dharmsastra* was speciously as well as improperly understood or conceived by the British colonial rule as the law of the land and administered as personal law to Hindus as such in colonial rule in India, and as such bringing the disastrous consequences by belittling its sustained significance. This seemed British colonial concoction to a false perception that *Dharma* has little or no connection to law. This misconception or wrong notion has inhibited the inquisitive that *Dharma* as law is conceived as jurisprudence of the training and disciplining of lawyers, judges, and thinkers in how to think legally reasonably as well as rationally. Therefore, law goes with *Dharma* and similarly influences other conceptions, and is a legal way or lawful manner to put it into practice or actions or to give actions meaning. Transgression of *Dharma* as law is crime, violent crime, adultery, recidivism, delinquent, and legal transgression (*sastraviruddhacara*) that produces sin (*dosa*). Besides, *Dharma* has moral notions in terms of law, viz., above bias, attachment, love, affection, emotions, prejudices, etc. For example, *Ramayana* gives a juristic example of *Dharma* when Rama rebukes his younger brother Lakshmana's suggestion prior to his submission to their father Dashratha's command to renounce his claim to the throne and to take up fourteen years period exile so that his younger brother Bharat may become king: "I well know, Lakshmana, the profound affection you bear me. But you fail to understand the real meaning of truth and self-restraint (*sama*). Righteousness is paramount in the world and on righteousness is truth founded (*Dharme satyam pratisthitam*). This command of father's is based on righteousness and is absolute. Having once heard a father's command, a mother's or a Brahman's, one must not disregard it. ...So give up this ignoble (*anarya*) notion that is based on the code of the *Ksatriya and Ksatradharmasritam*; be of like mind with

51. *Supra* 154; Dr. Ludo Rocher, *Vacaspati Misra Vyavaharacintamani* A Digest on Hindu Legal Procedure, 1956.

me and based your actions on righteousness, not violence (*taiksnyam*)." This example seems to be a rich model of *Dharma juristic* aspect. Rama does not want to be swayed away by the love, affection, or attachment of his mother and brother, because such influences are prejudicial in taking righteous decision decisively. Therefore, his rational reasoning to explain *Dharma* as law-morals correlative is imperative for him to be a Jurist. *Dharma* is conceived as a *Rashtra* Law as an embodiment of *Rashtrabhakti*, viz., national interest is above individual interest: *Api swaranmavyi Lanka naa shobhate Lakshmana, Janani janambhumisca swaragadapi griyasi.* This shows Rama's filial duty; this shows *Dharma's* conceptual framework of duty. Similarly, *Bhagavad Gita* is also a juristic explanation to *Dharma* as righteous action for righteous cause, viz., to achieve righteous cause (ends) a righteous action (means) is the only alternative the performance of which howsoever painful it may be. Arrayed person (Arjuna) has to be brought back to the righteous path to performing duty as unattached, unbiased, and non-prejudice person, and that alone helps to arrive at judicious decision decisively. This example from *Bhagavad Gita* shows Krishna as a great Jurist in explaining juristic-moral correlations of *Dharma*. The main argument of it is to show the insights of the legal side and objective reality of *Dharma* is not conspicuously absent, and it shall be absurdity to supersede it by the vocabulary of *rituals, cultic, communal, religious, and unscientific* rhetoric. Therefore, morality and law are intimately connected conceptually and largely not distinguished from each other.

M. Rama Jois explains the concept of *Dharma* as law (*Dharamswarupa Nirupanam*) as the legal system (*Vyavahara Dharmasastra*) of the country having widest import and has no corresponding word in any *lingua fauna* of the world.[52] It means law, justice (*Nyaya*), moral, religion, pious or righteous conduct, being helpful to living beings, giving charity or alms, natural qualities or characteristics or properties of living beings and things, duty, obligation, law and usage or custom having the force of law, and a valid *Rajasasana* (royal edict for good/sustainable governance/management with transparency

52. Legal and Constitutional History of India, Vol. I, 1984, p. 3.

and accountability).[53] According to *Mahabharata-Shantiparva-Dharma*, as asserted by Yudhishtra, which helps the upliftment of living beings, or which ensures welfare of living beings, or which sustains is *Dharma*.[54] According to *Taittiriya Samhita: Dharmo Vishvasaya Jagataa Pratishtha, Loke Dharmishtham Praja Upsarpanti, Dharme Sarvam Pratishthitam: Dharma* constitutes the foundation of all affairs in the world; people respect one who adheres to *Dharma*. *Dharma* insulates man against sinful thoughts and actions. Law (*Dharma*) is the foundation of the universe.[55] According to Jaimini *Dharma* is conducive to the highest good.[56] *Dharma* is that which sustains and ensures progress and welfare of all in this world.[57] *Dharma* is promulgated in the form of commands.[58] *Dharma, Artha and Kama (Trivarga)* are ordained for the welfare and happiness of the people and the ruler is entrusted with a responsibility/duty/obligation of enforcing *Dharma*.[59] Anger (*krodha*), passion (*moha*), greed (*lobha*), infatuation (*mada*), and enmity (*matsarya*) are the natural impulses recognized enemies of man and if allowed to act like unruly horse may instigate him to entertain evil thoughts resulting in deviant as well as recidivist actions causing civil and criminal injuries to others.[60] Succinctly, *Dharma* as law regulates the mutual obligations of individual and the society, and, therefore, the protection of *Dharma* is in the interest of both the individual and the society: *Dharmaiv hato hanti dharmo rakshati rakshita*.[61] *Dharma* as law has been recognized as the king of kings; nothing is superior to law; the law aided by the power of the king enables the weak to prevail over the strong, viz., kings are subordinate to *Dharma* Law, to the Rule of Law,[62] and then

53. *Ibid.*
54. *Ibid.*
55. *Id.* pp. 4-6.
56. *Ibid.*
57. *Ibid.*
58. *Ibid.*
59. *Ibid.*
60. *Ibid.*
61. *Ibid.*
62. *Ibid*, see Dr. S. Radhakrishnan, *op. cit.*

alone Rule of Law becomes the Rule of Life. This definition of *Dharma* as law also enunciates its enforceability.

Dr. Nagendra Singh in his *Juristic Concepts of Ancient Indian Polity* gives beautiful exposition of the concept of *Dharma* asserting that *Dharma* as law has been expounded rationally and not theologically.[63] He opines that ancient Indian literature describes *Dharma* as sacred law; *vyavahara* or secular law; *charitra* or customary law; *rajasasana* or royal edict for good/sustainable governance/management, transparency as well as accountability, and these laws have been conceived to governing family—*Kuladharma*—and the State—*Desadharma*.[64] Law *lex* has been supreme as king of kings *rex*. He urges, quoting from authoritative sources like *Shantiparva of the Mahabharata, Rigveda, Kautilya's Arthasastra, Sukraniti, Manusmriti, that Dharma* is a code of law to restore conditions of order, law, justice, and security to prevent anarchy or *arajaka* for the protection of all in the world. This could be achieved by the State with its principles of statecraft as its protecting branches, with its four beautiful flowers of *sama* (conciliation), *dana* (concession), *danda* (force), and *bheda* (dissension), and its three fruits of *dharma, artha, and kama* (law, religion, social, economic welfare), which encapsulate the entrenched concept of access to justice and distributive justice, viz., law, morals, justice—economic, social, political, human dignity, fraternity, and integrity.[65] [*Namo'stu rajyavrksaya sadgunyaya prasakhine, samadi charupuspaya trivarga phaladayine: Let us bow to the State for the sake of dharma and artha—social and economic well-being—which may be regarded as the aims of the State.]* In the backdrop of this, it seems that *Dharma* as law as well as constitutional law constitutes Constitutional functions of the State and secures social, economic, political justice, viz., welfare and well-being, as the objects or aims or ideals of the State. *Dharma* as law aims at attaining good governance/management with ample transparency as well as accountability so that each individual is able to enjoy his/her life and property; good governance/management alone prevents anarchy or *arajaka* :

63. Dr. Nagendra Singh, Juristic Concepts of Ancient Indian Polity, 1980, p. 48.
64. *Id*. p. 7.
65. *Id*. pp. 12, 13.

Arajake hi lokesmin, sarvo vidrute bhayat, raksârthamasya sarvasya, rajanamasrjat prabhuh.[66] It unequivocally discerns that the supremacy of *Dharma* as law and subordination to law and morality have been recognized and he who acts contrary to it or disobeys it shall get ruined or destroyed.[67] Therefore, obedience to the laws of *Dharma* seems apparently to be enforced by all—the ruler, the ruled. It seems perceivable that *Dharma* as law is the king of kings, and it stands in sharp contrast to the Western theory, "king can do no wrong."[68]

Dr. A.S. Altekar opines that the ancient Indian concept of *Dharma* includes rules and laws of morality and prudence.[69] He asserts that it was not a scheme of life evolved and determined by cultic priests who conceived *Dharma* as mere religious and ritualistic in their interests, but *Dharma* as law, morality and prudence contained rules which made a liberal allowance for the changes in the customary, civil, and criminal law, as sanctioned by popular usage and moulded by the State guidance.[70] For example, the practice of levirate (*niyoga*) [conceiving a child by the brother of the deceased husband or conceiving the child through other sources other than the legal spouse] stamped out of existence because its practice was conceded to be immoral, unethical, and contrary to all canons of law of *Dharma.*[71] Similarly, succession over the entire patrimony is wrong and as such questionable morality. *Dharma* enjoins duty to right such wrong. Be that as it may, the State sought to encourage *Dharma law* by promoting piety, righteousness, by extending equal patronage to all sects and establishments and by financing public utility services not as a theocratic or theological State but as a social welfare State making *Dharma* as one of its aim.[72]

---

66. *Id.* pp. 14, 15; *Manusmriti*, VII, 3.
67. *Id.* pp. 17, 18.
68. *Id.* pp. 20, 21.
69. Dr. A.S. Altekar, State and Government in Ancient India, 1955, pp. 254-255, 45-47.
70. *Ibid.*
71. *Ibid.*, see Manu's Code of Law *Manvadharmasastra, op. cit.*, pp. 197-198, *Chapter 3.173, Chapter 9.57-70, 120-121, 143-147, 167.*
72. *Ibid.*

In the same vein quintessential of *Dharma* as law has been acknowledged by many thinkers, scholars, and jurists in their scholastic writings. Dr. P.V. Kane summarizes the law of *Dharma* as follows:[73]

> The *Dharmasastra* authors hold that *dharma* was the supreme power in the state and was above the King who was only the instrument to realize the role of *Dharma*.

Dharma, thus, is the sovereign of the State as true law and constitution which is enforced by the State and its machinery.[74] In the backdrop of this, the *raison d'être* of *Dharma* conceptually as law and morality correlative is the upholding of law and the creation of conditions of peace, order and happiness for which Divinity has prescribed *Dharma* as the doctrine, the ruler as the executor of it and *moksa* (salvation) is attained by *Dharma* as the ultimate goal of all.[75] *Dharma* as law, justice, morals, legal and moral duties have been founded on the conceptual framework of "right" and "wrong", and, therefore, all laws being deemed to be grounded in *Dharma* or law and moral duties which is a law throughout ancient Indian literature and perceptions thereby.[76] *Dharma* is the universal principle of law, order, harmony, truth, pure reality, law of humanity and human dignity, law of human happiness, law of sustainability, law of human as well as all creatures good, law of good/sustainable governance/management, and law of property and property-bearer (*Dharma and dharmin*).[77] *Dharma* is also known as *purusharthas*, viz., *Dharma* does not permit sycophancy because that is against fair approach to take righteous action. *Dharma* conceptually is law, morals, duty (*kartavya*), actions and activity (*karma and pravriti*), *varna*

73. Dr. P.V. Kane, History of *Dharmsastra*, Vol. III, p. 241.
74. See Dr. R.K. Mukherji, Chandragupta Maurya and his Times, p. 49.
75. See Dr. Nagendra Singh, India and International Law, Vol. I, pp. 1-22.
76. See N.C. Sen-Gupta, Evolution of Ancient Indian Law, Tagore Law Lectures, 1950, 1953.
77. See *Dharma* Wikipedia Encyclopedia, http://en.wikipedia.org/wiki/Dharma dated 17.10.2007 pp. 1-12; see also concept of *Dharma* in *Ramayana*, http://schools-wikipedia.org/wp/r/Ramayana.htm dated 17.10.2007.

shramadharma (nothing to do with castes because that is not included in *varna*), justice (*Nyaya*), rules of conduct, code of conduct, mores, customs, religio-legal-ethical code and rationality, logic and reasoning (*Yukati*), and as such *Dharma* surely serves the stabilization of society. Justice has not been identified with blind justice as a blind guide to the solution of disputes because Indian Goddess of Justice is not blindfolded; rule-of-thumb decisions have been avoided and mutual adjustments favoured as court practices (*Dharma vyavahara*), which in the modern legal language is called 'mediation', 'conciliation', and 'arbitration'.[78] This unequivocally is the global concept of *Dharma* as law.[79]

Dharma (law) and *Danda* (force, sanction, and punishment) are inasmuch as integrated that if it is ignored then there shall be the law of jungle, viz., *matsyanyaya* where big fish swallows the small fish. This in essence is the law of punishment (virtues of *Dandaniti*). *Danda* must be wielded discretely for the governance of the State as well as means of its protection with the sole object of happiness of all and the progress of the realm, because *Danda* keeps awake when all are sleeping, viz., it is the ever vigilant *Danda* with its all pervading force which keeps thieves, criminals away and hence *Danda* is *Dharma* : *Danda sashist praja sarva danda aivbhirakshati, danda supteshu jagriti danda dharmam vidurbudha. Danda* prevents *arajakta* (lawlessness); it is a contributory factor in the promotion of an orderly society, because it is *Danda* who is the king and it is *danda* who is the regulator of the universe: *sa raja puruso dandah san eta sasita ca sah.*[80] *Manusmriti, Sukraniti und Kautilya Arthasastra* also enjoin that it is because of fear of *Danda* alone that the world observes the laws of *Dharma* and each

78. See Varghese Manimala, The Four Goals of Life in Hindu Thought as Principles for a Civil Society, http;//www.crvp.org/book/Series)1/1-16/chapter_xvi.htm, chapter XVI, pp. 1-14 dated 17.10.2007.

79. http://www.dharmaconference.org dated 17.10.2007, every sect of Hindu or Vedic *Dharma*, viz., Hinduism, Jainism, Buddhism, Sikhism (*Taji sabh bharam bhajio paarbrahm, kaho Nanak attal ih Dharma*); see also Sri Aurobindo, Integral Yoga Literature, Vol. 13, Essays on the Gita.

80. *Manusmriti*, VII, 17; see also M. Rama Jois, *op. cit.*, 324-347.

individual is able to enjoy his life and property.[81] *Danda* or punishment or sanction or force behind the State is the most valuable device for the benefit of mankind: *Sarvo dandajito loko, durlabho hi sucirnarah, dandasya hi bhayat sarvain, jagad bhogaya kalpate.*[82] Same is the thematic thrust in *Sukraniti* that unequivocally states that the fear of *rajadanda* compels individuals to stick to their duty and respect the laws of *Dharma*, so essential for human happiness: *Rajadandabhayal lokah svasvadharmaparo bhavet.*[83] It is asserted in *Manusmriti* that there is a direct connection between *Danda* and *Dharma* and all objects—animate or inanimate—observe *Dharma* or duty because of *Danda: Tasya sarvani bhutani sthavarani carani ca, bhayad bhogaya kalpante svadharmanna calanti ca.*[84] Therefore, the validity of all laws have their intrinsic conformity to the standards of equity as propounded by *Dharma* coupled with the sanction/punishment/ *danda* of social usage. It, therefore, discerns that law without the authority of *Dharma* and *Danda* is impotent.[85] It may be submitted that the condition of law without *Dharma, Morals, and Danda* shall be the same as that of a person/ruler/king who is voluptuous, partial and deceitful.[86] Therefore, the significance of *Danda* has been acclaimed by the *Dharmasastras* as a great gift given to mankind for the reasons that punishment or fear of punishment protects *Dharma, artha and kama* (the law, the lawful wealth and lawful desires of human beings): *Danda sanrakshate dharmam tathaivartham janadhip, kamam sanrakshate dandistrivago dand ucayate.*[87]

---

81. As quoted in Dr. Nagendra Singh, Juristic Concepts of Ancient Indian Polity, *op. cit.*, p. 15.
82. *Ibi; Manusmriti*, VII, 22; see also M. Rama Jois, *op. cit.*, pp. 10-11.
83. *Sukraniti*, I, 23.
84. *Manusmriti*, VII, 15, 14.
85. *Supra* note 186 at p. 110.
86. *Id.*, p. 114.
87. *Mahabharata Shantiparva*, 15-3; M. Rama Jois, *op. cit.*, p. 324; James L. Fitzgerald, *op. cit.* at pp. 195-205 and pp. 470-478 transcribes the concept as well as significance of *Danda* as enjoined in The *Shantiparva of Mahabharata*: "The king's rod of punishment governs all creatures, the rod of punishment protects them, the rod of punishment stands watch while everyone sleeps—the wise know that the rod is Law. The rod of punishment guards Law and likewise Profit, overlord of men,

ii. *Dharma* and the Concept of State: Sovereignty, *Rajdharma, Rajayadharma, Rajasasana Rajyasastra:* Good/Sustainable Governance/Management

The State polity in ancient India was known by several expressions such as *Rajdharma, Rajayadharma, Rajasasana, Rajyasastra, rajnitisaastra.* These expressions ascribe the 'science

---

and it guards Pleasure—the rod of punishment is said to be the whole group of the three pursuits. Grain is protected by the rod of punishment; wealth is protected by the rod of punishment. . . . Law, which has punishment as a name, was established in the world so mortals would have no confusion, and so riches would be protected. . . . If there were no rod of force in the world, these creatures would perish; the stronger would roast the weaker on a spit like fish. [Some time in the past this truth was spoken by Brahma: 'The rod of punishment protects creatures, when applied well. Look how fires go out when they are not afraid; but when scolded, they blaze up from fear of punishment'.] If punishment did not exist in the world, separating the right and the wrong, all that is here would be like blind darkness; nothing at all would be perceived. . . . If the rod did not rule, the celibate student would not study Veda, the lovely cow would not give milk, and a girl would not marry. If the rod did not rule, everything would be neglected, all barriers would be shattered, and men would not recognize individual possession. ...All creatures stand within the sway of the rod of punishment. Wise men know that fear is the rod. Heaven and this human world as well, stand firm upon the base of the rod of punishment. Where the enemy annihilating rod is active and well administered, deceit, evil, and fraud are not seen. ... Law was promulgated in the world just so the world could function. The most excellent summary statement of Law is 'Doing no injury and the rightful inflicting of injury'. No one is absolutely virtuous, and no one is absolutely devoid of virtue. Both right and wrong are seen in everything that must be done. Men castrate animals, and they punch holes in their noses, and they tie them and tame them; and many animals pull heavy loads. ...(The) rod of punishment is the one thing in this world upon which everything depends. "Judicial process" is regarded to be a name of Law. The very proceeding of judicial process is directed to this end: "How may this Law, *Dharma*, the whole collectivity of Meritorious Deeds, which applies to the populated realms, not be interrupted?" It is called "judicial process" in this world because there is in it an accounting of a lawsuit. The rod of force supreme is a divine being: It is like a blazing fire in physical appearance".

of the kingdom'/State/Nation State/governance/management.[88] These expressions are believed to have been derived from *Niti/Nitisastra*, which popularly concern with the science of government, good/sustainable governance aiming at securing all round progress and prosperity of society.[89] *Sukra* in *Sukranitisara* asserts that *Rajdharma and Rajyasastra* are *sine qua non* for the stability and progress of society in all directions. *Kautilya* in *Arathasastra* contends that *Arathsastra* is also the science of government as well as good/sustainable governance which deals with the acquisition and protection or governance of territory.[90] These expressions are not the product of imagination, but concretely lay down the principles of the administration of polity or State comity or civil administration through the doctrines of *Rajdharma*—the law of the constitution—, *Rajyadharma*—the law of administration—, *Rajyasasana*—the law of governance/good governance. These terms deal with the duties and responsibilities of all and also describe the nature and functions of the different *Prakritis* (phenomenon) of the State to attain harmony, happiness, peaceful lives on account of their innate virtuous disposition.[91] The phenomenon of the State is linked with the principles of statecraft, viz., *Sandhi* (agreement); *Vigraha* (hostilities); *Yana* (marching or mobilization); *Asana* (readiness to attack); *Dvaidhjbhava* (division of troops or double dealing); *Asraya* (subordinate alliance); the State has been conceded to perform a variety of functions, viz., *Sama* (conciliation), *dana* (concession), *danda* (force, sanction, punishment), *bheda* (dissension) to assure the dignity of the human being in the avowed aspects of the State *dharma, artha, and kama* (juristic, moral, social and economic welfare).[92] This unequivocally reveals that the nature of State was pure as well as virtuous welfare State and not a theocratic or theological. *Mahabharata, Kautilya, Manu, Sukra* have conceived State as an

88. Dr. A.S. Altekar, *op. cit.* p. 1; see also M. Rama Jois, *op. cit.*, pp. 575 *et. al.*
89. Dr. A.S. Alteker, *Id.*, pp. 2-4.
90. *Ibid.*
91. *Id.* 23 *et. al.*
92. See Dr. Nagendra Singh, Juristic Concepts of Ancient Indian Polity, *op. cit.*, pp. 12-13; see also M. Rama Jois, *op. cit.*, pp. 575 *et. al.*

organic unit that cover republics (*Gana Rajya*), Oligarchies (*Parmastya*), Kingdoms (*Samrajaya*), empires (*Chakravartins*), vassal kingdoms (*Samant Rajyas*), protectorates (*Samsryaraja*), and the State has been constituted of seven limbs (*angas*), namely, the king as its *atman* or soul, *amatyas* or ministers, *kosa* or treasury, *dand* or force, *mitra* or allies, *janapada* or provincial units, and *puras* or cities.[93] Similarly, they have conceived seven elements of the stable State for stability and sustainability, viz., king or *svamin*, minister or *amatya*, village communities or *janapada*, forts or *durga*, treasury *or kosa*, armed forces or *danda*, and allies or *mitra*, with an aim to constitute inter-State as well as intra-State relations for existence and co-existence.[94] This seems a significant advancement of the organic conception of *rastra*, State, political State, nation state of which territory, population, government and sovereignty are the important constituents. The basic function of the functionaries of the State has been conceptually articulated to act in conformity with *Dharma*—law, morals, *danda*, justice, truth, good governance, rule of law to serve rule of life. *Dharma*, therefore, seems to be perennial, everlasting, entrenched and immutable though its neglect as a strong foundation of law and nature, and law and morals has been exercise in futility to dry up its richness, because the soup and sauce of *'Dharma priyaatmana' or 'Nyaya mam priyaatmana' or 'Sruti smriti sadacara svasya ca priyaatmana, samayakmangkalpaja kamo dharma mulmidam smritam'* has not evaporated *Dharma* as soul of State. Therefore, it discerns that *Dharma* has been an infallible instrument of State polity. *Dharma* in relation to State has been considered to hold priority over all laws, and it has been the law most in use that is based on its intrinsic utility and accepted as valid as "equity, justice and good conscience" answering fully the basic requirements of justice or *Dharmanyaya*.[95] Not *ipse dixit* but empirically *Dharma* in relation to State polity has never been static but dynamic, ready to meet the challenges of the age, and, therefore, it has proved to be a living organism as well as a perennial foundation source of laws,

93. Dr. Nagendra Singh, *Id.*, pp. 29-30.
94. *Ibid.*
95. *Id.*, p. 100.

morals, ethics, justice to govern the vast governments, and for that reason alone the rulers could not enact despotic laws and get away with them. For instance, the concept of State changed from the basis of "war drum" (*bheri-gosa*) to "*Dharma-ghosa*: peaceful moral life."[96]

State in relation to sovereignty is not an isolated or abstract concept operating in vacuum, but it has the attribute of absolute supremacy, and accountable to none is a constant, ever present factor associated with sovereignty. Therefore, sovereignty encapsulates that fundamental authority which controls, restraints and protects man as a member of the society. Therefore, it seems that the concept of sovereignty from the dawn of human civilization has been linked to the concept of State or an organized society having a political entity.[97] Sovereignty in political entity has the attributes of *Praja* or the citizen-body or the populace; *Rashtra* or the State and its territory; *Rajan* or the king or the ruler as the wielder of *danda* or the power, or the authority, or sanction; *Dharma* or the laws of *Dharmasastras, such as sruti, smriti, etc.; Parameshwara* or the supreme creator. This close affinity between State and sovereignty has been contributory for the establishment of *Rajdharma* or the law of constitution, *Rajyadharma* or the law of administration, *Rajsasana or* the law of good/sustainable governance coupled with accountability and transparency for *Rajyotpattihi* or for the origin of State, State polity and its aims as well as purposes.[98] Consequently, the State administered with the aid of *Dharma* through the assistance of sagacious ministers secures *Nite falam dharmarathakamavapitiah*, viz., and the goal of State polity *Rajniti* is the fulfilment of *Dharma, Artha, and Kama.*[99] This is the incisive insight of *Rajdharma, Rajyadharma, and Rajsasana. Rajdharma* is the law of the constitution and is also known as *Rajnitisara, Nitisara, Dandaniti, Arthasastra, Shantiparva of Mahabharata,* relates to the constitution of the State and State polity, which is necessary to maintain the society in a state of *Dharma*, namely, all laws are merged in *Rajdharma*—compatible

96. *Id.*, p. 54.
97. *Id.*, pp. 104-107.
98. See M. Rama Jois, *op. cit.*, pp. 575-590.
99. *Ibid.*

to the constitution—and it is supreme *Dharma.*[100] According to Manu *Rajdharma* is indeed the constitutional law of the State, State polity.[101] It has been conceded to be one law, one constitution, one people, and one nation with many States, viz., as a society, the entire Indian population constituted itself into one homogeneous unit; political divisions of the country coming under the control of different rulers did not result in the division of the Indian society into separate nations.[102] The *Rajdharma* constitutional law nevertheless fundamental in the governance of the country has, therefore, uniform application throughout the territory of Indian Nation State as one composite unit, and it has been the duty of the State actors to apply it uniformly. This also *a multo fortiorari* spells out that *Rajdharma* is a rule compatible with *Dharma;* the law of administration, namely, *Rajyadharma,* conceives the application of laws, constitution, and justice. *Rajsasana* (royal edict) means law of good governance/ management coupled with accountability and transparency in accordance with *Rajdharma and Rajyadharma,* and declare all laws and actions (legislative as well as administrative) which are opposed or contrary to the constitution as invalid or void *ab initio: Tasmadharmam. yamikshtekshu sa vyavasayanradhpah, anikshtam capayanikshtekshu tam dharmam na vicalayath: Let no man transgress that law which the king decrees including the direction to do any act which he favours or desist from doing acts which he prohibits or disfavours; all should obey the king's decrees.*[103] *Rajsasana* explains the behaviour of the ruler since the 'ages (*Yugas*) are the results of the ruler's behaviour"[104] revealed through his *Rajsasana* governance, which is the preserver and upholder of *Dharma,* and the conserver of social traditions as well as the transformer of tradition.[105]

---

100. P.V. Kane, History of Dharmsastra, Vol. III, 3-9 at p. 3.
101. See Patric Olivelle, Manu's Code of Law: A Critical Edition and Translation of the *Manava-Dharmsastra,* 2005, VII-1, pp. 613-658, at p. 613.
102. M. Rama Jois, *op. cit.,* pp. 580-581.
103. *Supra* note 205, VII-13, at p. 614.
104. K.M. Pannikar as quoted in M. Rama Jois, *op. cit.,* pp. 629-630.
105. *Ibid.*

iii. *Dharma* and the Concept of Person/Man/Human Being

Sariatim and illuminating concept of *Dharma* in deep relation to person/man/human being is entrenched in *Dharmavidhi* (rules relating to *Dharma*), *Prayaschittavidhi* (rules relating to penance), *Manavadharma* (rules relating to persons/men/human beings and their conduct as well as behaviour compatible to *Dharma*). These are the rules of actions in normal times (*anapadikarmavidhi*), and rules of actions in times of adversity (*apadikarmavidhi*).[106] These splendid rules of actions are the laws of the social classes, viz., *Dharma* of the four *Varna* (*Chaturvarnyasya Dharmah: Dharmavidhi*).[107] The fruits emanating from the actions are ultimately for the consummation of all those who perform the actions and are enjoined in *Naihsreyasahkarmavidhi* (Rules of actions for securing the supreme good).[108] The purpose of supreme good is the securing of an orderly society—work for the good of the people—that expect men/women do not deviate from the said laws.[109] Any deviation from the prescribed laws, occasions reasons for litigations and, therefore, justice delivery system has been evolved (*Vyavaharapada*: Titles of Law for litigation and dispensation of justice).[110] It seems vividly that the aim of *Dharma* laws (*Vidhis*) is to present a blueprint for a properly ordered society with regard to areas of human activity—ritual, food, marriage, inheritance, adoption, debts both personal and commercial, judicial procedure, taxation, punishment, penance—shows that it was not divorced from reality[111] or did not work in vacuum as an abstract entity, rather it has been heuristic, empiricist. These *Vidhis* explicitly narrate that *rindana* (non-payment of debts—personal or commercial) must have

106. See Patrick Olivelle, Manu's Code of Law a Critical Edition and Translation of the *Manavadharmasastra*, 2005, pp. 1-73; see also *supra note 297*.
107. *Ibid; see also supra note 297.*
108. *Ibid.*
109. *Ibid.*
110. *Ibid.*
111. *Ibid.*

been the most common reason for disputant litigation[112] culminating into individual and group disputes concerning criminal law, civil law, familial relations law, public order and safety, arising out of litigious issues/causes such as non-payment of debt (*madana*); deposits (*niksepa*); sale without ownership (*asvamivikraya*); partnership (*sambhuyasamuttahana*); non-delivery of goods (*dattasyanapakarma*); breach of contract (*samvidvyatikarma*); cancellation of sale or purchase (*krayavikrayanusaya*); disputes between owners and herdsmen (*svamipalavivada*); boundary disputes (*simavivada*); verbal assault (*vakparusya*); physical assault (*dandaparusya*); theft (*steya*); violence (*sahasa*); sexual crimes against women (*strisamgrahana*); law concerning husband and wife (*stripumdharma*); partition (*vibhaga*); gambling and betting (*dyutasamahvaya*).[113] The

---

112. *Ibid.*
113. *Ibid.* In *Arthasastra Vyavaharapada* terms are used as *stripumdharma* (law concerning husband and wife); *dayavibhaga* (partition); *vastuvivada* (property disputes); *samayasyanapakarma* (breach of contract); *madana* (non-payment of debt); *aupanidhikam* (deposits); *dasakarmakalpa* (rules regarding workers); *sambhuyasamuttana* (partnership); *vikritakritanusaya* (cancellation of sale or purchase); *dattasyanapakarma* (non-delivery of gifts); *asvamivikraya* (sale without ownership); *sahasa* (violence); *vakparusya* (verbal assault); *dandaparusya* (physical assault); *dyutasamahvaya* (gambling and betting); *prakirnaka* (miscellaneous); *Yajnavalkya* uses these terms as *madana* (non-payment of debt); *Upanidhi* (deposits); *dayavibhaga* (partition); *simavivada* (boundary disputes); *svamipalavivada* (disputes between owners and hersmen); *asvamivikraya* (sale without ownership); *dattapradanika* (non-delivery of gifts); *kritanusaya* (cancellation of purchase); *abhayupetyasusrusa* (breach of contract of service); *samvidvytikrama* (breach of contract); *vetanadana* (non-payment of wages); *dyutasamahvaya* (gambling and betting); *vakparusya* (verbal assault); *dandaparsuya* (physical assault); *sahasa* (violence); *vikriyasampradana* (non-delivery after sale); *sambhuyasamutthana* (partnership); *steya* (theft); *strisamgrahana* (sexual crimes against women); *prakirnaka* (miscellaneous); and *Narada* expresses the terms as *madana* (non-payment of debt); *niksepa* (deposits); *sambhuyasamutthana* (partnerships); *dattapradanika* (non-delivery of gifts); *abhyupetyasusrusa* (breach of contract of service); *vetanasyanapakarma* (non-payment of wages); *asvamivikraya* (sale without ownership); *vikriyasampradna* (non-delivery after sale); *kritanusaya* (cancellation of purchase); *samayasyanapakarma* (breach of conventions); *ksetrajavivada* (land disputes); *stripumsamyoga* (relations

vayavaharapadas (rules of litigation— civil, criminal, familial) are for the orderly conduct of individuals and the duty of the ruler and his servants has been directed to work for the good of his people.[114] Therefore, anything that obstructs the orderly conduct must be eradicated as a matter of policy of "eradication of thorns" (*Kantaksodhana*).[115] In the orderly conduct of man and society, and the ruler (in democracy the elected representatives and executive heads) and his servants (in democracy citizens), it has been imperative not to accept gifts because that amounts to misuse of office or position and such allurement may be an offence or wrong or breach of trust or breach of office or abuse of office by intrusion of bribe, corruption, illegal gratification. Therefore, it is unworthy of a person/man to receive gifts that makes him as well as his office position impious and impure.[116] This unequivocally states the concept of person/man/human being *vis-à-vis Dharma*, viz., "No one should transact any business with uncleanness sinners; and under no circumstances should anyone abhor those who have been cleansed"[117] otherwise his/her "proclivity to virtue becomes weaker."[118] In the backdrop of this discussion, it seems that the basic aim of *Dharma* is to enhancing the personality of the person/man from cradle to grave (ashes), which depends upon the perspectives of conduct, behaviour, and life pattern. It depends on two aspects, first, "listen" (*sruyatam*), and, second, "learn" (*nibodhata*). Both "listen" and "learn" develop assimilation that culminates into decisive nature of justice and *adhivakta* (Advocate/Lawyer). *Dharma* the law has been disseminated by *Manu* to his son *Bhrigu*, the great sage, for human beings, and *Bhrigu* has handed it down delightedly for the assimilation of human beings: "Learn the Law always adhered to by people who are erudite, virtuous, and free from love and hate, the Law assented to by the heart":

between husband and wife); *dayabhaga* (partition); *sahasa* (violence); *vakparusya* (verbal assault); *dandaparusya* (physical assault); *dyutasamahvaya* (gambling and betting); *prakirnaka* (miscellaneous).

114. *Ibid.*
115. *Ibid.*
116. *Ibid;* see Chapter 11 cantos 68-71.
117. *Ibid;* Chapter 11:190.
118. *Ibid.*

Tatas tatha sa tenokto maharsir manuna bhriguh, tan abravid risin sarvan pritatma sruyatam iti, vidvadbhih sevitah sadbhir nityam advsaragibhih, hridyaendabhyanujnato yo dharmas tam nibodhata.[119]

In the backdrop of the above, it is apparently clear that *Dharma* and the concept of person/man/human being has been in existence that *Dharma* the law is for the present and the future generations to the effect that all human beings as well as human order must conform to the supreme and entrenched immutable law (*Dharma*). *Dharma* separates right from wrong; it recognizes the institution of right (righteousness) and discourages the institution of wrong (sin) and develops concept of punishment (*Danda*) and penance (*Pryacshchit*) for the wrongdoers—those who commit sins [wrongs]: civil, criminal, familial, filial and societal civility; *Dharma* creates duties, obligations and rights; it creates an orderly human conduct; it creates a welfare society for the good of the people; it lays down a code of conduct for the ruler and the ruled; it is not an abstract entity to operate in vacuum; it is a recipe for human beings to be humane; it is a prescription for the cure of arraying people; it is for the creation of notions of sovereignty, democracy, citizenship, domiciles; and is a mandate for the rule of law to serve the rule of life; it does not recognize the institutions of slavery or bonded slavery (*Bandhak*). Aquinas's *Lex humana* (humanly posited law)[120] seems identical to *Dharma* and the concept of person/man/human beings, and both are for humans to be humane. *Dharma* in relation to human beings is *a proprio vigore gubernaculums* (absolute prerogative) and *jurisdiction* (absolute legal restraint). It seems that humanitarian aspect has deeply been recognized in the field of human behaviour both in peace and war times. This seems to be the concept of *Privya Aatmana*, an infallible instrument of justice, being the greatest contribution of *Dharma* not only of age, but for all times perpetually.[121] *Privya Aatmana* does not mean what pleases one or pleasing voice, rather it is *Nyaya Dharma* based on what is agreeable to one's good conscience and an appeal to one's inherent sense of justice which

119. *Ibid*. This shows the element of fairness in the dispensation of justice delivery system.
120. Discussed critically *supra*.
121. See Dr. Nagendra Singh, *op. cit.*, pp. 97-99.

provides the widest measure of flexibility devoid of rigidity and an avenue of progressive development of the law, society and human beings, thus contributing to the longevity of the legal system which it is intended to serve[122]—State, citizens and the nation. Statehood and citizenship are closely associated with nationality and as such interacted as well as integral aspects of juristic concepts of *Dharma* – person/man/human beings.

iv. Dharma and the Concept of Human Dignity

The term human dignity defies any precise definition or meaning. This expression like *Dharma* is the most difficult, vexing and complex one. Human dignity like *Dharma* signifies a concept that is one of the most key and significant topics of thought and discussion in *Vedic literature—Vedas, Sastras, Dharmsastras, Ramayana, Mahabharata, Bhagavad Gita.* Human dignity spells out in detail the variety of behavior patterns that are the relationship of *Dharma* and real life. It is variety of behavior pattern that is *Dharma* for different people. Human behavior is an action of body, mind, heart, and life each persuading another for good or bad/evil. Human behavior is or is not *Dharma* depends upon attitude and aptitude, motives, ethical sensibilities, the general quality of his or her life, actions, deeds, needs, passions, compassions, issues of hypocrisy, of true virtue as opposed to apparent virtue, of inner virtue as opposed to outer virtue, and together is the mystery of the concept of human personality inasmuch as human dignity.[123] *Dharma of Acara, Vayavahara, and Sadacara* in brevity is the conceptual framework of human dignity. Together, it demonstrates the systematic, methodological and scientific growth and development of the concept of human dignity.

Human dignity is the cornerstone of *Dharma* that itself is the governing principle of entire juristic culture and outlook on life which is so beautifully summed up (brevity is beauty) as per *Vedic* traditions and literature: *Svasaya ca Priya aatamana.* The

---

122. *Ibid.* Flexibility is the dynamic aspect of the legal system and the rigidity could easily dry up the entire legal system.

123. See James L. Fitzgerald, *Dharma and Its Translation in the Mahabharata*, Vol. 32, 2004, Journal of Indian Philosophy, pp. 671-685.

Vedic tradition emphasizes removing imbalances in human nature and develops its full potential. Once imbalances are removed in human nature, human being excels in his potentialities not allowing his weaknesses to overpower him, because human weaknesses are obstacles in the development of human personality which is *sine qua non* of human dignity.[124] The *Vedic* tradition of India *a proprio vigore* is concerned about human dignity and human dignity, according to the *Vedic* traditions, is located in an order in human nature which values principles that promote that order on the level of the individual and of society. The method for promoting order is not only the following of ethical and legal standards or the use of a particular system of reasoning, but the culturing of individual human nature to attain a unique state of human enlightenment where imbalances in intellect, mind, emotions, and senses have been removed and full potential is lived in life.[125] The principle that is deduced from this *Vedic* perception is that a person with a developed intellect, clear mind, balanced emotions, and full perceptions is best placed to fulfil his or her society's highest ideals of ethical and lawful conduct.[126] It unequivocally seems that developed intellect, clear mind, balanced emotions, and full perceptions enhance the personality of the human beings in the society, which consequently promote his dignity. This contributes in developing rich cultural and scholarly heritage of mankind.[127] The *Vedic* literature encapsulates the vision and perception on the formulation of the concept of human dignity. The basis of such perceptions is the *Vedic* literature that embraces works of architecture [*Vastu Sastra*], astronomy, astrology, mathematics, medicine [*Ayur-Veda*], education, law, music, defense, and philosophy contributing towards the nourishing of intellect, clear mind, balanced emotions, and full perception to flourish his or her personality in the utmost dignified way in the

124. See J. Krishnamurthy, The Kingdom of Happiness.
125. See Maharishi Mahesh Yogi, On the Bhagavad-Gita: A new Translation and Commentary, 1967; Michael S. King, *Natural Law and the Bhagavad-Gita: The Vedic Concept of Natural Law,* (15 & 16) 2002, Ratio Juris, 399-415.
126. *Ibid.*
127. *Ibid.*

society.[128] The *Vedic* traditions are helpful in the growth of self-development or reclusive or alternative lifestyles. The *Vedic* traditions of medicine—*Ayur-Veda*—are one of the dominant systems of health care, because healthy physique and healthy mind develop human personality. It seems that such a rich cultural and scholarly heritage known to humanity has been the common heritage of mankind.[129] This shows the practical wisdom in the nourishing as well as flourishing of human dignity.

The practical wisdom and heuristic value of humanity is vividly visible in the *Bhagavad Gita*: "The *Bhagavad Gita* presents the science of life and the art of living. It teaches how to be, how to think and how to do. ... It narrates differing aspects of human functioning. ...It describes the human psyche and discrete higher states of consciousness, the introduction of a technology for the development of these states, and the empirical [or heuristic] means [—action *Karma Yoga*—] of testing the technology."[130] The empirical or heuristic means help to correct the arrayed or drifted mind. The *Bhagavad Gita* explains the basis the arrayed or drifted person [*like Arjuna*] may have the inquisitiveness to know how he can act in accord with natural law, act in accord with his *Dharma*, since *Dharma* is "one's natural duty, which includes all moral goodness, right action, freedom, justice, and lawfulness—all the principles that uphold and support life."[131]

Arrayed person's both mind and heart lack coordination, which consequently becomes his weakness that overpowers him and obstructs him to excel in his potentialities. Coordination of mind and heart is imperative in the development of human personality. The *Bhagavad Gita* assigns five reasons for mind-heart coordination to overcome weaknesses and excel in one's potentialities, because every human being has hidden potentialities in him. The first three reasons are familiar or similar to Western thought.[132]

---

128. *Ibid.*
129. *Ibid.*
130. *Ibid.*
131. *Ibid.*
132. *Ibid.*

a. The justification of action by reference to what is perceived to be in accord with human nature, in accord with natural law or law and morality;
b. Action in terms of the actor's relationship to others;
c. An analysis of the consequences of actions;[133]
d. Although there is fear of death, but there is a part of human nature, the spirit, that does not die with the body;
e. There is a state of human functioning, a state of inner equanimity where he would be able to act rightly. This state is described as one where the intellect is established. This is the state of enlightenment cherished in *Vedic* thought, a state where the individual is fulfilled, and herein is the idea of state of human functioning where an individual is by nature able to make right decision decisively.

These five reasons together make the full personality of human beings helpful in the enhancement of his human dignity to be decisive in arriving at right decision, right action, and right reasoning. This also has heuristic value inasmuch as extensive test by empirical means. This *a proprio vigore* shows that the human nature need not be static, as the state of enlightenment can be systematically cultivated harmoniously enabling the individual to enjoy life using his or her full mental potential.[134] This also demonstrates that human life is naturally ordered, and this orderly human life is consequently the human personality of humanity *vis-à-vis* human dignity.

133. As to natural law reason, Lord Krishna guides arrayed Arjuna that it is right for a warrior to kill in battle that destroys evil and upholds society. It was in accord with his *Dharma*, in accord with his nature as a warrior to act in this way. In terms of his relationships with others and the consequences of Arjuna's action respectively, failing to fight would bring him humiliation and derision while fighting would advance his own progress in life. Indeed this *Vedic* concept of action according to natural law requires that it be natural, that it produces a beneficial effect and that it be in harmony with other people. It is not only a matter of right choosing that is essential, but also right acting. It is *Trimurti—Triumvirate*—right decision, right action, and right reason.

134. *Supra note 368.*

The human life and its enlightenment is embedded in the concept of "self" which must be devoid of vices like lust, hatred, dishonesty, and malice, because such vices are ajar to humanity. The "self" must not be perceived, as Western thought, in terms of the basic goods that an individual acquires through action guided by practical reason,[135] but in the *Vedic* traditions to developing his full personality.

> Self has two connotations: lower self and higher self. The lower self is that aspect of the personality which deals only with the relative [changing] aspect of existence. It comprises the mind that thinks, the intellect that decides, and the ego that experiences. This lower self functions only in the relative states of existence—waking, dreaming, and deep-sleep.[136]

This *Vedic* model of human psyche of "the self" has most broadly been explained in the *Bhagavad Gita* that gives the model for the development of individual, his individual self that is *sine qua non* of human dignity.

> [T]he higher Self is that aspect of the personality which never changes, absolute Being, which is the very basis of the entire field of relativity, including the lower self. . . . It is the source of functioning of the other levels of the psyche—ego, intellect, mind, and senses. However, entire field of relativity means not only the individual self but also the entire universe. ...There is a universal source of life, a universal field of consciousness that is the basis of human existence and that of the entire material universe. It is an underlying field of intelligence, the basis of the different laws of nature that structure and maintain the universe. Together they comprise natural law [or law and morality *vis-à-vis* human personality, human dignity, and the human self].[137]

---

135. See Finnis, *op. cit.*, p. 124.
136. Maharishi Mahesh Yogi, *op. cit.*, p. 339.
137. See Maharishi Mahesh Yogi, *op. cit.*, p. 339.

In sum and substance, the mind-heart coordination—psychological balance—result in inner happiness, fulfilment, enlightenment, decisive attitude; deficiency in the functioning of mind-heart coordination—psychological imbalance—result in errant, deviant and recidivist behavior. Psychological balance results in increased intelligence, creativity, improved intellectual performance in language, literature, life, and law, and decreased aggression, anxiety and recidivism. Psychological imbalance results in increased crime, conflicts, accident rates, deteriorated health, and shambled economic conditions. Psychological balance shows that "individual is skilful in action and takes delight in doing good to all creatures."[138] This ideal of life in accord with *Dharma*—Natural law or Law and Morality—is the gist of human personality and human dignity. This shows the role of law and cultural norms which is indeed crucial as is violation of law and cultural norms (natural law) is seen the creation of imbalance in the body-mind-heart coordination resulting in stress, strain, anxiety, and fatigue that inhibit the development of full potential providing the basis for errant behavior.[139] In the backdrop of this, it is clear that law and morality or natural law and its promulgation as well as enforcement shall promote right action, happy and fulfilled individuals and a harmonious as well as prosperous society. This delineation is, of course, the conception, perception, vision and view of human dignity *vis-à-vis Dharma*.

v. *Dharma* and the Concept of Justice—Social, Political, Economic, Distributive, or Access to Justice

Justice is one of the nuances of *Dharma*. Justice refers to the family of *Dharma* moral concepts. Some scholars make a difference between justices and doing what is just, and to such scholars justice is a legal term; just implies moral dimensions. But 'justice' and 'just' are actually within the framework of *Dharma* that is law and morals both. As discussed earlier, justice may be referred to *Priya Aatmana* having reference to one's own

---

138. The Bhagavad-Gita, Chapter 2, Canto/Verse 50.
139. See J. Krishnamurthy, and Maharishi Mahesh Yogi, *op. cit., notes 382 and 383.*

soul or conscience is the very essence of the overall concept of justice or *Nyaya Dharma* as conceptualized by Kautilya. Therefore, *Priya aatmana or Nyaya Dharma* is an infallible instrument in judicial process as one of the greatest contribution of *Dharma* not only in ancient India or only of ages, but for all times perpetually. Sense of Justice in adjudication has been high and well known to be so, because justice has not only to be done but also shown to be done has been the principle of administration of justice and decision-making process, as well. This principle has to be in the conduct as well as behavior of the judges in the dispensation of justice. The guiding principle in the rendition of justice is the judicial propriety as to how the verdict is to be reached in the decision-making process as just, fair, and equitable. The decision-making process involves the observance of right proportions in the awards, decrees, and punishment concerning civil, criminal, and familial relations matters. In this process an element of discretion has been present and required to be exercised judiciously, that is, application of just, fair and equitable means to reach just ends. This aspect has been the fountainhead of justice delivery system. Justice delivery system devoid of harsh and inhuman elements has been conceded to be humane. It has been voiced that if the sum and substance of the judicial exercise in the pursuit of adjudication was to be fair, just, equitable, and answerable to a sense of correct balance and proportion, the resultant judicial administration could not, on the whole, be harsh and inhuman.[140] This shows the flourishing concepts of accountability, transparency, and answerability that have inherent aspects of good court/judicial governance. Thus, *Priya Aatman* has been conceived the pulse of healthy legal life in ancient India, which helped to serve the ends of justice. Manu in *manavadharmasastra* observes:

> Where justice, wounded by injustice, approaches and the judges do not extract the dart, there (they also) are wounded (by that dart of injustice). Where justice is destroyed by injustice, or truth by falsehood, while the judges look on, there they shall also be destroyed. Justice, being violated,

140. See Dr. Nagendra Singh, *op. cit.* at p. 136.

destroys; justice, being preserved; therefore, justice must not be violated, lest violated justice should destroy us.[141]

It has been discussed earlier that *Dharma* is a "Code of Law" to "regulate human conduct", and to restore conditions of order, law, justice, and security to prevent anarchy or *arajaka*. This could be accomplished with its principle of statecraft as its protecting branches, with its four beautiful flowers of *sama* (conciliation), *dana* (concession), *danda* (force), *bheda* (dissention), and its three fruits of *dharma, artha, kama* (law, religion, social, economic, welfare), which encapsulate the entrenched concept of justice, access to justice, distributive justice, viz., law, morals, justice is the *Trimurti or Triumvirate* conceptual relationship between *Dharma* and justice. *Nyaya and Yukti* are compasses of *Nyaya Dharma. Dharma Devta* is the personification of dispenser of justice, viz., Justice, who is not blindfolded, that is, a detached or non-prejudice or unbiased or impartial personality entrusted to dispense or render justice in accord with *Dharma* Law.

Yato Dharmastato Jaya: where there is law (righteousness), there is victory: has been the ennobling concept of Justice.[142] This shows that the concept of State, statecraft, and justice were closely intertwined inasmuch as the ancient Indian polity was ennobling. Had it not been so, "the innate avarice of man would lead to *matsanyaya*"[143]—big fish swallows the small fish—the weak being devoured by the strong. Therefore, the existence of

---

141. See Chapter VIII, verse or canto 12, 13, 14, 15 of Manu's Code of Law: *Manavadharma. Cf.* J. Barnes, Ed., The Complete Works of Aristotlem 1825, 1984: "When men are friends they have no need of justice". Some would also contrast justice between "corrective justice" and "distributive justice". Corrective justice involves rectification between two parties where one has taken from the other or harmed the other. For instance, disputes in contract law. Distributive justice involves the appropriate distribution of goods among a group—'giving each person his or her due'.—Most of the better known modern discussions of justice, which usually treat justice primarily as about the proper structuring of government and society, are basically discussions of distributive justice.
142. This ennobling concept of the sovereignty of justice is the emblem of the Supreme Court of India along with the *Dharmacakara*.
143. *Supra note 378* at p. 176.

Dharma (law) and *Danda* (authority or force or punishment) have been imperative for the sustenance of the sovereignty of law and justice.

The explanation to the concept of justice is related to the quest of: What is the justice delivery system? What is the pursuit of justice? The answers are conceptually conceived in the constitution of court, grounds for litigation and legal proceedings.[144] Conception of Court: When the king (here in modern constitutional set-up the king should be understood as the Chief Justice) is going to try a case, he should enter the court modestly accompanied by Brahmins (here in modern constitutional set-up the Brahmins should be understood as puisne judges) and counsellors (legal advisors) who are experts in policy (*Dharma: law and Justice*). Seated or standing there, dressed in modest clothes and ornaments, and raising his right hand, he should look into the cases of the plaintiffs or litigants or disputant parties every day in accordance with the standards of the region and those specified in the legal texts, lawsuits that fall individually under the eighteen avenues of litigation.[145] *Manavadharmsastra* identifies eighteen grounds for the institution of litigation, because these are the most litigation prone areas in which disputes among people arise, and the king should decide such cases based on the eternal Law, that is Natural Law, viz., (i) non-payment of debts; (ii) deposits; (iii) sale without ownership; (iv) partnerships; (v) non-delivery of gifts; (vi) non-payment of wages; (vii) breach of contract; (viii) cancellation of a sale or purchase; (ix) disputes between owners and herdsmen; (x) the Law on boundary disputes; (xi) verbal assault; (xii) physical assault; (xiii) theft; (xiv) violence; (xv) sexual crimes against women; (xvi) Law concerning husband and wife; (xvii) partition of inheritance; and (xviii) gambling and betting. The classifications of the various kinds of litigation seem to have come into vogue from time to time and place to place, and certainly do not seem to have been as rigid as the forms of

---

144. See Patrick Olivelle, Manu's Code of Law: A Critical Edition and Translation of the *Manvadharmasastra, op. cit. Chapter VIII and IX, Sanskrit Verses*, pp. 659-809 and translation, pp. 167-207.
145. *Id.*, p. 167.

actions in ancient Roman law or the writs of English Common law.[146]

The objective of litigation is only pursuit of justice, which has unequivocally been explained in *Manavadharmasastra* as follows:

> When Justice (*Dharma*), pierced by Injustice (*adharma*), comes to the court for redress and the court officials do not pluck out that dart from him, then they are themselves pierced by it. A man must either not enter the court or speak candidly; by refusing to speak or by speaking deceitfully, he commits a sin. When Justice is struck by Injustice, and Truth by Untruth, while the court officials remain idle onlookers, then they are themselves struck down. Stricken, Justice surely strikes back; defended, Justice defends. Therefore, never strike at Justice, lest Justice, stricken, wipes us out. Lord Justice is truly the bull (*vrsa*), and a man who impedes (*alam*) him the gods call a low-born (*vrsa-la*). Therefore, one should never trample Justice. Justice is the only friend who follows a man even in death; for all else perishes along with the body.[147]

The consequences of the above delienation have been spelled out in *Manavadharmasastra* as follows:

> One-quarter of an Injustice goes to the perpetrator, one-quarter to the witness, one-quarter to all the court officials, and one-quarter to the king. The king, on the other hand, becomes sinless, the court officials are freed, and the sin falls squarely on the perpetrator, when a man deserving condemnation is condemned.[148]

The decision-making process shall be in accord with reasoning, and attention shall be paid on two imperative aspects of reasoning, viz., what is and what is not in accord with the

146. See N.C. Sen Gupta, Evolution of Ancient Indian Law, 1953, p. 45.
147. *Supra note 364, pp. 167-168, verses 12-17. Dharm ev hato hanti dharmo rakshati rakshita, Tasmadhamo na hantavao maa no dharmo hato vadheet.*
148. *Ibid., Verses 18 and 19.*

provisions of polity (*artha*), and what is not in accord with the Law (*Dharma*).[149] Dispensation of Justice has not been an easy task because it is inasmuch as complicated as the complex character of a person. Therefore, it seems to be psycho-legal, since the dispenser of justice, in his judicial conduct, requires to discover the internal disposition of men by external signs—voice, color, expression, bearing, eyes, and gestures; inner thoughts are discerned by the bearing, expressions, gait, gestures, and manner of speaking, and by changes in the eyes and face.[150] Judicial conduct and reasoning have been explained that he who knows the Law should examine the Laws of *Chaturvarna*, regions, guilds, and families, and only then settle the Law specific to each; even men living far away endear themselves to the world when they stick to the activity specific to each and carry out their specific activities.[151] One of the cardinal principles of administration of justice has not been that neither the king nor any of his officials shall initiate a lawsuit independently; nor shall he in any way suppress an action brought before him by someone else.[152] In the backdrop of this, it discerns that the methodology applied in the rendition of justice has been deductive method that speaks about the heuristic value of the administration of justice. It is mentioned that as a hunter traces the location of an animal by the trail of blood, so a king [Justice or dispenser of justice] should trace the location of justice by deductive reasoning; when he is conducting judicial proceeding, he should pay close attention to the truth, the object of the suit, himself, the witnesses, the place, the time, and the appearance.[153]

In the backdrop of the above, it is pertinent to mention that the judicial authority of the dispenser of justice—the king—is not founded on any fiction but upon *Dharma* Law, and for the purposes of maintaining *Dharma*—social and moral order—he is endowed with the power of *Danda*—punishment.[154] It is

149. *Ibid., Verses 23 and 24.*
150. *Ibid., Verses 25 and 26.*
151. *Id.,* p. 169, *Verses 41 and 42.*
152. *Ibid., Verse 43.*
153. *Ibid., Verses 44 and 45.*
154. For critical study see N.C. Sen Gupta, *op. cit.,* pp. 37-81.

emphasized that *Danda* is looked upon as the weapon to enforce obedience to *Dharma*, and conceived as *Dharma—Dandaniti—* itself: *Dharmo hi dandrupen Brahmana nirmitam pura.*[155] *Dandaniti* or law of punishment is conceived as a most essential part of the administration of justice as this helped in the maintenance of social and moral order.[156] The king as the dispenser of justice is not the repository of this law but the upholder of this law as his obligation, duty, and as such he has to ascertain this law from several competent sources such as learned men in *Dharma* Law and from the *Kulas* and guilds.[157] This shows that as dispenser of justice, the king should not only know the law *Dharma* but should also be educated as well as informed about the law *Dharma* so that he acted impartially, unbiased, and non-prejudicial in the rendition of justice. King's authority to administer justice is exercised with fetters of constitutional limitations with resulting important developments in the administration of justice and as such he has to get his law from three sources:

1. The scriptures, including the *Veda, Dharmasutras, Vedangas, and Puranas;*
2. Customs and usages of countries, communities and *Kulas* unopposed to sacred texts; and
3. Customs and laws prevailing among cultivators, traders, herdsmen, moneylenders and artisans determined by each community in matters relating to themselves.[158]

It thus emanates that the king, the dispenser of justice, has to ascertain the law from those who have authority to decide about the law.[159] *Shantiparva of Mahabharata* prescribes the recipe regarding the quality, qualifications and personality traits of persons to be appointed as judges thus:

---

155. *Ibid. See Manavadharmasastra, op. cit., Chapter VII Verse 14.*
156. *Ibid.*
157. *Ibid.*
158. *Ibid. Gautama Dharmasutra, S. XI, 19-21.*
159. *Ibid.*

Vayayahareshu dahrmeshu yokatvyashav bahushrutaa
Prmananagaya mahiipal nyayasastrabalambinah
Vedarath tatvid rajan taraksastrabahusruta
Mantre ca vayayahare ca niyokatvya vijanatah

"A person who is (i) well versed in Vyavahara (law regulating judicial proceedings) and *Dharma* (law on all topics), (ii) a *Bahushruta* (profound scholar), (iii) a *Pramananjana* (well versed in the law of evidence), (iv) *Nyayasastravalambinah* (law abiding), and (v) has fully studied the *Vedas and Tarka* (logic) should be appointed to carry on the administration of justice".

Dharmakosha and Nardasmriti also give the similar provisions, viz., let the king appoint as members of the court of justice, honourable men of tried integrity (*Sabhyas*) who are able to bear the burden of the administration of justice and who are well versed in the sacred laws, rules of prudence, who are noble and impartial towards friends and foes : *Raja tu dharmikanh sabhayan niyunanjayat suprikshitaan, vayayahardhuram vodum ye shakta sadbhava iv, dharmasastraartha kushala kuleena satayavadeena, sabha shastrou ca mitre ca nripate sayu sabhasadah.* In *Sukraniti*, an ancient treatise on polity, also prescribes illuminating provisions prescribing quality as well as qualifications of judges, viz., one who is well versed in civil and criminal law and law of procedure, sprightful, of sterling character, impartial towards friends and foes, of *Dharma* abiding nature, truthful, ever active and who has established control over anger, desire and greed and pleasant in speech and demeanour should be appointed as judge: *Vayayaharvigaya pragaya vritsheelgunanavinta, ripou mitre samaa ye ca dharmagayasa satayavaadinah, niraalasaa jitkrodha kaam lobhaa priayavandaa, ragaya niyojit vayaste sabhayaste sabhayasarvaasu jatishu.*

These imperatives are essential just means to arrive at just ends of justice, viz., justice done by just means shall only unveil that justice is not only done but appears to have been done. This also unequivocally speaks about the independence of the judiciary; transparency of the judiciary; fairness in the administration as well as rendition of justice; courts are right not because they are superior but superior because they are right; accountability as well as answerability of the judiciary; and justice at the face value, that is, fair, impartial, unbiased, minus pre-conceived notions, and non-prejudicial justice. This is the picturesque of good/sustainable judicial governance/ management as per *Dharma* edict. *Sukraniti* enjoins that the dispenser of justice must be unbiased, impartial and fair giving fair hearing: *Dharmasastraanusaaren krodhlobhvivarjitah, rahsi ca nripah prgaya sabhashcaev kadachan* and also *Pakshpataadhiropasaya kaaranani ca panch vae, raaglobh bhayadvesha vadinoshcha rahshrutihi,* viz., judge should try cases adhering to law and uninfluenced by anger or greed and should not hear the party in secret. There are five causes which give rise to the charge of partiality against the judge, viz., *raga* (affection in favour of party), *Lobha* (greed), *bhaya* (fear), *Dvesha* (ill-will against a party), and *vadinoscha rahashrutihi* (the judge meeting and hearing a party to a case secretly). Besides, in the case of any doubt or difficulty—*Vipratipati* —, the king as the dispenser of justice is required to ascertain the law from aged persons who are experienced as well as learned in sacred lore of the law—*Dharma*.[160] In the backdrop of this, it is apparent that there is obligation on the part of the king the dispenser of justice to know the law and sacred lore of *Dharma* from the competent authorities or persons or constitutional authority to advise him in the shape of his *Sabha* so that proper, right and just justice—social, economic, distributive and equitable—is done, and there is access to justice or the doors of justice are not ajar to the 'lowly and the lost' and the affluent equally. As a dispenser of justice, the king may delegate his judicial functions to his puisne judges to render justice as delineated above. It may be inferred that the constitution of *Sabha* is necessitated of respectable members (*Sabhyas*) of good conduct, aged, experienced, wealthy, and free from greed who are held in high esteem whose advice is reliable for the decision-makers.[161] It also emanates that this is necessitated to place an important constitutional limitation on possible remotest of the remote whims and caprices of dispenser of justice, the king, and the decision-makers.[162] This also helps in

160. *Ibid.*
161. *Ibid.*
162. *Ibid.*

eliminating the probability of any type of influence on the decision-makers, for influence of any type belittle the sense of justice.

Legal procedure, a lawsuit or a case, in respect of the forms of litigation, as stated earlier, is described in four parts, viz., plaint/complaint, reply, trial, and decision, the object of which is truth and to establish truth.[163] This procedure has been laid down for the multitude of regular courts, which are classified as: (1) *Pratisthita* Courts in the cities and villages; (2) *Aparatisthita* is a travelling court not sitting at a fixed place, and is significant in the sense that justice at the door steps so that the litigants and others have not to face the hardships of exorbitant costs of travelling and others; (3) *Mudrita* the court of the *Pradvivaka* a person assisting the king in the dispensation of justice; (4) *Sasita* the court over which the king presides.[164] It is generally asked as to when the legal procedure has originated. It is unanimously opined by *Narda, Manu, Brihspati, Vishnu, Katyayana,* and a host of others that the legal procedure has originated like this: "At the time when men were disposed towards the sacred law only and when they spoke nothing but the truth, there was no legal procedure, nor was there hatred or covetousness. ...When people violated the sacred law, legal procedure was revealed, and the examiner of legal procedure was the king who himself holds the rod of punishment that means that he is the foremost chastiser."[165] It may discern that the administration of justice system of the age and time seem to be of scientific classification, systematic exposition, developed with farsighted vision, perception and comprehension, far from inferior in the wealth, length and breadth of details, founded on practical knowledge of law and its administration devoid of prolonged litigation, delay, and other vices in the justice delivery system. The legal procedure seems to be a fine illustration of the kind of development that the law had in the hands of practical jurists. Therefore, those who say that India has not produced jurists is a specious presentation of India's rich ancient literature in art,

---

163. *Ibid; see also Dr. Ludo Rocher, Vacaspati Misra Vyavaharacintamani, 1956, op. cit; Manu's Code of law Manavadharmasastra, op. cit.*
164. *Ibid.*
165. *Ibid.*

language, law, and life, and unnecessary trying to make us believe the truth of their lies. This may be proved by the 'Rule of Justice' that is a striking point of Justice and Jurist, which requires the decision-makers to determine cases according to the substance of the thing (*Bhuta or res*) by eliminating all false pleas (*Chhala*); *Chhalam nirsaya bhuten vayaharanayannrippa.*[166] This unequivocally shows that decision should be according to the justice of the case irrespective of technical flaws. This also shows that the judicial process or decision-making process or administration of justice does not suffer from the interstices of technicalities, adversarial process, and *plus petitio.* The rule of *plus petitio* says that the original case in the Plaint shall not be departed from or new case made out at the trial.[167] This shows that multiplicity of suits/cases has been incompatible with the justice delivery system because that unnecessarily causes prolongation of litigation as well as delay. This also shows that if the defendant or opposite disputant denies the whole claim, then, if a part of it is proved, there would be decision/judgment for the whole.[168] This also unfolds that sensible rules are laid down for nullifying litigation or vexatious litigation for force or fraud. It indeed indicates that administration of justice or judicial process or decision-making process by trained practical lawyers or jurists had been fully established.[169] It also appears that in the Indian law there has always been an undercurrent of sound common sense and justice wearing down rigidity of rules without any outside interference. There seems to be a convincing conceivable argument in it, because law has been evolved brick by brick like Rome was not built in a day, and there is a long sound history of laborious works of forces/jurists breaking down senseless forms and bringing out the sensible essential rules of justice, and there is nothing pretentious or fallacious about it.[170]

In the administration of justice there is another provision that is imperative injunction to escaping justice which is called

166. *Ibid.*
167. *Ibid.*
168. *Ibid.*
169. *Ibid.*
170. *Ibid.*

Asedha and that works as an injunction prohibiting the litigants or disputants to escape justice.[171] The basis of justice is measured by *Tula* a balanced scale with two pans on both sides indicating that the justice has no scabbard and justice has to be balanced one and not tilting on either side, viz., favoring or disfavoring any side of the litigation. This balanced scale is seen in the Western concept also with one difference that the Indian Goddess of Justice holding the balanced scale is not blind-folded, whereas the Western Goddess of Justice holding the balanced scale is blind-folded. But what is the origin of it no one knows. May be that this practice is borrowed by one community from another, or it may be that it was the institution common to all races inhabiting the area from India to Babylon.[172] Be that as it may, when we look at the growth of procedural and evidence laws in the decision-making process or judicial process, their development is very largely due to the works of men who have specialized in law, that is, *Vyavahara, Achara,* and the whole sacred law as well.[173] It seems that the learning in law and tradition—dissemination and assimilation—might have been handed down from generation to generation in the schools (known as *Parisad, Panchalas*) of sages and finally have come to be embodied in works like *Dharmsutras, Vyavahara Matrika,* etc. But, without any pretension, it may be submitted that these schools must have special organized law institutes or colleges or *Parisads* of learned men who might have specialized in the study of law—*sacred law, Dharma, Nyaya, Yukti, Vyavahara, Achara, Sadachara*—giving advice on questions of law as non-partisans and impartial (*Ripau mitra cha ye samah*), and certainly contributors in the scientific, systematic, and methodological development of administration of justice, judicial process, decision-making process with one aim search of truth and establishment of justice in accord with *Dharma: Yato Dharmastato Jaya*.

171. *Ibid.*
172. *Ibid.*
173. *Ibid.*

vi. *Dharma* and the Concept of Information and knowledge: A Roadmap for Good/Sustainable Governance/ Management —Accountability and Transparency

Information and knowledge coordination as well as correlation may be described as substantiating the distinguishing idea of natural law or law and morality. The concept of information and knowledge is impregnated deep in *Dharma* in *Vedic* vocabulary *aa no bhadra kratvo yantoo visvata:* Let noble thoughts come to us from every side; *tamso maa jyotirgmaya:* Lead me from darkness to light/enlightenment, knowledge; and *Om sanghgachhdhvam, samvadhvam. . .*: Let us sit together, discuss together, share with each other together, and participate in discussion openly so that there is free flow of information from one to another for disseminating and assimilating knowledge for the benefit of all humanity: "Assemble, speak together; let your minds be all of one accord. The place is common, common the assembly, common the mind, so be their thoughts united. One and the same be your resolve, and be your mind of one accord. United be thoughts of all that may happily agree". The importance as well as significance of this *Vedic lingua fauna* is inasmuch as seen that *Dharma* is a science whose aim is knowledge and information. This coordination and correlation is truth and an *'ecole de verity' (the school of truth)* which enriches the 'solution of solutions' and offers the scholar of critical capacity the opportunity of finding the 'better solutions' for his time, space and place, viz., this coordination and correlation is extremely useful of law reforms, and a scholarly pursuit for law, society and development. This coordination is scientific correlation in *lingua fauna of Dharma* of causation and necessity. For example when a legislature enacts a proposed law, the law is called a statute or statutory law; when a scientist validates a hypothesis, he or she confirms a scientific law;[174] when a legal-moralist validates a statutory law, he or she confirms it heuristic and empirical tested law. This coordination suggests a novel account of natural law or law and morality

174. See George P. Fletcher, Basic Concepts of Legal Thought, 1996, pp. 28-38; Carl F. Stychin and Linda Mulcahy, Legal Method, 2003, p. 4.

perspectives. The importance and significance of this coordination seems imperative in the modern polity and comity of good/sustainable governance/management, information technology, intellectual property law (its use and misuse), TRIPs, new economic market (WTO), inasmuch as it has been renowned in the rich historical as well as classical roots. The inventors of astronomy, astrology, mathematics, medicine, music, art, literature, etc. must have farsightedness of this coordination not as a mere cosmology but the impetus of it in new emerging scenario of legal cosmology which is felt in the new technological and economic order. This coordination, therefore, calls for an in-depth probe, in the modern scenario, on the function of law and morality or natural law rather than spiteful about the controversies of doctrinal issues that now lay far behind, for *de novo* future where dissemination and assimilation of information and knowledge from all angles may *lead us from darkness to gleaming wings of light where new vistas of knowledge await to ring the bell*. This coordination undoubtedly helps to fill the gap or vacuum to meet the urgent need of the present development for the future growth and posterity systematically. This is evident from the recent judicial dictum of the Supreme Court of India which has unequivocally recognized the significance of this coordination while interpreting a statutory law with the help of *mimansa rules of interpretation*. The Supreme Court said: "It is a matter of deep regret that *Mimansa* principles have rarely been used in our law courts. It is nowhere mentioned in our Constitution or any other law that only Maxwell's principles of interpretation can be used by the court. We can use any system of interpretation which helps us solve a difficulty, ambiguity or incongruity. . . ."[175]

Though the proverb is blessed are merciful as well as ignorant, and ignorance is bliss, but ignorance is an inescapable consequence in terms of legal *lingua franca* of *Dharma*, information and knowledge *triumvirate/trimurti*. In the modern scenario, the information technology has advanced and as such there has to be respect for information technology and

175. *Mimansa* Rules still Relevant, The Hindu, Tuesday, December 18, 2007, www.hindu.com dated 18.12.2007.

knowledge of scientific technology for the common good of the mankind, but this information technology not to be used as brutal instrument for oppression, as have been used in the World War II and its perennial use against civilly human beings by the brutal human beings. This coordination precisely is in order to prevent a repetition of the horrors that the concern about the human beings through the Universal Declaration of Human Rights was born, and as such "we must beware lest the Stone Age return upon the gleaming wings of science".[176] Science and technology though have held the key to an age of ease and plenty, but it has evaporated the soup and sauce of elementary decency that is the integral part of law and morality knit and the coordination of *trimurti Dharma,* information and knowledge. Science and technology must be unlike the 'despotic power of husbands over wives';[177] science and technology must be used in its direct influence on human happiness, which is the real kingdom of happiness where every human being gets equal chance to flourish, nourish and prosper in relations. Therefore, the quest for knowledge lay in the hidden treasure of information, which must be shared regardless of spatial countries, traditions or creeds. Dissemination and assimilation of information is the oxygen of human beings' creativity, innovation, novelty, and basic skills in human intercourse/ interaction, understanding, and the development of the intellect. To impart as well as receive information through any media is the domain of civilized governance not for suppression but for the advancement of education not as an empty phrase rather to 'equip every individual with freedom of the word, the ability to read and write'.[178]

Dissemination and assimilation of information as well as knowledge bring transformation in the development of the intellect and the skill to excel, and, that, seems to be the intellect

176. Winston Churchill as quoted by John Polanyi, a Nobel Laureate in Chemistry (1986), in Yael Danieli, Elsa Stamatopoulou and Clarence J. Dias (Eds.), The Universal Declaration of Human Rights: Fifty Years and Beyond, 1999, p. xi.
177. John Stuart Mill, On the Subjection of Women, 1868, as quoted by M.F. Perutz, a Nobel Laureate in Chemistry (1962), in *Id. ix*.
178. Nadine Gordimer, a Nobel Laureate in Literature (1991), in *Id*. p. vii.

meaning conveyed in the above mentioned *Vedic lingua franca Aa no bhadra kratvo yantoo visvata; tamso maa jyotirgamaya; sangh gachhdhavam...*, because in the pursuit of information and knowledge there must not be barrier of territorial boundaries; there must be free flow of information from any where and from any source of media irrespective of country, creed or traditions. The objective is the pursuit of true knowledge that is helpful in the development of perception formulation, conception of vision, penetrating reasoning, and conclusive perceptual knowledge.

Knowledge is not mere logic but experience, and, therefore, knowledge and experience together enable to develop understanding to attain enlightenment and to act rightly. This is the gist of *"Sankhya" (knowledge) and "Yoga" (experience)* embedded in immutable *Bhagavad Gita* which is imparted to arrayed person "Arjuna", drifted from his part of "duty", to prepare the arrayed to receive instruction on how to attain a state where he would be able to imbibe/gain understanding that there is an ideal state of equanimity or enlightenment to act rightly.[179] This coordination helps to balance the different levels of the psyche and gives them a stable basis.[180] For stable basis, one must stay aloof from the world of three qualities: be indifferent to pairs of opposites, forever fixed in clarity, non-acquisitive, self-possessed.[181] Then alone one can perform right action and one is only entitled to the action and not to its fruits;

179. Michael S. King, *Natural Law and the Bhagavad Gita: The Vedic Concept of Natural Law, op. cit., Yoga in Bhagavad Gita* should not be mistaken as Yoga of Patanjali or Hatha Yoga or Kundalini Yoga. *Yoga* is derived from *Yuj*, which means to yoke. The expression *Yoga* occurs 150 times in *Bhagavad Gita* which always refers to strenuous effort to which a person has committed himself. It means self yoking to a particular effort to win or conquer a goal. It denotes a broader concept than discipline or method. It implies the process of a difficult effort; a person committed to it; the instrument he uses; the course of action chosen; and the prospect of a goal.

180. *Bhagavad Gita*, Chapter Two, *Sankhya Yoga (Theory)*, Mind confused with the law and morality seek refuge in seeking knowledge to take decisive action, and he who shirks from decisive right action incurs guilt and shame, shame is worse than death. Verses 7, 23, 34, 39, 47.

181. *Ibid.*, Verse 45.

one should not let the fruits of action be his motive, and by this one should also not attach to non-action.[182] Knowledge is awareness of this coordination which helps the complete individual development and short of this is inevitably some deficiency in psychological functioning that adversely affects the functioning of the intellect, feeling level, and the senses, and impetus upon the ability to perform right action.[183] Deficiency is a lack of coordination between heart and mind that results in an inability to act rightly in crucial situation that demands decisive action. It may also seem that deficiency culminates into errant behavior and all errant behavior, including crime, arises due to some deficiency in the functioning of the psyche.[184] The *Bhagavad Gita and the Vedic lingua fauna* emphasize that the psychological imbalance between heart and mind can be minimized or eliminated by the eradication of fatigue of nervous system due to stress that is beyond the power of reasoning alone to resolve.[185] One striking aspect of the above mentioned *Vedic lingua fauna* is that it is not religio-legal coordination but it relates to *Dharma*'s foundation in reason, which recognizes the sources of knowledge and authority in matters relating to *Dharma* to be human beings.[186] The above mentioned *lingua fauna* unequivocally demonstrates that the coordination of *Dharma*—information-knowledge deal with reality and does not operate in vacuum.

Knowledge and information are not the custody or repository of one individual alone. It is possessed by different people separately inasmuch as knowledge "never exists in concentrated or integrated form, but solely as the dispersed bits of incomplete and frequently contradictory knowledge which all the separate individuals possess. ... Each individual knows a number of useful facts that are not known to anybody else, ... practically every individual has some advantage over all others

182. *Ibid., Verse 47.*
183. *Ibid., Verse 41.*
184. *Supra 438.*
185. *Ibid.*
186. See Donald R. Davis, Jr., *Dharma In Practice: Acara And Authority In Medieval Dharmasastra,* Vol. 32, 2004, Journal of Indian Philosophy, 813-830, at p. 815.

in that he possesses unique information of which beneficial use might be made. ...The unique knowledge is often very important but unorganized knowledge includes the knowledge of the particular circumstances of time and place".[187] Knowledge has several important implications, such as knowledge accumulated by society as a whole is not held by any one individual or the sum of the knowledge of all individuals exists nowhere as an integrated whole or each individual is ignorant of a great number of facts that are known to others and this ignorance cannot be escaped or it would be impossible for one mind to grasp all the relevant information. How to profit from this knowledge that exists only dispersed as the separate, partial, and sometimes conflicting beliefs of all men? It depends upon the ability of the man to make use of such dispersed information and access to all that knowledge is *sine qua non* for social life inasmuch as—

> Most of the advantages of social life, especially in its more advanced forms which we call "civilization", rest on the fact that the individual benefits from more knowledge than he is aware of. It might be said that civilization begins when the individual in the pursuit of his ends can make use of more knowledge that he has himself acquired and when he can transcend the boundaries of his ignorance by profiting from knowledge he does not himself possess.[188]

Be that as it may, it unequivocally seems that the societies on the whole do succeed in benefitting from dispersed information as espoused in the above mentioned Vedic *lingua fauna.* The analysis is that sharing of information is imperative for the quenching of inquisitiveness of the seekers of knowledge and necessary condition for the existence of society as well as survival of man.

> Living as members of society and dependent for the satisfaction of most of our needs on various forms of co-operation with others, we depend for the effective pursuit of our aims clearly on the correspondence of the expectations

187. See Erik Angner, Hayek and Natural Law, 2007, pp. 50-51.
188. *Ibid.*, p. 51.

> concerning the actions of others on which our plans are based with what they really will do. This matching of the intentions and expectations that determine the actions of different individuals is the form in which order manifests itself in social life. [189]

The analysis shows that information and knowledge inculcate the sense of freedom, liberty and the absence of coercion; freedom against serfdom and fiefdom. What is the use of information and knowledge in society? The safe answer may be that the coordination enables individuals to be decisive in taking right actions for the unforeseeable and unpredictable events; it gives opportunities to individuals to realize their aims, just ends by just means; it also enables individuals to take wisest decisions in competitive environ. The analysis also shows that information and knowledge is not the privilege and monopoly of the privileged as well as monopolistic that have the habit to prevent others to do better or excel in their potentialities. However, there is one problem as to how to secure the best use of resources or how to utilize knowledge not given to anyone in its totality? There can't be any readymade are spontaneous answers to such problematic questions because of the complexities of free economic markets, economic liberalization, globalization, privatization; artificialities; global warming that is the bane from human beings to human beings; domestic violence; child abuse; child labor; girl child another kind of bonded labor; non-transparent and non-accountable governance shorn of good governance; refugees, migrants and internally displaced persons and socio-economic-politico-education problems attached to such persons; questions of decency, humane and humanity; environment and sustainability; gay pairs and lesbianism; global lawlessness; militancy, terrorism, impetus of traumatic happenings, and victims of such recidivists as well as torture survivors; indigenous and aboriginals; housing and living conditions; non-armed conflicts and impediments as well as implications in the implementation of human rights in such situations; disabilities or mental as well as health infirmities

189. *Id*, p. 53.

and care giving as well as rehabilitative modalities; old aged persons, care giving and rehabilitative modalities; victims of rape and adultery, care giving and rehabilitative modalities; victims of crimes, care giving and rehabilitative or resocialisation modalities; surrogating and surrogate mother, fetus, abortion and women; divorce and care giving: why not the father who fathers the child and why only the mother who mothers such child should look after the child and the traumatic impetus on the child; etc. Another perplexity seems attached to this scenario is whose law and whose morality? There can be a way out of this perplexity and that is to search for perpetual answers in the knit work of *Dharma* law and morality in using the information and knowledge that may be a legacy for everyone. This could be by an analysis of information and knowledge acquired from anywhere for the ultimate use of human beings and human good where everyone lives terror free by creating a world without violation of human happiness: *Sarve bhavantoo sukhina sarve santoo niramaya. . ., sarv dharmsambhav and vasudev kutumbakam.* It may also discern that proper use of information and knowledge coordination in interaction with *Dharma* law and morality as a tool kit may help to dismiss hypocrisy to enhance sustainable governance in democracy.

Another area in the above mentioned *triumvirate or trimurti* is the enhancement of good governance or management or sustainable governance in the bribe/corruption ridden societies where no body knows or dares to know what transpires under the red carpet of the wonderland of bureaucracy in democracy. How to change the process for our country's progress where everything is transparent and everyone is accountable or answerable? How the above mentioned *trimurti* is a workable roadmap for good governance or management or sustainable governance? The roadmap for good governance or good management or sustainable governance depends upon the *modus operandi* of changing the process in the empowerment of citizens that would be a meaningful way in decision-making process. This tool kit shall be an effective instrument in our country's progress. This tool kit includes right to information helpful in the advancement of dissemination as well as assimilation of knowledge, information technology as well as e-governance, and that seems to be the modern and scientific way of approaching *aa no bhadra kratvo yantoo visvata; tamso maa jyotirgamaya; sanghgachhdhavam sanghvadhavam....* What is good governance or good management or sustainable governance? It is like defining the truth: "Man can embody the truth, but he cannot know it."[190] Good governance is both a goal and a process which involves three main actors, the State, the Civil Society, and the Private Sector for the sustainable governance. The challenges to it are bribery/corruption, poverty, inequality, insecurity, lethargy, indecisiveness that brings unpleasantness, delay in the disposal of cases, non-work culture. The main actors, the State, the Civil Society, and the Private Corporate Sector, are expected to create an environment for the development and the management of their respective spheres.

Good governance or good management or sustainable governance, as enjoined in *Atrismriti*, requires the obligatory functions of the State as moral behavior and ethical conduct thus:

> *Dushtsaya danda sujnasaya puja nayayen koshsasya ca Sampravridhi*
> *Apakshpatooarathishu rashtraraksha panchaiv yagya kathita nripnaam*

"To punish the wicked, to honor (protect) the good, to enrich the treasury (exchequer) by just methods, to be impartial towards litigants and to protect the kingdom" are the five *Yajnas* (selfless duties) to be performed by a King (ruler and, now, in democracy, by the elected kings/rulers).

The same principle has been incorporated by *Kautilya* in his *Arthasastra* who sums up the objects and purposes of the exercise of sovereign power by the king in the attainment of good governance or good management or sustainable governance thus:

190. Vide William Butler Yeats, Nobel Laureate, 1923.

Prajasukhe sukham rajaya prajanaan ca hite hitam
Naatampriyam hitam rajaya prjanaam tu priyam hitam

"In the happiness of his subjects (now citizens in democracy) lies the happiness of the King (now elected kings/rulers of democracy); in their welfare his welfare; he shall not do what pleases him; he shall do what pleases his subjects (now citizens).

The above mentioned *Dharma* serves as beacon light for all those who desire to exercise their power of office which they come to occupy under the constitutional system honestly and sincerely and inspire them to discharge the powers and duties in a selfless manner so that good governance or good management or sustainable governance is translated into action. The analysis also shows that the assumption of office should not be regarded as assuming power for the sake of power, but it must be regarded as undertaking a selfless duty to be performed for the benefit of the people. Power is *Diksha*, a dedication, and a *Vrati*, a person devoting to a cause to wit the services of the people. This analysis shows that power is service. Otherwise, power corrupts and absolute power corrupts absolutely, which is a cause of mismanagement, maladministration, abuse and misuse of office. This aspect is proved in the theorem of Manu's *Manavadharmasastra:*[191]

Adharmeinai dhatetaavat tatobhadrani pshayati
Tataa spatnaanjayati samoolsayatu vinshayati

"Those who indulge in *adharma* (for acquiring wealth or power by unlawful or illegal means) may attain success quickly, may over-power their opponents, but ultimately their ruin to the root is certain".

Besides, the expression governance is derived from the Greek word *'kybernan' and 'kybernetes'*. It means to steer and to pilot or be at the helm of things. While the term government indicates a political unit for the function of policy-making as

191. Manu's Code *Manavadharmasastra, op. cit., Chapter IV, Verse 174.*

distinguished from the administration of policies, the term governance indicates an overall responsibility for both the political and administrative functions. It indeed conveys moral behavior and ethical conduct in the task of governance. It ensures the continuous ethical exercise of authority on both the political and administrative units of governments. It indicates the more integral, balanced and interdependent the State, the Civil Society and the Private Corporate Sector are the better it is for the society and also a direction of the societies economic and social flight path. It is described to achieve the desired objective of a nation-state's political development. Good governance is accountable, effective and efficient, participatory, transparent, responsive, consensus-oriented, and equitable. As already observed, for good governance to exist in both theory and practice, citizens must be empowered to participate in meaningful ways in decision-making processes; to have a right to information and to access. Though widespread accessibility remains a barrier for many countries, but one of the ways to access information is through Information and Communication Technology (ICT) applications such as the Internet.[192] Be that as it may, good governance is integral to economic growth, the eradication of poverty and hunger, and sustainable development. Besides, E-governance has emerged as a viable means to address development issues and challenges because citizens find empowerment through access to information. This shall eradicate or wither sub-rosa of wonderland of bureaucracy and its hypocrisy. However, a doubt about its achievement remains, because it is the man who is to develop e-governance in the system, and if the electronic apparatuses remain non-operative for the lair of the dust to pile and used as sophisticated typewriters alone then what would be the cumulative result! It is a paradox. It is conceptualization of man and machine like law and morality in the above mentioned *triumvirate.*

The green principles of good governance globally identified are: all people are neighbors; build partnerships; commitment to care for others to the higher quality of behavior among human beings; democracy and equality; environmental protection;

192. See United Nations Outline of good governance at the World leaders at the 2005 World Summit.

fundamental values; co-operative global approach; universal sense of human identity; improved understanding; core values of respect for life, liberty, justice and equity, mutual respect, caring and integrity; pooling information, knowledge and capacities; larger, long-term mutual interest; meeting basic material needs; new vision for humanity; people should treat others, as they would themselves wish to be treated (*aatamvat sarvbhuteshu yaa pshayati saa pshayati*); principles of consultation, transparency and accountability; commitment to core values concerned with the quality of life and relationships; human rights; shared vision and destiny; working together; using collective power to create a better world; vision of one world; new world; flexible and fluid process; dynamic process; and global citizenship. The State, the Civil Society, and the Private Corporate Sector have to perform good governance or sustainable governance within these parameters. The State constitutes as well as assures to provide the foundation of Equality, Equity, Justice and Peace, creating a conducive political and legal environment for development by (i) maintaining the rule of law; (ii) regulating socio-economic standards; (iii) developing social and physical infrastructure; and (iv) ensuring social safety nets and civic protection. Civil Society ensures to secure the foundation of Liberty, Equality, Responsibility and self-expression through (i) organizing the communities; (ii) educating the communities; (iii) mobilizing groups to participate in the economic and social life of the city; (iv) facilitating political and social interaction; (v) supporting solidarity actions and watch-dog/ombudsman functions; and (vi) fostering the cultures. Private Corporate Sector promises to promote the foundation of economic growth and development through (i) employment and income generation; (ii) production and trade; (iii) human resource development; (iv) service delivery; and (v) setting and constantly upgrading corporate standards.

Sustainable Governance is the cumulative impact that the interaction of the above mentioned three actors, The State, The Civil Society and The Private Corporate Sector in nation's political, economic and administrative domains will have on the lifestyles and living standards of its citizens. These actors constitute the governance system through many different and complex mechanisms, institutions, and partners, processes and relationships which citizens use on daily basis to (i) articulate their needs, problems and aspirations; (ii) exercise their rights and duties; (iii) obtain redress or solutions; and (iv) mediate to maintain law, order, and justice.

Ultimately, results of good governance or good management or sustainable governance in sum and substance are (i) the orderly organization of country's/society's predominant political thought, vision, perception, and action; (ii) the administration of events and processes leading to the realization of the vision; and (iii) the maintenance of ethical rhythm and equity in the distribution of the fruits of realized vision as well as perceptions to the satisfaction of all.

The cumulative result of good governance is development that 'gives priority to poor, lowly and lost, advances the cause of women and other disadvantageous or marginalized groups of society, sustains the environment adversely affected by man-made excesses and militancy/terrorism effect and cause, creates conducive environment for the refugees as well as internally displaced persons, creates opportunities for the resocialisation of victims of crimes, recidivism and administrative recidivism, creates healthy environment for the disables and their rehabilitation, creates respectful resettlement of old aged persons affected by the persecution of kiths and kins, and creates needed opportunities for employment and other livelihoods.

Good as well as sustainable governance is good and effective when it subscribes to the promotion of participation, strategic vision, rule of law, transparency, responsiveness, consensus orientation, equity building, effectiveness and efficiency, and accountability. The *mantra* of good governance is growth, equity and sustainable governance that shall lead to economic growth, human development, and development of the whole society. Without good governance, by might and craft, a few will appropriate to themselves the best of the products of economic growth leading the way to greater economic and social disparities. Transparent, responsive and accountable governance systems and processes upholding the rule of law to serve the rule of life can prevent such polarization of resources, both material and human, to a very great extent. Good governance is not an accident. Process towards good governance too must be planned meticulously and pursued systematically. Good governance is a result of good planning, efficient investment of managerial resources, effective partnership and sound decision-making. Some of the major steps towards effective governance may be: understanding and appreciating the potential of efficient and effective governance for equitable development; identify critical pastures, overcoming distrust among them and gaining mutual respect; consensus building on core principles of partnerships, formalizing partnerships and assigning specific responsibilities; creating a vision for basic infrastructure development—municipal development—, planning basic infrastructure progress, setting objectives and targets, setting the governance upgrading programmed in motion; reviewing local self-government revenue and mobilizing new resources; reviewing and upgrading management tools for assessing governance and partnerships; setting up systems for functionaries to upgrade their managerial skills, information and knowledge on a regular basis; regular review of performance, revision of procedures and legislation and mid-course corrections; constant search to further improve good governance practice. It is the belief that this delineation can be translated into action if just ends of good and sustainable governance are arrived at by just means of *Dharma triumvirate/trimurti* outlined above.

In the backdrop of the above, information technology or information and communication technology or information technology and telecommunication, and right to information are incredible background characteristics for a progressive movement of good governance/management to sustainable governance. Information technology is the study, design, development, implementation, support or management of computer-based information systems, particularly software applications and computer hardware. It deals with the use of electronic computers and computer software to convert, store, protect, process, transmit and retrieve information, securely. Information and Communication Technology or Information Technology and Telecommunications are inclusive of

Information Technology expression to broaden its horizon. E-governance is another tool kit of the term information technology that has ballooned to encompass many aspects of computing and technology, and the term is more recognizable than ever before. The information technology umbrella can be quite large, covering many fields. IT professionals perform a variety of duties that range from installing applications to designing complex networks and information databases. A few of the duties that IT professionals perform may include data management, networking, engineering computer hardware, database and software design, as well as the management and administration of entire systems.[193] *Aa no bhadra kratvo yantoo visvata, etc. triumvirate/trimurti* may be conceded to encompass within its fold or umbrella the above mentioned scientific explanation of information technology.

Right to information is *sine qua non* of *Aa no bhadra kratvo yantoo visvata, etc. triumvirate/trimurti,* which helps to know what transpires under the red carpet of the wonderland of bureaucracy. This also enriches the citizens to acquire information about the functioning of the governments in democracy, and consequently provides an opportunity to the growth as well as development of participative governments in democracy. This also provides a platform for transparency, accountability and answerability. This also helps to minimize/eradicate/evaporate corruption, maladministration, mismanagement. More the access to information most is the proximity of having good governance and sustainable governance. Information means acquiring of knowledge from different sources about the functioning of the governance including records, documents, memos, e-mails, opinions, advices, press releases, circulars, orders, logbooks, contracts, reports, papers, samples, models, data material held in any electronic form and information relating to any private body which can be accessed by a public authority under any other law for the time being in force but does not include "file notings". This unequivocally tells that secrecy should not be the rule but

193. Retrieved from http://en.wikipedia.org/wiki/information technology dated 20.12.2007.

exception in governance and that only conveys the theme of sustainable governance. As such, right to information includes the right to (i) inspect works, documents, records; (ii) take notes, extracts or certified copies of documents or records; (iii) take certified samples of material; (iv) obtain information in form of printouts, diskettes, floppies, tapes, video cassettes or in any other electronic mode or through printouts. However, the right to information may not be conceded if it infringes copyright of any person other than the State, and/or if it affects the sovereignty, defense, and integrity of India, the security, strategic, scientific or economic interests of the State, relation with foreign State or lead to incitement of an offence; if the information which has been expressly forbidden to be published by any court of law or tribunal and the disclosure of which may constitute contempt of court; if information, the disclosure of which would cause a breach of privilege of Parliament or the State Legislature; and if the information, the disclosure of which may impede the national interest.

Be that as it may, the above mentioned scientific explanation to information, knowledge, and information technology may not have the meaning of *triumivirate/trimurti*: *aa no bhadra kratvo yantoo visvata; tamso ma jyotirgamaya; sangh gachhdhvam...* as understood in this scientific age, but, nevertheless, it may have not less meaning to understand as we understand it in the above mentioned scientific explanation. Therefore, the above mentioned scientific approach to *triumvirate/trimurti* is obvious existential umbrella or tool kit of *Dharma* and the concept of information, knowledge, and information technology in the furtherance of good governance, good management and sustainable governance.

vii. *Dharma* and the Concept of Democracy, Polity and Synergetic Comity

The ancient Indian intellectual history of *Dharma* enjoins the role of *Dharma* that intends to serve as a comprehensive, *Vedic*-inspired basis for living a good life in a good society in a good polity, and that is the coordination between *Dharma* and the concept of democracy, polity, society, and synergetic comity.[194] *Dharma* and the concept of democracy, polity and synergetic comity are ordained in the *lingua franca* of constitutional law as well as constitutional morality. This unequivocally conveys that the constitutional theory of ancient Indian polity duly recognized the State and its functionaries have had to function in accordance with *Rajdharma as well as Rajayadharma* which is the tool kit of *Rajyasastra* for *Rajsasana,* i.e., the supremacy of *Dharma* or Law. This unequivocally conveys that all the segments of modern concept of democracy, which means rule by the people, rule for the people, and rule of the people, have their roots in these *Vedic* concepts. There did not exist either the absolute monarchy or the spirit of absolutism as the system worked under sufficient checks and safeguards in the form of either

---

194. See Sri Aurobindo on the nature of true democracy which streamed from the intuitive plane and originated from the Rig Veda; and which emanated from the Sattvic plane of clear reason. It nurtured great social ideals; the ideal of social honour remains its main legacy. Vedic age considered individuals not as social, but as spiritual beings undergoing evolutionary process. This is the key to that *Dharma* based society, for which its unique form of democracy streamed from the high planes of the intuitive mind. This is called ethical age. The ethcal age that followed corresponded to that of the *Upanishads,* viz., *Hradye Guhayam,* i.e. it dwelled in the secret and sacred heart of every being. The *Sanatana Dharma* as the evolutionary principle of society as a quest for self-perfection that fashioned the whole Indian civilization for millennia. It combines *Dharma,* democracy, polity and society, and transnational together, which is the language universalisation and globalization. It is based on *Svabhava and Svadharma* as culmination of three *gunas*: clarity (*sattva*); dynamism (*rajas*); inertia (*tamas*) and are primal qualities of being. The binding role of *Dharma in self-governed polities is the message* that shows peoples' wish/will/opinion on the ruler, viz., peoples' participation in ruler's ruling so that the ruler did not derail or stray in his decision-making power. It means, in peoples' happiness/satisfaction lay the happiness/satisfaction of the ruler; it mean integration, unity; it means the true principle of democracy and not the way it is being put forth by some these days leading to disintegration and disunity. It shows the coordinative and cooperative federalism; it shows unifying political rule; it shows the centre-state unifying political rule, yet without destroying the self-governance of the autonomous polities. Retrieved from http://www.auroville.org dated 9.01.2009.

Samitis or Sabhas known as Assemblies or Councils to see that whenever a ruler (king) became tyrannical, or he did not render justice to his people, he was either dethroned or banished or executed. *Samitis or Sabhas* known as Assemblies or Councils convey the modern concepts of Parliamentary system of government in the shape of the House of People (Loksabha) and Council of States (Rajyasabha). However, ruler's powers were not unlimited and he was invariably guided by his Ministers, *Samitis and Sabhas* to attain good governance as well as sustainable governance.

Dharma is Law and Morals both created for the sole purpose to restore conditions of order, law, justice and security in the State against *Matsyanyaya*, i.e., against greed and selfishness that shall sway the human mind to permeate anarchy or *arajaka*. *Dharma* helps to liberate the State or society from chaos and to create cosmos—an orderly society or State—in accordance with *Dharma* through the instrumentality of the institution of the king. *Shantiparva* of *Mahabharata* mentions that the creation of the State with its king as head of the State has an obligation or profound responsibility to protect, guard and defend (*raksanti/raksana*) the subjects or citizens (*praja*). This unequivocally conveys the constitutional culture and constitutional morality ordained in *Rajdharma, Rajayadharma, Rajsasana, and Rajsastra*. This is the royal science of *Dharma* as law, moral and constitution and has been ordained as The Yoga of the Kingly Science and the Kingly Secret in *Bhagavad Gita:*

> *Raajavidyaa raajaguhyam pavitramidamuttamam,*
> *Pratyakshaavagamam dharmyam susukham kartumavyam.*[195]

This royal science, the royal secret is the complete science of *Rajdharma, Rajayadharma, Rajsasana, and Rajsastra*, the ultimate institutional instrument to attain sustainable governance in accordance with *Dharma*, i.e., law as well as constitutional law that helps to prevent anarchy or *arajaka*. It shows *Dharma* is law as well as constitutional law to prevent anarchy or *arajaka* and to protect all beings in the world as *arajaka* or anarchy is devoid of

---

195. *Bhagavad Gita, Chapter IX, Verse 2.*

the State polity of *Lokhita* (the protector of the people), i.e., the law that worked as mercenary of all beings.

> *Arajake hi lokesmin, sarvato vidrute bhayat,*
> *Raksarthamasya sarvasya, rajanamasrjat prabhu.*[196]

It is, thus, clear that the democracy has been at the root of good governance and sustainable governance inasmuch as a wise ruler did not act without the approval and cooperation of his Council of Ministers known as *Mantrins*. This constitutional theory of the State which has advocated consultation with the Council of advisers has been acknowledged in *Sukraniti*,[197] *Shantiparva* of *Mahabharata* as well:

> *Mantrinaa mantramulam hi rajayae rastram vivardhate.*

> "The prosperity of the State is directly proportionate to the ability of *Mantrins*".

Kautilya also acknowledges the functioning of democracy as a tool kit of good governance as well as sustainable governance within the virtuous kit of *Dharma* as Law and Constitutional Law and Democracy.

> *Sahaya sadhayam hi rajtvam cakramekam nh vartate.*[198]

> "State cannot function on a single wheel".

In the backdrop of the above, it is clear that the democracy has been at the root of the governance of the State. The Council of Ministers (*Mantrins*) and the *Sabha* (the Assembly or Parliament) have always worked in all matters of the State as its watchdog—checks and balances in the modern *lingua fauna* vocabulary—so that the ruler should not have arrayed or strayed or drifted or absolutism or despotic as powers concentrated in

---

196. *Manu's Code of Law, Manavadharma, op. cit.,* Chapter I, Verse 13.
197. *Sukranitisara, II, 2, 3 and 4.*
198. *Kautilya's Arthasastra, vii: 15.*

few or in one hand permeates misuse or abusive use of office and gives room for anarchy or *arajya* that is the root cause of corruption or absolute corruption. Power corrupts and absolute power corrupts absolutely. This culminates in self, the State and the citizens ruinous. This in brevity is the message of *Om sanghachhadhavam, sanghvadhvam.* ... Therefore, the *mantra* of democracy, according to *sage Sukra,* is: "Without the *mantrins* matters of State should never be considered by the king alone, be he an expert in all the sciences and versed in policy. A wise king must always follow the opinion of the members of the Council of *Adhikarins* of ministers with portfolios, of the president of the *mantra-parisad.* He must never follow his own opinion. When the sovereign becomes independent [of his council] he plans for ruin. In that event he loses the State and loses the subjects".[199]

The quintessence of the above indicates that the king who has no faith or belief in democracy for good as well as sustainable governance, according to *Shantiparva in Mahabharata* must be "shunned like a leaky ship on the sea", because such a ship has no shore to reach.[200] This *Raajvidya* ordains *sastra* (military science), *shastra* (political science), *duta* (science of law of diplomacy), which unequivocally convey the principle of democracy within the structure of *Dharma,* viz.; rule of democracy is inasmuch as skilful with the pen as with the sword. *Sama (conciliation), dana (concession), danda (force), and bheda (dissention)* are inasmuch as effective devices of democracy as of carrying out an effective as well as efficient foreign policy through the instrumentality of diplomacy assisted by *duta* with its renowned maxim:

> *Upayantaranasetu tato vigrahamacaret.*
>
> "War is the last resort of diplomacy when all other methods have failed."

The constitutional theory of ancient Indian polity has laid down the functions of the Nation State in accordance with the

---

199. As quoted in Dr. Nagendra Singh, *op. cit.*, pp. 60-61.
200. *Mahabharata, Shantiparva, LVII, 43.*

concept/notion of *Dharma*. It is not possible to mention as to how the idea of the formation of State has sprung up from the *Rigveda* period to *Mahabharata, Kautilaya's Arthasastra, Sukranitisara, Vidurniti, Yuktikalpattaru* of king *Bhoja* (1025 A.D.). But, suffice it to submit that the Indian Nation State in ancient India has to perform a variety of functions to develop polity and synergic comity. Thus, the State's constituent functions have been the maintenance of law and order, security of person and property, defence against aggression, restoring rule of law to serve rule of life from chaos and anarchy, and administration of justice.[201] Be that as it may, *Sukraniti* gives an outline of the tree of State that ordains its six principles of statecraftsmanship as its protecting branches: *Sandhi* (agreement), *Vigraha* (hostilities), *Yana* (marching or mobilization), *Asana* (readiness to attack), *Dvaidhjbhava* (division of troops or double dealing), *Asraya* (subordinate alliance), with its four beautiful flowers of *Sama* (conciliation), *Dana* (concession), *Danda* (force), and *Bheda* (dissention), and its three fruits of *Dharma, artha, and kama* (legal, social and economic welfare).

> *Namo'stu rajyavrksaya saadgunyaya prasakhine,*
> *Samadi charupuspaya trivarga phaladayine.*[202]

> "Let us bow to the State for the sake of *Dharma and artha* (social and economic well-being) which may be regarded as the aims of the State."

---

201. See in particular Dr. Nagendra Sing; N.C. Sen Gupta; Dr. A.S. Altekar, *op. cit.;* Dodwell (ed.), Cambridge History of India, 1934; Max Muller, History of Ancient Sanskrit Literature, 1860. It is difficult to fix a firm date from which the *Vedic* period may said to have begun. However, the available evidence merely proves that the *Vedic* periods extends from an unknown past, say x to 500 B.C., none of the dates 1200-500 B.C. or 1500-500 B.C. or 2000-500 B.C. or 1500-1000 B.C. or 3000 B.C., which are usually assumed, being justified by facts. It may, however, be submitted, as a result of recent researches, that 800 B.C. may probably be taken, millennium before Christ, or as per Altekar it may be regarded as 2500 B.C. See Winternitz, M., *Die Geschichte der indischen Litterattur*, Vol. I, 2nd. Ed., 1909, p. 258.

202. *Sukranitisara.*

This is the constitutional theory of *Dharma*, which is at the foundation of *Rajdharma and Rajayadharma*. It shows that social welfare and economic well-being are the mainstream functions of the State as its objects or ideals. The State has been empowered with *Danda* (force, sanction, punishment) so that laws of *Dharma* are observed and each individual is able to enjoy his life and property. *Danda* or punishment which has its sanction in the 'force behind the State is the most valuable device for the benefit of mankind.[203] From this constitutional polity it discerns that the loose democracy brings chaos and anarchy, whereas *danda* (stern actions) alone has the power to restore cosmos or orderly State out of chaos. This also shows that democracy is successful if the laws of *dharma* are observed in practice that is necessary for the salvation of mankind. From this it also appears that *danda* and *dharma* together are the principle ingredients of statecraft in the constitutional polity of ancient India, and are, nevertheless, equally significant in the modern Indian polity so that all objects—animate or inanimate—observe their *dharma* or duty so essential for good governance as well as sustainable governance to achieving human happiness.

In the backdrop of the above, it seems that code of *Dharma* is meant to regulate the king's powers so that the king enforces obedience to avowed *Dharma*, and if the king's government failed in its duty it permitted the people to remove the king. This is a device to check royal absolutism, chaos and anarchy. From this it seems that the king has had to work democratically devoid of totalitarianism. This clearly indicates the constitutional concept of democracy or federal democracy as well as federal comity. *Dharma* as law and constitutional law is ranked supreme in the constitutional polity/morality/culture and ordains the State, its organs and the king responsible for the enforcement of *dharma*, i.e., constitutional functions and political duties. This includes conduct of external relations, declaration of war and peace, maintenance of internal law and order, dispensation of justice, interpretation of laws of *dharmasastra*, development of laws to meet the just but changing needs of the society, constantly watch the working of the State to maintain its efficient

---

203. *Supra* 202; and also see *Manu's Manavadharmasastra, op. cit.*

existence. It indicates that it is the imperative function of *dharma* or law and constitutional law to check the absolutism of the king, his office and his organs which gather enormous powers. The gathering of enormous powers leads to emergence of uncontrolled despotism, tyranny, and the eradication of rule of law. Therefore, *dharma* or law or constitutional law is imperative checks upon such uncontrolled despotism in democracy.

Dharma, besides law and constitutional law, as religion acts as the greatest deterrent to law-breaking or *Dharma*-breaking inasmuch as the "the ruler who collects his dues from his subjects [citizens] but fails to offer them protection [here State as provider] and to do his duty sinks into hell".

> *Yo raksanbalimadatte karian sulkain ca parthivah,*
> *Pratibhbhagam ca dandain ca sa sadhyo narakam vrajet.*[204]

Besides, if the king acts contrary to the laws of *dharma* would result in his destruction whereas if he acts in accordance with *dharma* he would be entitled to a place in heaven.

> *Adharmadandanain svarga kirti lokamca nashyet,*
> *Samyakut dandanain rajnah svarga kirti jayavaham.*[205]

From this it infers that the laws of *dharma* threaten the unworthy king. It also discerns that the fear of *dharma* is a proper check and control on the unruly king who acts as an unruly horse. *Dharma* does not protect the king if he transgresses *dharma* or law or constitutional law; the law or constitutional law or *dharma* protects when it is cherished. From this it appears that during monarchy democracy has been the rule in accordance with *Dharma,* and why it would not be the rule in democracy to act in accordance with the laws of *Dharma* to save the society from the shadow of new serfdom as well as fiefdom!

It is an imperative element of democracy and its polity that the rulers or the head of the State always acts with the aid and advice of his Council of Ministers as it helps to arrive at just as

---

204. *Manu's Manavadharmsastra, op. cit. Chapter VIII, Verses 307, 309.*
205. Yajnavalkyasmriti, XIII, 357.

well as judicious decisions. It is said that collective decision is better even if it may sometimes produce bad results, because it gives chance to correct the decision collectively. It has been emphasized that it is in the interest of the prestige of the king itself if he acts with the advice of his Council of Ministers in letter and spirit. It appears from the records of the history that the king invariably consulted his council before acting. The constitutional functions and the position of the council in relation to the king have been described at length in *Sukranitisara* and *Arthasastra.* Council of Ministers has been an effective constitutional device to check royal absolutism, as the powers of the Ministers of State included deposition of a prince or king and electing another as mentioned in *Patanjali, Samvara, and Sonaka Jatakas.* This shows the prevalence of the principle of call back of the ruler/prince/king if he strayed from the prescribed constitutional norms in the functioning of the governance. This imperative of law and morality needs to be accepted in the present scenario of political and constitutional polity to strengthen democracy. It shows that a king/ruler/prince may be selected from outside the royal family, and this unequivocally shows an effective check to absolutism because an individual with a tendency to indulge in vices was prevented from coming anywhere near the divine office of the king/prince/ruler. This also indicates that single family rule as a matter of hereditary could be discouraged. It is submitted that this is required to be followed in democracy as a rule rather than an exception if the democracy and rule of law have to flourish.

A further legal and constitutional check through the instrumentality of *samiti* and *parishad* (Assembly of the People) on regal power has been prescribed as mentioned in *Vedas* and *Upanisads. Atharva Veda* states that there has had to be a proper amity between the regal and the Assembly. If the regal has become a source of woe or violated the laws of *Dharmasastra* the Assembly could expel, outcast and even execute him and appoint a good man as a king. From this it is clear that the king's divinity did not necessitate passive obedience to unworthy and wicked sovereigns. From this it also seems that better governance has been preferred to ill-governance. This is mentioned in *Sukraniti:*

Adharmasilo nrpatir yada tain bhisayejjanah,
Dharmasilatibalavadriporasrayatah sada.[206]

The right of the people has been recognized to dethrone a king if he becomes tyrannical and oppressive and enthrone a suitable non-tyrannical as well as non-oppressive ruler.

Araksitaram hartaram vilotparam nayakam,
Tam vai rajakatnim hanyuh prajah samnahya nirghrnam.[207]

It is thus evident from the above that the *sabhas* and *samitis*, the popular Assemblies of People, have provided a constitutional check on regal absolutism in the ancient *Vedic* literature, which seems to be accepted principles of democracy in monarchical State. This also seems to be the evidence of flourishing of States as well as people during such periods of history of ancient India. This indicates that democracy permeates participative governance as a rule of sustainable governance if adequately and properly exercised within the recipe of *Dharma* as law and constitutional law. In the backdrop of this, it is evident that the supremacy of the laws of *dharma* must have provided an effective constitutional check for efficient governance.[208] The regal power appears to be subservient or subject to the laws of *Dharma* lest he becomes autocrat or despot. He whosoever ever tried to be wicked was driven away by their subjects, i.e., people or citizens in the modern polity language. This shows the clearest and unmistakable proof of constitutional devices for the establishment of righteous, law-abiding, benevolent, and Social Service State that is democratic in the modern sense of the term of democracy.

Another check to regal absolutism is to be seen in the concept of *Dharma* as his duties to himself and to others in the governance of State affairs. He must be free from vices which result from *Kama* (pleasure) and *Krodha* (wrath) which are mischief. The intrinsic and urgency of this is that he must always

206. *Sukranitisara, IV, 1.3.*
207. *Mahabharata, XIII, 86, 35-6.*
208. See *Supra* note 202.

be kept out of mischief inasmuch as that there is little room to deviate from the path of *Dharma* as law and constitutional law of sustainable governance. This seems to be preventive measures against maladministration or bad governance. This seems to be identical to the institution of ombudsman or watchdog. It is intriguing to note that the modern rulers of democracy in India seem to be ignorant about the intrinsic value of this institution may be due to the witch-hunt of corruption, maladministration, and the emergence of new despotism in democracy. This also indicates that the regal government is responsive to the voice of the people or public opinion. From this it may discern that the regal government is responsible to the people or public of the day. It may also be inferred that there has been a chance of successful opposition or dissention to the regal if he or his government has had acted oppressively and contrary to law or *Dharma*. From this it is clear that the imperial structure of the regal State has been essentially democratic in character. From this it may be inferred that the imperial State in ancient India has rarely degenerated into military despotism. It also indicates that the institution of regal has been so completely interwoven with the concept of law of *Dharma* that everyone who ascended to that office bowed to *Dharma* first and last.[209] The aim of the regal State has been *triumvirate*, viz., *Dharma* (law, individual and social morality), *artha* (economic well-being), and *Kama* (enjoyment of life with dignity), and the successful attainment of this *triumvirate* has been possible through the instrumentality of *Danda*, i.e., sanction, force, punishment.

The concept of the political nation State has been conceived as an organic unit. According to *Mahabharata* the nation State is constituted of seven limbs, namely, the king as its *atman* (soul), *amatyas* (ministers), *kosa* (treasury), *danda* (force or sanction), *mitra* (allies), *janapada* (provincial or federal units), *puras*

---

209. *Ibid.* The regal was required to adhere to the oath throughout, the regal could hardly be described as an autocrat or an oriental despot: "Between the night I am born and the night I die, whatever good I might have done, my heaven, my life and my progeny may be deprived of, if I oppress you to become tyrannical". This royal science unequivocally shows the democratic characteristic of the regal governance.

Cities).[210] *Kautilya* in his *Arthasastra* also gives seven elements of a stable nation State, viz., *Swamin* (king), *Amatya* (minister), *janapada* (village communities), *durga* (fort), *kosa* (treasury), *danda* (armed forces), *mitra* (allies).[211] *Manu* also mentions the seven constituent organs of a stable Nation State, viz., *Swamin* (king), *amatya* (minister), *pura* (capital), *rastra* (country), *danda* (armed forces), *suhrd* (allies).[212] This concept of a Nation-State is conceived as *Saptanga* concept of an organic State. These elements of a nation State are conceived imperatives for inter-State and intra-State relations, and as such essential for the growth as well as development of international law and the strengthening of the concept of the political Nation-State or federalism as it exists today in the modern context, which contains four segments territory, population, government, and sovereignty. Thus, modern theory of a Nation-State is *Caturanga*. In *Sukraniti* the relative importance of a Nation-State has been narrated as: king or *swamin* is the brain, ministers or *amatyas* are the eyes, allies or *suhrd* the ears, treasury or *kosa* the mouth, forts or *durga* the arms, territories or *rastra* the legs, and force or *bala* the strength of the man himself.[213] Besides, the organic conception of the Nation-State has been compared to a tree, the roots are the king, ministers are the stems, the commander-in-chief and the armed forces are the branches, leaves, and flowers of the tree, *praja* or subjects or citizens are the fruits, and the territory the seed:

> *Rajayavriksasya nripatirmulam skandhasah ca mantrinah,*
> *Shakha senadhipah senah palvah kusumani ca,*
> *Praja falani bhubhagya vijayam bhumiah prakalpitah.*[214]

---

210. *Shantiparva of the Mahabharata, LXIX, 65: Atma matyas ca kosas ca dando mitrani caiva hi, tatha janapadas caiva purain ca kurunnandana, etatsaptatmkain raijain paripalyain prayatnatah.*
211. *Kautilya's Arthasastra, VI, 1: Swamya amatya janapada durga kosa dandamitrani Prakrtayah.*
212. *Manu's Code of Law Manavadharmsastra, op. cit., IX, 294,* p.801.
213. *Sukranitisara, 1, 60, 61, IV, 1257-58.*
214. *Sukranitisara, IV, 1257-58.*

This organic concept of a Nation-State, which is classified as *Gana rajya* (republics), *Parmastya* (oligarchies), *Samrajaya* (kingdoms), *Chakravartins* (empires), *Samant Rajayas* (Vassal kingdoms), *Samsrayaraj* (protectorates), [broadly classified as monarchies and republics], indicates the feeling of closest affiliation, brotherhood, fraternity of the citizens in allegiance to the Nation-State and as such the existence of 'nationalism' in the modern sense as a part or segment of nation polity.[215]

Though democracy, rule of law, rule of law to serve the rule of life, the laws of *Dharma* have been operative in the imperial system, but imperial tendency and ambition of expansion with military might through the instrumentalities of *Asvamegha and Rajasuysa* to establish a universal empire have not been missing. It indicates that imperialism is born of armed strength and ensures the further employment of the armed might with the result that military might and expansion become its characteristic features is noticeable in the Indian Nation States of ancient time.[216] Be that as it may, this tendency has been operative within the Indian Nation-State, and the Indian Nation-State has never the ambition of expansion to establish a universal empire across or beyond its national territory.

The basis of democratic governance has been to adhere to the sacred precept of *Dharma* for sustainable governance or *rajasasana*. The *rajasaśana* polity has a place among sources of law, which could not be arbitrary law, but propounded in conformity with *Dharma* coupled with the sanction or *danda* and social usage by the regal and its government in the good governance of the country or *rastra*. This is the legislative function of the regal governance in accordance with democracy, polity and comity. Besides legislative functions, the regal has certain specified executive/administrative/governmental functions, both civil and defence or military, to perform, viz., appointment of ministers, priests, superintendence, correspondence with the Council of Ministers or *mantri parisad*, security of secret information gathered by spies or *dutas*,

215. *Supra* note 202.
216. See H.H. Dodwell, The Cambridge Shorter History of India, p. 10.

receptions of envoys or diplomats or *rajdutas*, planning strategies of defensive measures for the safety and protection of his kingdom or *rajya* in consultation with Commander-in-Chief or *Senapati*, conduct of public affairs through secretariat or *sacivas* and ministers or *amatyas*, and performance of these functions with the aid, assistance, advice, and consultation of Council of Ministers or *mantri-parisad*. Cumulatively, if the State, the people, the army, the exchequer, and the regal monarch do not grow, or the enemy is not broken through the policy of the ministers, the ministers do not justify their existence and have to be relinquished.[217] This is the *raison d'être* of the democratic set-up of the system that flourished in accordance with the laws of *Dharma* or law and constitutional law and constitutional polity. Besides, the constitutional powers of the Council of Ministers have been propounded by *Kautilya's Arthasastra* and endorsed by *Sukranitisara* as: (1) deliberation on the policy of State and its strategy (*mantra*); (2) realization of the result of that policy and strategy; (3) execution of business; (4) the business concerning income and expenditure; (5) army and its leading role; (6) providing army against enemy and wild tribes (*atavi*); (7) maintenance of government; (8) providing army against national degeneration; and (9) protection of the princes and their consecration (*coronation*).[218]

The republic as well as democratic characteristic of the State unfolds the equality, military skill, and financial administration ubiquitous to the policy of "live and let live". From this it may be seen that the system has been "as skilful with the pen as with the sword". It may also seem that the Indian Nation State in ancient India ordains the civil element of the constitution, constitutional polity, constitutional culture and constitutional morality. It is significant to mention that the republican form of government in ancient India has distinguishing characteristic of fertile territory and virile people.[219] The ennobling character of Indian polity

---

217. *Sukranitisara, II, 82: Raiyain prajabalain kosah sunrpatvain na vardhitam, Yanmantrato narinasas tair mantribhih kim prayojanam.*
218. *Kautilya's Arthasastra, VIII, 127; Sukranitisara* as mentioned in Jayaswal, Hindu Polity, 1934, p. 311; *Supra* note 202.
219. However, as per Dr. Altekar, imperialism is said to have given the death blow to republican principles. The decline and downfall of

ordains *ath dharmarthfalaya rajayyya namah,* i.e., "State is the source of all life and spirit" and as such it is revered.[220] This concept is further witnessed in *Mahabharata Shantiparva:*

> *Sarve tayaga rajdharmeshu drishta sarva diksha rajdharmeshu yukata,*
> *Sarva vidhaya rajdharmeshu couktah sarve loka rajdharme pravishtah.*[221]

> "In the politics of the State are realized all the forms of renunciation. In the political State are united all the sacraments. Politics combines all knowledge; in the concept of the State are centered the very heavens and all the worlds."

From this it unequivocally seems that the State alone has been conceived an indispensable institution in the orderly existence and progress of society. This has been possible only if the Nation-State adhered to the laws of *Dharma*—law, moral law, constitutional law, constitutional morality, and constitutional culture that takes care every form of human activity. In the backdrop of this, it discerns that the State has thus to be served by those ennobling souls dedicated to serve humanity:

> *Na tvaham kamye rajayam na svargam n punrabhavam,*
> *Kamye dukham taptanaamah pranninaamam aartnaasham.*

> "I seek no kingdoms nor heavenly pleasures nor personal salvation since to relieve humanity from its manifold pains and distresses is the supreme objective of mankind".

Besides, the democracy ordains the character of the *Samitis and Sabhas* as 'representing the whole people': "*Raja na satyah*

---

republics was due to the fact that they had ceased to be popular because monarchy or anarchy or absolutism had become the order of the day.

220. *Niti Vakyamrit.*
221. *Mahabharata Shantiparva, 63.28.29.*

samitiriyanah", viz., "like a true king going to the samiti".[222] This is the most distinguishing feature of democracy, Indian polity, Indian Nation State, which conceived through this instrumentality the process of consultation, participative governance, and law-making as well as decision-making have been subject to the basic requirement of consultation. This shows the origin, growth, and development of constitutional organism of the *Samitis and Sabhas* as the Parliamentary form of government for sustainable governance. This *triumvirate* of constitutional law, constitutional morality, and constitutional culture ordains *Bhagavad Gita* conception as well as vision: "Where there is firm morality there are surely fortune, wealth, prosperity, victory, sound policy, expansion, happiness and righteousness as mediums of sustainability":

> *Yatra yogeshvara Krishno yatra Partho dhanurdhara,*
> *Tatra shrivijayao bhutidhruvah nitirmatirmam.*[223]

viii. *Dharma* and the Concept of Logic and Reasoning—Practicality and Heuristic

Dharma or the law of ideal living embraces the imperishable relationship between law and morality as the law and custom of society. It is based on *nyaya or tarka-sastra* the science of logic or reasoning. Reasoning has main place in *nyaya-dharma,* which is not pure theoretical but encompasses the values of heuristic practicality. It helps to confirm the inseparable relationship between law and morality; it clears doubts of the faith in *dharma* through reasoning. Logic or reasoning is indispensible to the

---

222. As pronounced in *Rigveda*.
223. *Bhagavad Gita,* Chapter XVIII, Verse 78. This is as per *Aadi Shankaracharya's* reading and translation; see text and translation of *Bhagavad Gita by* Annie Besant, 19th reprint, 2002; Lars Martin Fosse, 2007; Swami Chinbhavananda, The Bhagavad Gita, 2000, pp. 980-984; Commentary by Paramahamsa Swami Shivananda Saraswati, The Divine Life Society, www.astrojyoti.com, 18.10.2007; A.C. Bhaktivedanta Swami Prabhupada, 1972, 2007 edition; Boris Marjanovic, Abhinavagupta's commentary on the Bhagavad Gita Gitaratha-Samgraha, 2004, 365.

study of *dharma* as the law of ideal living and *sanskara* an immutable truth emanating from *Vedas* affirmed by *Upanishdas* and determined by *Mimamsa* to its meaning.[224] This shows that *dharma, nyaya, taraka-sastra, law and morality* are truth, and are not unjust laws, and are subject to tests (heuristic) so as to confirm their practicality.[225] The heuristic tests show their acceptance with logical reasoning rooted in authority.[226] The heuristic acceptance is based on logical arguments, which must not be of carping character, stemming from the urge to be merely contrary.[227] Succinctly, it means that one must give up the habit of captious arguments and that in dealing with a question one must employ proper reasoning, duly respecting the views of *dharma, nyaya, taraka-sastra* as the fountainhead of law and morality.[228]

Logic or reasoning or *nyaya or taraka-nyaya* has four *parmanas,* i.e. instruments of scientific knowledge, viz., *"pratyaksa"* [direct perception, i.e. what is perceived by the eyes and the ears]; *"anumana"* [inference that is central to *nyaya or taraka-nyaya* and is the ends of *hetu as sadhya and sadhana*]; *"upamana"* [this is *manana,* i.e. going over an idea again and again in the mind, making use of our own ability to reason]; and *"sabda"* [the language as a thirst and ever-yearning to restore, retain, preserve, observe and promote values, purity and sanity in personal and public life]. In the backdrop of this, it is a quest for knowing interrelationship and interdependence of *Dharma-nyaya* logic or reasoning to sustaining imperishable law-morality relationship that expounds through logical reasoning that all these are transient.

---

224. See Science of Reasoning from the chapter of *Nyaya,* in Hindu Dharma, retrieved from http://www.kamakoti.org dated 9.01.2009.
225. *Ibid.*
226. *Ibid.*
227. *Ibid.*
228. *Ibid.* This is based on the *Upadesa* of Sankara to his disciples at the time of departure to the heavenly abode by the name of *"Updesa-Pancaka or Sopana-Pancaka: Dustarkat suviramyatam—Srutimatastarko'nusandhiyatam".*

4

CONCLUSION

In conclusion, I must not hesitate to say that I have all along been wondering what the legal system can do to an individual hapless enough to be caught within its soul murdering gears while living on a borrowed legal system. The borrowed law system, howsoever, good it may be for the insiders, but how its results would make one to feel right emotionally to those who are neither its insiders nor cast members. Besides, I have an enlightened vision that I stand on the shore of a deep as well as unfathomable sea unfamiliar with its behaviour pattern and thinking how to dive into it to separate sand and pebbles from the pearls. *Dharma* as law and morals is unfathomable and full of pearls as a treasure house of values + ethics + morals + law + action + duties + obligations + justice and together constitutes the "science of law"; life and literature as well as the repository of civil society that man seeks to have civility. In the backdrop of this, I have made a modest attempt as a most ignorant person, since my knowledge on the subject is far from nearly complete, in laying down the foundation for the building of an Indian concept of law and morality ingrained in infallible expression *Dharma*. He, who has his own concepts of law, has the potentialities to flourish in law, life and wealth alike, "he who has wealth has friends, he who has wealth has relatives, he who has wealth is a man in the world, and he who has wealth is a learned expert".[1] I wish some scholar(s) may take up the task to develop India's own law concepts, law perceptions, and law visions from the rich treasures of Indian literature for the posterity so that India would be rich in producing legal wealth unlike "all the undertakings of a stupid man who has no wealth dissolve intonothingness, like puny little rivers in the summer."[2] Why "(I)t never occurred to the lawyers that they should suggest or insist on any improvements in the system"[3] should not be the cause of grieves, rather law, love, wealth, riches and heaven come from *Dharma* should be the yearning to developing the Indian law concepts. I have no religious/theological/cultural/ism obsessions in writing this write up.[4] I teach law

1. James L. Fitzgerald, The Mahabharata, *op. cit.*, p. 183.
2. *Ibid.*
3. Franz Kafka, The Trial.
4. *Bhisma* in *Shantiparva of Mahabharata* counsels *Yudhisthira* who seeks about the Law from *Bhisma* "A man of vile understanding could not even think of acquiring in a whole day as much of these goods as a man of excellent understanding could get in a moment. Law has jealous as its stain, Riches have concealment as its stain, and Love has excessive pleasure as its stain—when the particular quality of each is carried to an extreme." James L. Fitzgerald, *op. cit.*, p. 479, and at pp. 518-544 a succinct and a very subtle point about Law in Times of Distress has been made out: "Hunger corrupts Law". "There are friends who appear to be enemies, and there are enemies who appear to be friends. Those that have been wooed with conciliation are not taken into account, for they are under the sway of passion or greed". "No one is one's enemy by birth; no one is one's friend by birth. Friends and enemies are produced through the application of people's different capabilities". "When someone sees his own interests served while another is alive, then that one stays alive just that long; he will be that one's friend just as long as there is no change in the situation". "There is no friendship that is really lasting, nor any enmity that is permanent. Friends and enemies are born the appropriate fit among their interests". "A friend becomes an enemy at some change of circumstances, or an enemy becomes a friend. Self interest is what is most powerful". "Father, mother, and sons are understood in terms of the appropriate fit of interests, and mother's brothers, sisters' sons, and other kin and relatives." "A father and mother will abandon a dear son who has fallen. Everyone in the world protects himself. See how essential one's own interests are". "One becomes dear to another for a reason; and one becomes an enemy to another for a reason. Every

students with a deeper law and moral insights as well as awareness of what law lacks and this alone has encouraged me to take up this write up.

My write up is based on some paradoxes, which have developed in a span of about four decades of teaching and research in law and literature. My paradox is based on an inquisitive what we expect and what we actually get from our courts. This paradox shows moral deficiency and moral bleakness in a legal system that citizens and courts are at odds. A paradox stems from a story between wife and husband over a minor dispute where from the sun arise. There was an argument between the wife and the husband, the wife pleading that the sun rises from the east and whereas the husband insisting that the sun rises from the west. This led to an altercation with no end result. Both decided to go to the village headman to decide the wrangle. The headman heard both wife and husband and concluded that the wife was right in her contention and the husband was wrong in his contention. Both asked the village headman to give in writing his decision which the village headman declined urging that he had no authority from the village court [*Panchayat]* and the matter needed to be referred to the village court for decision. The dispute was thus referred to the village court [*Panchayat]*. The village court heard the contentious arguments of both the wife and the husband and arrived at the conclusion that the wife's contention was right. And, when asked to give in writing, it also declined to give its verdict in writing urging that it had no authority under the law to give its verdict in writing. The village court advised both the wife and the husband that they should go to the district court for appropriate orders. Consequently, both engaged their respective lawyers to refer the dispute to the district court for the resolve. The disputant-matter when pleaded before the district court judge the arguments of the lawyers of both the side went like this. The lawyer of the wife's side presented that the sun rises from the north instead of the east and prayed for the relief

---

living being in the world sees his interests". "A modest man does not boast a lot to anyone when he has done something superb. He is always quiet in mind and quiet in speech, while modesty is gained from doing Lawful Deeds".

accordingly. Whereas, on the contrary, the lawyer of the husband made a plea before the judge that the sun rises from the south instead of the west and prayed for the appropriate relief in favour of his client accordingly. The case lingered on, as usual under the common law legal system, for years together without any seemingly remedy. On one evening, the judge and his wife were on the dining table, and while feeding her judge-husband the wife pleaded that her friend from the village had a case pending in his court which he must decide in her favour that the sun arise from the east. The judge told his wife that there was no dispute before him like the sun rises from the east rather the disputant case pending in his court was either the sun arise from the north or the south and all the documents presented before him related to that only. Therefore, it was difficult for him to please his wife. The wife was unhappy over the behaviour of her husband that he did not oblige her, and as such both went for sleep. Next morning the wife did not serve her husband either with the breakfast or the lunch, and the judge-husband had to leave for the court unfed. The judge was upset in the court. He accordingly called for the records of the disputant case and dictated the court order, thinking that it may please his wife, that a commission was appointed to examine where from the sun arise—east, west, north or south—and report the court for appropriate judicial order. This example speaks volumes about law and morals deficiency and bleakness and also shows a disparity between what we expect and what we actually get from our courts.

Another paradox stems from the facts that demonstrate that citizens and the legal system are at odds. People living in fear psychosis due to internal displacement by loosing homes and searching for own sweet homes as a consequence of terrorism. Besides, the victims of militancy are the worst sufferers. For example, the child who suffers in his/her rights of dignity, grooming as well as grilling, flourishing, education, nourishment, etc., and he/she pleads for the rights because of the changing image of the childhood. There are problems of fair sex exploitation; girl child abuse; girl child as domestic servant another kind of bonded labour; internally displaced persons and problems of hearth and home, women, their children; begging;

immoral human trafficking; victims of domestic violence; victims of democracy; disabled persons; refugees; migrants; children (particularly victims of sexual harassment and unnatural offences); sexual harassment of women at working places; old aged persons/parents; disadvantaged groups of society; aboriginals; minority groups; evil of despotic power of husbands over wives *vis-à-vis* human happiness are not exclusive social or legal problems but problems that are within the domain of law and morality and need *de novo* thinking in new world order in the realm of law and morality. Perspectives of victims of crimes, victims, particularly children, of terrorism and militancy, children who have lived a war and fight to survive to the changing images of their childhood appear to be the challenges to law and morality in the present scenario unless the shadows of the evils are evaporated or completely eclipsed or eradicated. Besides, new thinking in the liberalization and globalization, WTO and the challenges to copyright, trade, design, TRIPs, Corporations and international trade procedure and practices, new consumerism *vis-à-vis Caveat Venditor vis-à-vis Caveat Emptor*, implications and implementation of International Humanitarian Law in non-armed conflicts, that is terrorism/militancy and the victims of such conflicts (terrorism as a challenge to international humanitarian law), non-state actors—rebels, insurgents, belligerents, national liberation movements, rebel groups, armed opposition groups, parties to internal armed conflicts, mercenaries—rights, accountability, human rights and human dignity abuses, etc. open a flood gate for law and morality debate.

The concepts enshrined in constitutional vocabulary and law-sociology coordination like 'legality', 'due process', 'procedure established by law', 'life and liberty', 'reasonableness', 'equality before the law and equal protection of the law', 'human dignity', 'the rule of law', 'the rule of law to serve rule of life', 'the legal order', 'judicial activism', 'judicial creativity', 'judicial innovation', 'judicial craftsmanship', 'justice, access to justice and distributive justice', 'disadvantaged groups of the society', 'marginalized groups of the society', 'neglected segments of the society', 'aboriginals', 'minority', are value terms/expressions and appear to be very near or like or actually assimilable to *Dharma* as law and morality or natural law expressions and rarely, seldom as well as insufficiently investigated by socio-legal eagles heuristically and empirically with social sciences research methodologies. These expressions nevertheless do not lie far away from the eternal as well as internal morality, and in this area law and morality of *Dharma* can play its part.

However, the debate on *Dharma* and law and morality and its insights is illustrative of inconclusive discussion. In the backdrop of the emergence of new world culture, new constitutional as well as legal culture, it is in need of new approach. It seems that we have reached a point of functional approach to law and morality interaction, which may be helpful for reshaping as well as rehabilitation of *Dharma* as law and morality or natural law for the emerging millennia that encounters a number of challenges. Each and every challenge has genuine questions of morality—hidden or apparent—in search of genuine answers to such genuine moral questions. Sound and not arrayed human behaviour shall help to develop a new law and morality or natural law or *Dharma law* culture. Western law culture is in conflict of "is" and "ought" and searching conceivably for 'ought' from 'is' convincingly. *Dharma* law or law and morality culture has no such conviviality. This may alone be possible if we are determined:

> *Ya nisa sarvabhutanam tasyam jagarti samyami,*
> *Yasyam jagrati bhutani sa nisa pasyatah muneh.*[5]
>
> That which is night to all beings, in that the disciplined man wakes, that in which all beings wake, is night to the sage.
>
> 'In the darkest night
> The sage is wide-awake
> When all are awake by day
> It is night for the sage.'[6]

5. The Bhagavad Gita, Chapter 2, Verse 69.
6. See Alan Jacobs, The Bhagavad Gita, 2003, p. 37.

His perspective is wakefulness in the night of ignorance where other beings are still subject to divine hypnosis, or the power of illusion. The accomplishment of it is possible if:

Na karmanam anarambhan naiskarmyam puruso snute,
Na ca samnyasanad eva sidhim samadhigacchati.[7]

Man gains not actionlessness by abstaining from activity,
Nor does he rise to perfection by mere renunciation.

'Perform your duty!
Actions are better than
No actions.
Even saving life
Is impossible
Without action.'[8]

Dharma is born of the belief that law and morality is ingrained in it and has its roots and its analog in traditional Language of Law, Life, Literature, Morals, Ethics, Actions, Justice, Right, and Wrong, that is about the requisites of morality, viz., "the good life". Strip away these terms, plumb the inarticulate debates of stating problems, clarifying questions, determining facts, interpreting language, formulating and analysing concepts, perceptions and visions, and indecisive conclusions concerning justice delivery system. I can only submit that positive law, in fact, cannot survive without a "therapy" of *Dharma* Law and Morality.

7. The Bhagavad Gita, Chapter 3, Verse 4.
8. See Alan Jacobs, The Bhagavad Gita, 2003, p. 41.

BIBLIOGRAPHY

A.S. Altekar, State and Government in India, 1955.

Alan Jacobs, The Bhagavad Gita, 2003.

Andrew Clapham, Human Rights Obligations of Non-State Actors, 2006.

Annie Besant, The Bhagavad Gita, Text and Translation, 2002.

A.L. Harding, A Reviving Natural Law.

Anthony J. Lisska, Aquinas's Theory of Natural Law: An Analytic Reconstruction, 1996.

A. Passerin D' Entrenes, Natural Law

Austin, John, Province of Jurisprudence Determined 1832.

A. Ross, On Law and Justice.

The Basic Law of the Federal Republic of Germany.

Constitution of India.

Bentham, Jeremy, Of Laws in General, 1782.

Bentham, Jeremy, An Introduction to the Principles of Morals and Legislation.

Berman Harold J., Law and Revolution: The Foundation of the Western Legal Tradition, 1983.

Boris Marjanovic, Abhinavagupta's Commentary on the Bhagavad Gita Gitartha-Samgraha, 2004.

Brian H. Bix, A Dictionary of Legal Theory, 2004.

Brian Bix, Natural Law; The Modern Traditions, 2002.

C. Joseph Chacko, India's Contribution to the Field of International Law Concepts, Recueil Des Cours, 1958.
Carl F. Stychin and Linda Mulcahy, Legal Method, 2003.
Capps, Being Positive about Positivism, 2000.
Charles Covell, The Defence of Natural Law, 1992.
Charles P. Curits, Law As Large As Life, 1959.
City of God Book 4, iv.
C.K. Allen, Law in the Making.
Erik Angner, Hayek and Natural Law, 2007.
David Braybrooke, Natural Law Modernized, 2001.
David Kretzmer and Human Rights Eckart Klein, The Concept of Human Dignity in Discourse, 2002.
Donald P. Kommers, The Constitutional Jurisprudence of the Federal Republic of Germany, 2nd Ed. 1997.
Dyzenhans, Positivism's Stagnant Research Programme, 2000.
Erik Wolf, Analysis of *Das Problem der Naturiechtslehre, 1955.*
Fali S. Nariman, India's Legal System: Can It Be Saved?, 2006.
Francis Biddle, Justice Holmes, Natural Law, and the Supreme Court, 1961.
Finnis, John, Natural Law and Natural Rights, 1980.
Finnis, John, Natural Law, Vols. I and II, 1991.
Fitzgerald, James L., The Mahabharata, 1, 2, 3, 11, 12, 2004.
Guest, Why the Law is Just, 2000.
H.A. Oberman, The Harvest of Medieval Theology.
H.H. Dodwell, The Cambridge Shorter History of India.
H.L.A. Hart, The Concept of Law, 1951, 1994 Ed.
H.L.A. Hart, Essays on Bentham.
H.L.A. Hart, Positivism and the Separation of Law and Morality, *Harv. L. Rev.*, 1958, 593.
Handerson, Lynne, Whose Nature? 1990.
Hans Kelsen, Pure Theory of Law.
Hans Kelsen, General Theory of Law and State.
J. Bell, French Legal Cultures, 2001.
Jolly Julius, Hindu Law and Custom, 1928.
Fuller, Lon L., Anatomy of Law.
Fuller, Lon L., The Morality of Law.
John Locke, Two Treatises of Civil Government.
George C. Christie and Patrick H. Martin, Jurisprudence Text and Readings on the Philosophy of Law, 1999.

George P. Fletcher, Basic concepts of Legal Thought, 1996.

Hubert Rottleuthner, Foundations of Law, 2005.

Jean Porter, Nature As Reason a Thomistic Theory of the Natural Law, 2005.

J.A.B. van Buitenen, The Bhagavad Gita in the Mahabharata, 1981.

J.A.B. van Buitenen, The Mahabharata, The Book of the Beginning, 1973.

J.A.B. van Buitenen, The Mahabharata, 2, The Book of the Assembly Hall, 3, The Book of the Forest, 1975.

John Macdonnel, Great Jurists of the World, 1914.

J.D.M. Derrett, Religion, Law and the State in India, 1968.

J. Krishnamurthy, The Kingdom of Happiness.

J.W. Harris, Law and Legal Science.

James L. Fitzgerald, The Mahabharata, 11, The Book on Women, 12, The Book of Peace, Vol. 7, 2004.

K.L. Bhatia, Juris Vicissitude Law and Change Towards 21st Century, 1995.

K.L. Bhatia, *Main aur meri anubhooti, (Poems)*, 2007.

Kautilya's Arthasastra (English).

Kautilyeeatha Sastram (Sanskrit), Mysore University, 4th Ed., 1960.

Knud Haakonssen, Grotius, Pufendorf and Modern Natural Law, 1999.

Lars Martin Fosse, The Bhagavad Gita, The Original Sanskrit and an English Translation, 2007.

Ludo Rocher, *Vacaspati Misra Vyavaharacintamani, 1956.*

Mark E. Graham, Josef Fuchs on Natural Law, 2002.

Maharishi Mahesh Yogi, On the Bhagavd Gita: a New Translation and Commentary, 1967.

Mark C. Murphy, Natural Law in Jurisprudence and Politics, 2006.

Mark C. Murphy, Natural Law and Practical Rationality, 2001.

Michael Bertram Crowe, The Changing Profiles of the Naturai Law, 1977.

Michael H. Hoffheimer, Justice Holmes and the Natural Law, 1992.

Michael J. Seidler, Natural Law and Enlightenment Classics, The Present State of Germany, Samuel Pufendorf, 2007.

Michael King, Nature's Intelligence or Human Reason? Natural Law in Maharishi's Vedic Science, and in Legal and Ethics Thought, 1997.

Michael Doherty, Jurisprudence: The Philosophy of Law, 2005.

M. Fry, Adm Smith's Legacy, His Place in the Development of Modern Economics, 1992.

M. Rama Jois, Legal and Constitutional History of India, Vols. I and II, 1984.

Nagendra Singh, India and International Law, 1973.

Nagendra Singh, Juristic Concept of Ancient Indian Polity, 1980.

Nan Seuffert, Jurisprudence of National Identity, 2006.

N. C. Sen Gupta, Evolution of Ancient Indian Law, 1953.

Nigel Biggar and Rufus Black, The Revival of Natural Law, 2000.

Notre Dame Law School, Natural Law Forum, 1956.

——, *Notre Dame Law Review*, Vol. 75, 2: 1999/2000.

Olivecrona, Karl, Law as Fact, 2nd Ed., 1971.

Olivecrona, Karl, The Imperative Elements in Law, 1995, *Rutgers Law Review*, 794.

Panchatantra

Philip Anthony Harris, The Distinction Between Law and Ethics in Natural Law Theory, 2002.

Patrick Olivelle, Manu's Code of Law: A Critical Edition and Translation of the *Manava-Dharmasastra*, 2004.

Political Studies, 2000, Tony Burns: Aquinas's Two Doctrines of Natural Law, Vol. 48, 929-946.

Postema, Bentham and the Common Law Traditions.

P.V. Kane, History of Dharmasastra, Vols. I-V.

R.K. Mukherji, Chandragupta Maurya and his Times.

R.S. Pandit, *Kalhana's Rajatrangini.*

R.W. Dyson, Natural Law and Political Realism in the History of Political Thought, Vols. I & II, 2005.

Raymond Wacks, Understanding Jurisprudence: An Introduction to Legal Theory, 2005.

Robert P. George, Natural Law, 2003.

Robert P. George, In Defense of Natural Law, 1999.

Robert P. George and Christopher Wolfe, Natural Law and Public Reason, 2000.

Romans, 2, pp. 14-15.

Roscoe Pound, Jurisprudence, Vols. I-V.

Roscoe Pound, Justice According to Law, 1951.
Sarvadhikari, History of Hindu Law, Tagore Law Lectures, 1880.
S. Radhakrishnan, The Principal Upanishads.
Samuel Pufendorf, The Law of Nature and Nations, 1672.
Stephen Buckle, Natural Law and the Theory of Property, 1991.
Stephen E. Gottlieb, *et. al.*, Jurisprudence Cases and Materials: An Introduction to the Philosophy of Law and its Applications, 1993.
Summa Theologiae, Part 2, 1st Part, questions 94, 96, articles 2, 4.
Swami Chidbhavananda, The Bhagavad Gita, 2000.
Shantiparva, Mahabharata
Sukranitisara
Yajnavalkyasmriti
Vidhurniti
Niti Vakyamrit
Tur and Twining, Essays on Kelsen.
T.J. Hochstrasser, Natural Law Theories in the Early Enlightenment, 2000.
Thane Rosenbaum, The Myth of Moral Justice, 2005.
Tony Burns, Natural Law and Political Ideology in the Philosophy of Hegel, 1997.
T.J. Hochstrasser and P. Schroder, Early Natural Law: Theories Context and Strategies in the Early Enlightenment, 2003.
W. Freidman, Legal Theory, 1967.
Walter Farrell, O.P., The Natural Moral Law, 1930.
W. Morison, John Austin.
V.C. Govindraj, Judge Nagendra Singh of the World Court, His Contribution to the Development of Contemporary International Law, 1999.
Yael Danieli, Elsa, The Universal Declaration of Human Rights: Fifty Years and Beyond, 1999
Stamatopoulou, Clarence
J. Dias
Wisconsin Law Review, 2004, John R. Kroger, The Philosophical foundations of Roman Law: Aristotle, the Stoics, and Roman Theories of Natural Law, 905-944.
Ratio Juris, Vol. 18 (1), 2005. George Pavlakos, On the Necessity of the Interconnection between Law and Morality, 64-83.

Ratio Juris, Vol. 18 (2), 2005. Frank Haldemann, Gustav Radbruch vs. Hans Kelsen: A debate on Nazi Law, 162-178.

Ratio Juris, (15 and 16) 2002 and 2003, Michael S. King, Natural Law and The Bhagavad Gita, 399-415.

Ratio Juris 17 (2004), 156, Alexy, R., The Nature of Legal Philosophy.

Journal of Indian Philosophy, 32 (2004).

www.hindu.com date 18.12.2007.

The Bhagavad Gita, The Divine Life Society, Swami Sivananda Sarawati, www.astrojyoti.com date 18.10.2007.

Donald R. Davis, Jr., Hinduism as a Legal Tradition, *Journal of the American Academy of Religion*, www.jaar.oxfordjournals.org date 17.10.2007.

Sri Aurobindo, Essays on Gita, www.miraura.org Date 26.10.2007.

Werner Menski, From Dharma to Law and Back? Postmodern Hindu Law in a Global world, 2004, www.hpsacp.uni-hd.de

A.C. Bhaktivedanta Swami Prabhupada, Bhagavad Gita As It Is, www.asitis.com date 16.10.2007.

Ernest Valea, Possible Difficulties in the Philosophy of the Bhagavad Gita, www.comparativereligion.com date 17.10.2007.

Nagendra singh, History Of The Law Of Nations Regional developments: South and South-East Asia, 1984, 824-838.

Varghese Manimala, the Four Goals of Life in Hindu Thought as Principles for a Civil Society, www.crvp.org date 17.10.2007.

Hindu Forum of Britain, Hindu resources, www.hfb.org.uk date 17.10.2007.

Ramayana, www.schools-wikipedia.org date 17.10.2007.

Dharma, From Wikipedia Encyclopedia, www.en.wikipedia.org date 17.10.2007.

Jose Puente Egido, Natural Law, 515-520.

www.en.wikipedia.org date 20. 12. 2007: Information Technology.

Good Governance, www.issues.takingitglobal.org date 20.12.2007.

The Ideal of Ethics in the Upanishad, www.sriramkrishnamath.org date 17.10.2007.

Hinduism Rediscovered, www.srivaishnava.org date 17.10.2007.

www.home.at.net date 18.10.2007.

The Vedas, and Dharma, www.haryana-online.com date 17.10.2007.

Hinduism, www.haryana-online.com date 17.10.2007.

Sanatana Dharma or Hinduism, www.dharma.indviews.com date 17. 10. 2007.

Donald R. Davis, Jr., Hinduism as a Legal Tradition, *Journal of the American Academy of Religion*, 2007, Vol. 75, No. 2, pp. 241-267.

A.I.R. 1980 S.C. 1579

A.I.R. 1981 S.C. 1850

S.C.C. 1994

A.I.R. 1997 S.C.

A.I.R.1978 S.C. 597

A.I.R. 1993 S.C. 477

A.I.R. 1987 S.C. 1086

A.I.R. 1996 S.C. 1446

A.I.R. 1996 S.C. 2715

A.I.R. 1993 S.C. 2178

A.I.R. 1989 S.C. 2039

A.I.R. 1997 S.C. 1225

A.I.R. 1997 S.C. 568

A.I.R. 1996 S.C. 114

(1996) 5 SCC 125

A.I.R. 1996 S.C. 2426

A.I.R. 1996 S.C. 1234

A.I.R. 1997 S.C. 95

A.I.R. 1983 S.C. 803

A.I.R. 1986 S.C. 180

BVerfGE 61, 126, 137 (1982)

BVerfGE 87, 209, 228 (1992)

BVerfGE 7, 198, 204 (1958)

BVerfGE 45, 187, 229 (1977)

BVerfGE 75, 369, 380 (1987)

BVerfGE 93, 226, 293 (1995)

BVerfGE 87, 209, 228 (1992)

BVerfGE 61, 126, 137 (1982)

BVerfGE 45, 187, 229 (1977)

BVerfGE 75, 369, 380 (1987)

BVerfGE 93, 226, 293 (1995)
BVerfGE 30, 1, 25, 26 (1970)
BVerfGE 45, 187, 228 (1977)
BVerfGE 27, 344, 351 (1970)
BVerfGE 88, 203, 281 (1993)
D.H. and Others *v.* The Czech Republic, a case decided on 13.11.2007 by the Grand Chamber of the European Court of Human Rights, Strasbourg, concerning the Right to Education and discrimination.

Index